RE CODING

THE REAL ESTATE EXPERIENCE

THE MINDFUL GUIDE
FOR BUYERS & SELLERS

RE CODING
THE REAL ESTATE EXPERIENCE

THE MINDFUL GUIDE
FOR BUYERS & SELLERS

How aligning insight and intention turns real estate into a journey of clarity & control.

BY SLOAN HUNTER

Mindful
REAL ESTATE

ISBN: 979-8-9936331-0-7

eBook ISBN: 979-8-9936331-1-4

audiobook ISBN: 979-8-9936331-2-1

First Edition.

Printed by distributed print partners.

To my husband Dave and my children
Matthew & Avery—
Your love, patience, and unspoken sacrifices
built the foundation for everything I've accomplished.
While I dedicate myself to a career of
high standards and long hours,
you've given me space to grow, to serve, and (now) to write.
This book carries your quiet support on every page.
Thank you for letting me build a life helping
others find a home and build wealth.

To the buyers and sellers who don't know where to begin—
This is for you.

To the ones who've felt unsure, unprepared,
or unheard, and those never taught
that ownership is possible or that or that they are worthy of it—
You don't have to be wealthy to own.
You don't have to know everything to begin.
You just need the right support,
the right mindset, and the right relationships.

This guide was written to show you that
mindful, ethical professionals do exist—
real estate firms, brokers, agents and other industry partners
who want your success as much as you do.
May this book remind you that you are capable
and that real estate can be a powerful,
proud, and personal journey.
You can do this—and you're not alone.

The Download for Free

As a thank-you for purchasing this book,
I'd like to gift you free access to
the C.O.R.E. Foundations Course

The C.O.R.E. Foundations Course

A four-part video series introducing
Comprehension • Orientation • Relationships • Etiquette
The four pillars that align mindset with strategic awareness —
centering you, clarifying your approach, and elevating
how you participate in real estate for more sound decisions,
meaningful collaboration, and purposeful outcomes.

Go to Mindful-RealEstate.com to receive the free video series

Contents

RECODING THE REAL ESTATE EXPERIENCE

SATISFACTION is the feeling experienced
when one's wishes are met.

A state of mind in which one is free from doubt.

The quality or state of contentment,
gratification, and vindication.

MERRIAM-WEBSTER

If you've ever felt more like a passenger than a participant in a real estate transaction, you're not alone. Too often, buyers and sellers are rushed through a maze of negotiations, inspections, and financing hurdles—only to land at closing wondering what just happened. Frustration overshadows what should've been a milestone. Relief takes the place of celebration.

Let me ask you this, though: Do you know what you *should* feel when it's all said and done? Elated? Empowered? Confident in your decisions? Supported by professionals truly invested in your outcome, not just compensated for the closing but committed to protecting your interests the entire transaction? You deserve to move through your real estate process guided by insight, not confusion—by professionals who prioritize your outcome, not their platform. That's why I've written this book, to return representation to where it belongs: in the hands of real people, supported by real expertise so you can close your transaction not just relieved but truly satisfied.

What does one do after selling, managing, leading teams, and practicing real estate for over thirty-five years? She dumps her real estate transaction knowledge into a book and hopes it makes a difference to the reader in their next real estate experience. Real estate transactions have evolved dramatically over time, shaped by centuries of negotiation, legal refinement, and market forces. Yet, despite these advancements, I have witnessed the experience itself become increasingly impersonal—more about transaction volume than advocacy, speed than satisfaction.

I've spent over three decades earning trust—client by client, transaction by transaction, firm by firm—while helping to raise the bar for the kind of real estate industry I want to work in. What I've learned I'm passing on now because buyers and sellers deserve better. I've built careers, led offices, and earned market share with transparency, but what matters most is that I've never stopped learning, competing, and believing that real estate (when done right) changes lives. This book is part of that belief in action.

It's about more than buying, selling, and negotiating—it's about *REcoding* the real estate experience through mindful pillars and guiding principles that elevate the process, ensuring every party walks away not only with a closed transaction but also *REprogrammed* with assurance, clarity, and the satisfaction of a transaction done right. A first-time buyer, overwhelmed by online listings, hesitates to ask the right questions to prepare for expectations. A seller, eager to move forward, agrees to terms and obligations they don't fully understand. These are not just occasional missteps; they are symptoms of a real estate system that has become more complex yet less personal. My goal is to *REstructure* that.

This book is structured with intention, each section speaking directly to the needs of either the buyer or the seller while equipping you with the knowledge, terminology, and foresight to advocate for your best interest from entering the market to closing on a property.

If your time is limited or you prefer a high-level overview, note that The Download section is intentionally designed to stand alone—mindfully organized around four pillars that *REcode* the real estate experience. It distills key concepts, definitions, and strategies into one accessible resource, arming you with essential takeaways even if you read nothing else.

The remaining sections provide deeper insights and guiding principles tailored to your role—and to those who support you along the way—offering clarity, perspective, and a framework for intentional collaboration and lasting success.

Here's what truly *REcodes* the real estate experience: when every party reads every section, they gain the shared fundamentals to understand not only their own role but also the rationale and challenges of the other party involved. This shift in perspective fosters fewer misunderstandings, encourages patience in negotiations, and ultimately leads to more successful, satisfying transactions.

So, what needs *REcoding*? Agency. When and how firms and their brokers perform agency services—and how they are compensated—is redefined to align with true professional advocacy. In every real estate transaction, someone is representing someone; if you're not clear on who's representing *you*, you might not have the advocacy you think you do. That's why understanding agency matters. It's not just paperwork— it's the difference between being guided and being left to guess. (More details to come in The Download.)

What about *REcoding* the role of technology? While advancements in real estate technology have streamlined and made processes more efficient, it can inadvertently lead buyers and sellers to believe that digital tools alone are sufficient. The convenience of apps, websites, and automated systems can often mask what's truly needed—a personalized, human touch that offers expertise, guidance, and the context necessary for making informed decisions. Buyers may be unaware of the full picture, relying on digital platforms that do not offer advocacy, or provide due diligence insights and knowledge a professional can offer. Meanwhile, sellers, with their focus on quick digital transactions, might later feel that they've missed out on opportunities or didn't fully understand the process—missing out on more buyers. Technology should complement, not replace, valuable, proficient conversations and vested relationships that build trust and understanding throughout a real estate journey.

Apps now exist that claim to help you "buy a home in one click" or "sell without an agent," all under the promise of saving you money. What they don't advertise, however, is what's lost in the process: *agency, due diligence, contract fluency, skilled negotiation,* and the human competency and emotional intelligence required to navigate challenges, interpret nuance, and advocate for your best outcome—qualities a dedicated liaison brings to the experience. These platforms don't protect your interests; they protect their margins.

Not every party to a transaction will walk away overjoyed; this book isn't about achieving perfection but about eliminating ignorance, restoring trust, and ensuring every participant has control over their experience. For buyers, that means entering the process with sureness instead of uncertainty while knowing they have a clear path for advocacy and the support of industry professionals committed to securing the best possible result. For sellers, it's about knowing their interests are being protected, and their property is marketed to deliver the strongest possible return in the least amount of time.

Whether you're buying or selling real estate, you deserve an experience that is fair, transparent, and fulfilling. It's time to *REset* expectations, remove confusion, and *REstore* the integrity of the process—one transaction at a time. This book is designed to mindfully transform buyers and sellers into agentic participants in their real estate journey, empowered with knowledge, courage, and the ability to know their options and make informed decisions in their best interest. Rather than being swept along by the process, you will take an active role, initiate responsibility, anticipate challenges, and engage with professionals as a knowledgeable and prepared party. By *REcoding* the real estate experience, this guide ensures you step into every transaction with perspective on who to hire for representation, a process to engage, tools to strategize, and self-trust to close your next transaction without doubt.

Thank you for picking up this book and allowing me to be part of your real estate journey. Whether this is your first transaction or one of many, I hope my mindful approach gives you the competence, determination, and self-assurance necessary to navigate the process with ease. Real estate should feel empowering, not overwhelming; my goal, likewise, is to help buyers, sellers, and industry professionals move forward with certainty and satisfaction in a synergistic manner. Your time is valuable, and I'm honored you chose to spend some of it here. Wishing you success and a truly satisfying real estate experience!

THE DOWNLOAD

…an open channel providing clarity, insight, and truth in real time.
Much like updating software, this Mindful approach download allows buyers and sellers to process new perspectives, blend their wisdom, and take understanding past the limits of the mind and previous experiences.

When parties to a transaction are fully engaged, this gives way to trust in the process, alignment with purpose, and the ability to move forward with confidence. Whether in life, business, or real estate, those who stay open to receiving information remain ahead of the curve.

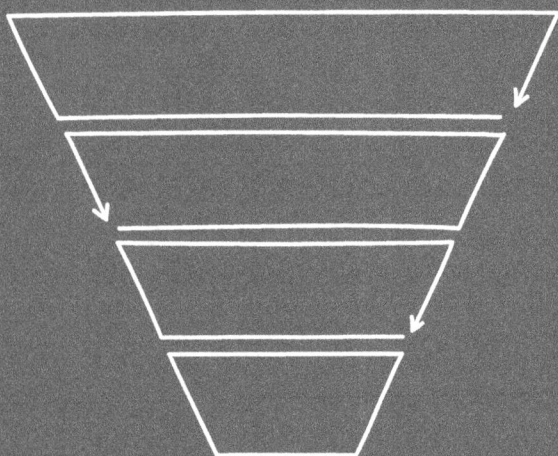

Knowing that each real estate transaction is inherently complex, this *Mindful Real Estate Guide* is designed to equip buyers and sellers with a shared understanding of terminology and outline clear expectations—ultimately leading to positive experiences for all parties involved.

First and foremost—congratulations! You're doing what 99% of buyers and sellers never do: taking the time to prepare, understand the real estate process, and make informed decisions before costly mistakes have a chance to surface. Scrolling through a property app may feel like research, but without context, intention, and perspective, it's really just entertainment.

True preparation begins here, *REdirecting* impending nervous energy and creating a plan with options so buyers and sellers align with minimized resistance so the transaction takes shape to be a satisfying experience. Shared insight and simplified language give perspective to the opposing party, balance emotional reactions, and streamline the process for all. Unlike other guides that focus on cookie-cutter steps involved with buying or selling real estate, this holistic approach features reliable and proven methods that feed proactive efforts to reduce anxiety surrounding sophisticated agency agreements and binding purchase and/or sale contracts.

Many buyers and sellers have a vision for what they want to achieve but may underestimate the challenges they'll face during the process. While both parties are of course responsible for fulfilling contractual obligations, many approach the transaction by "winging it" without guidance or any sort of clear strategy. This guide will likewise arm you with essential knowledge about factors influencing the pace of a transaction, when to act, and how to embrace professional support throughout the journey—avoiding the psychological stress of being passively pulled through the experience under demanding timelines.

So often when transactions go awry, buyers or sellers blame the real estate industry without reflecting on how their own personal choices contributed to an unsatisfactory experience. Complaints about real estate costs or skepticism about the value of what a broker (also known as an "agent") does, for example, often bog down the broader picture. Shared throughout this guide are details about what these invaluable professional services are all about, having been refined and executed with integrity for over a century now.

Corresponding buyer and seller content aims to shine a light on the real estate industry's commitment, one in which brokers serve millions of consumers to protect with honesty, diligence, and expertise every year. Just as these professionals work tirelessly to guide successful transactions, the very best outcomes occur when clients take responsibility for their decisions—steering clear of unfavorable results that happen when due diligence or contractual obligations are overlooked, reinforcing the importance of informed participation and respect for the process.

Brokers ride many professional and personal waves while juggling multiple transaction deadlines and legal complexities and tending to the emotional needs of their clients. Competent brokers make the work look effortless despite these changing tides to deliver meaningful client outcomes. Their market knowledge, legal compliance, and ability to orchestrate moving parts, however, are often minimized or misunderstood and rarely receive the credit they deserve.

One reason their value is misunderstood is most people have no idea how brokers actually get paid. Typically, their compensation is contingent upon the conclusion of a contract—meaning they dedicate significant time, energy, and expertise to their work without any upfront guarantee of payment. A broker's income reflects more than just effort. It represents years of experience, continued education, and a top-to-bottom, front-to-back understanding of agreements and contracts in addition to market expertise. This work goes far beyond marketing, showing properties, and facilitating paperwork. It's a continuation, one in which brokers refine negotiating strategies to match market pace, provide strategic planning designed to prep clients for due diligence, and advocate while serving to protect them throughout their real estate journey. The end goal? To meet contract obligations while advocating for clients at every transactional stage.

This guide seeks to *REcode* the real estate experience by fostering mutual understanding, accountability, and respect. My hope is to create a more informed, confident, and synergistic journey for all buyers and sellers while *REdefining* how they perceive and engage with the real estate process, resulting in better outcomes for everyone involved.

Whether you are buying or selling, you will feel the protection and avoid potential risks, meet contractual obligations, and arrive to a well-executed closing. After you absorb this <u>Download</u> section, I encourage you to head straight to your respective section(s) to improve your outlook and engage fully with the entire guide as you ready yourself for a complete transactional experience. By enhancing comprehension and restoring the importance of each party's contribution, this guide encourages a proactive and accountable flow to achieve desired intentions.

With over three decades of experience in the industry, I'm driven to help all parties to a transaction be stronger and smarter (#stronger&smarter) as my number-one goal. As you level up, you will be fully prepared to make informed decisions, take responsibility, and trust your choices.

We begin this download with CORE, the four pillars of the mindful approach: Comprehension, Orientation, Relationships, and Etiquette to establish balance, stability, and overall strength to improve the buying and selling experience.

CORE

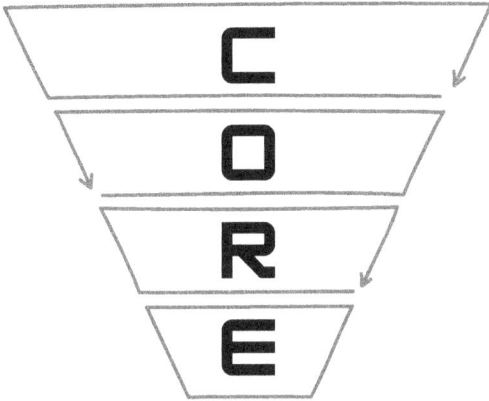

Real Estate Journey

COMPREHENSION

The most successful real estate experiences are born when buyers and sellers not only rely on professionals for guidance but indeed take an active role to comprehend relevant material and educate themselves. With this in mind, let's first discuss compensation and some key terms related to real estate representation.

Historical Compensation Experience

Historically, a seller would compensate a buyer's broker regardless of the level of care, skill, or expertise provided to the buyer—this industry norm limiting a buyer's ability to negotiate their own broker's fee or influence the services performed on their behalf. Compensation and representation, likewise, were confusing in terms of their roles and expectations.

What's Changed?

A series of class action lawsuits alleged that the National Association of Realtors (NAR)—the industry's largest trade organization, with over a million members called Realtors (licensed agents or brokers held to NAR's additional standards of professional accountability)—enforced a mandatory compensation rule requiring sellers to offer a buyer's broker fee. The lawsuits claimed that this practice, combined with the actions of several large franchise brokerages, conspired to keep commission rates elevated by discouraging brokers from showing listings that offered lower-than-traditional compensation, effectively keeping commissions artificially inflated.

The core argument: this rule created stable but inflated commission norms, leaving buyers with no incentive nor opportunity to negotiate the level of service or corresponding compensation. Worse, if compensation was reduced, the benefit went solely to the seller—not the buyer. The court found this practice in violation of federal antitrust laws, stating NAR created a system where all buyer brokers were paid similarly regardless of skill, care, or effort provided.

While I may not agree with how these changes were instigated—or with the claims made—the resulting shift is one I support. These updates reinforce professional standards by outlining services, compensation, and expectations from the start of a broker-client relationship, helping to eliminate any ambiguity that can arise from implied representation. By doing so and in strengthening the foundation of representation, this ensures both brokers and clients are on the same page and empowers clients to make informed, confident decisions.

Buyers deserve more than casual guidance; they deserve clear, accountable advocacy that includes a thoughtful discussion to negotiate representation, specify services, and understand broker compensation and what's expected from both sides of their agency relationship (just as listing agreements do for sellers). This level of transparency ensures that buyers are authorized to negotiate loyalty, attentiveness, and expertise from a broker who is genuinely invested in their success—not just the sale. Far more than a legal requirement, transparency serves as the foundation of a professional partnership built on trust, accountability, and advocacy.

The public demanded change, and the courts agreed. Real estate laws in many states—along with revised agreement and contract forms from multiple listing services (MLS) and professional associations—are quietly *REfactoring* the framework of agency, *REcoding* the sequence of representation to ensure a more informed, accountable and equitable experience for all parties involved. However, in response to these shifts, some firms, associations, and groups have introduced new policies, proprietary apps, and private MLS or IDX: (Internet Data Exchange) systems. While these innovations offer newfound options, they can also alter the dynamics of agency, compromise advocacy, and introduce complexities for both brokers and clients. It's important to recognize that technology, though beneficial, should never overshadow foundational principles of real estate representation such as advocacy and transparency. As we dive into the nuances of these changes, let's first clarify some key terminology to bridge legal and industry jargon with everyday language.

Agency refers to the formal relationship established between a buyer or seller and a licensed broker ("also known as agent and sometimes Realtor®") and their firm for real estate services, commonly known as "representation." Both buyers and sellers are entitled to and encouraged to seek professional agency as it provides crucial support before and throughout a transaction. Agency specifics vary based on a written agreement reflecting the circumstances, expectations, and complexities of the market. It's important to note that agency practices may differ by location, but they consistently offer significant benefits to both buyers and sellers (i.e., "principals" in a transaction).

The **principal** is either the buyer or a seller (the client) entering an agency agreement seeking advice, services, and advocacy and is the party to a purchase and/or sale contract. The firm and its brokers have responsibilities to represent their principals' best interests. This includes advocating for their needs, negotiating favorable terms, and protecting their rights throughout the transaction process.

Dual agency, also known as "limited dual agency," occurs when one (the same) broker represents both the buyer and the seller in a transaction. This arrangement requires the informed consent of both principals, which must be documented in their separate written agency agreements with both consents acknowledged in the purchase and/or sale contract. When performed with integrity, effective communication, and strict adherence to protocol, dual agency can be managed in a way that ensures both principals are fairly represented. However, this is a cautious balance that requires an experienced broker who can navigate the complexities without compromising their ethical boundaries. While limited dual agency may work in certain situations, it is important to recognize that it is not typical and should only be undertaken by a broker with the knowledge, experience, and commitment to maintaining the highest standards of professionalism.

No agency occurs when a principal chooses to waive their right to any representation, opting instead to advocate for and represent themselves. While this option is available, it is generally not advisable as it leaves the principal without professional agency, advocacy, or guidance and rarely serves their best interest.

Limited dual agency and no agency options are unique and not commonly employed due to their complexities, and I rarely recommend them—especially when professional buyer or seller representation is readily available. Limited dual agency, in particular, requires a sophisticated understanding as it limits the broker's ability to act solely in your best interest as the client. In some regions, laws and regulations strictly control or even prohibit limited dual agency due to potential conflicts of interest.

The **designated broker (DB)** has an important role and is typically a managing broker responsible for overseeing the practices of all brokers within a firm. To earn a DB license (also known as a Managing Broker's license in some areas), one must have over three years of full time experience as a licensed broker along with extensive additional education in areas such as brokerage management, business management, and advanced real estate law. The DB inherently acts as a dual agent when two brokers are under their supervision, each representing their principal in the same transaction.

Why a Buyer Agency Agreement?

For nearly a century and up until the late 1980s, brokers often performed services for both parties—buyer and seller—but were legally obligated only to the seller, with buyers going unrepresented in a transaction. Laws shifted, giving buyers lawful representation, starting in the early 1990s when agency disclosure laws went into effect (though the seller's written listing agreement continued to guide the compensation structure of most transactions).

As sellers have long recognized they can't sell and collect net proceed funds for their property without a willing and able buyer, it became common practice for them to pay a commission to their listing broker who then (via a cooperating agreement) offered a portion to a firm and their brokers for bringing in and representing the buyer. Sound familiar? If you've signed a listing agreement and sold a property before, this was likely how your last transaction was framed.

This pay-it-forward model benefited (and still does!) both parties: when a buyer purchased a property, their broker was compensated by the seller. Later, when that buyer (owner) became a seller, they would offer compensation to the next buyer's broker (with the cycle repeating when they became a buyer and purchased again). The updated framework has sellers entering into listing agreements to define their representation and compensation with the option to offer separate compensation to a buyer broker, but this must be negotiated and authorized in the terms—typically in alignment with current market conditions.

Mandatory changes now require all buyers to negotiate and sign a buyer agency agreement *before* receiving any professional services. This agreement outlines what services the broker will provide, what compensation is expected, and under what conditions the buyer may be responsible for covering that negotiated fee—particularly when a property doesn't offer compensation to a buyer's broker.

Until these changes took effect in 2024, dedicated buyer brokers offered professional guidance at all hours—advising, touring, managing contract timelines, and absorbing client emotions, all while protecting their buyer's earnest money— in the absence of an agreement, working tirelessly until the transaction successfully closed to receive the seller's offered compensation fee. These new changes now formalize the broker-buyer relationship, however, with a buyer agency agreement clearly stating the buyer's broker will act in good faith, avoid conflicts of interest, and commit effort toward the buyer's goals in exchange for the buyer's loyalty during the agreed-upon timeframe and compensation outlined.

Some buyers, however, may still assume they can't afford representation and attempt to navigate a purchase and/or sale agreement on their own (no agency): unaware of the legal intricacies, complex timelines, and financial risks involved. Without professional guidance, they're more likely to make costly mistakes that could've been avoided with clear, early representation.

Transparency

In the past, buyers and their brokers often did not have open conversations regarding how the broker would be paid if a property was purchased. Unless the broker and buyer entered into an agency agreement creating a representation discussion and arranging compensation before viewing potential properties, the buyer assumed they were viewing all inventory that met their *needs* and *wants* (#needs&wants), and their broker would be paid. What was not openly discussed between a broker and buyer without an agency agreement was that the broker could choose not to show a property if the seller wasn't offering a traditional buyer broker fee, therefore not acting entirely in the buyer's best interest.

This <u>does not</u> suggest such practices were widespread, just that brokers could choose not to show a property when their compensation was not protected by an agency agreement. Despite the expectation to perform as if they were being paid, no fee was guaranteed. If a buyer selected a property with the seller not offering a traditional broker fee, the burden fell on the buyer's broker to initiate an uncomfortable conversation: blindsiding the buyer with a request to negotiate their broker's compensation within their offer.

Buyer brokers caught in this scenario often hesitated to negotiate their fee, fearing it might cloud the buyer's purchase opportunity or diminish the overall experience. Without a transparent discussion about compensation and agency services prior to viewing properties, focus was split between the excitement of finding a property and the discomfort of addressing compensation after the fact. This is exactly why today's approach, *REquiring* a buyer agency agreement **before** services begin, is more effective, more professional, and better for everyone involved. This is the here and now.

Bridging Past Relationships in a New Era of Agency

If you've worked with a broker in the past and intend to again, don't assume loyalty alone will protect that relationship. Following the aforementioned changes to real estate law, brokers are now required to secure a signed agency agreement *before* providing services, including touring a property.

If, on a whim, you click "Schedule a Tour" through an app or website, you may be paired with a different broker who, by law, must present an agency agreement before showing you the property. In your excitement, whether you are a buyer or potential seller, you may sign without realizing you're now committed to that buyer's broker for that property—unintentionally bypassing the broker you trusted all along. Your past broker didn't do anything wrong beyond failing to inform you of the updated laws and protocol.

Some buyers are of course also inherently sellers, such as owners considering a move who must sell their property in order to buy. Satisfied with their last broker and planning on utilizing their services again (if and when they find the right property), they get a little excited when a special property hits the market but don't want to "bother" or "waste" their broker's time since they're only "curious" at that point. So, they decide to "schedule" a showing via an app while having no idea they're required to sign a buyer agency agreement to view the property—tying them to that specific app broker; if they choose to make an offer, they forfeit their relationship with their trusted broker for that particular property where it was love at first sight. It happens!

Have a past relationship you want to honor? *Pause before clicking.* Contact your broker first to protect that connection before the convenient click unintentionally cuts them out of your next transaction.

ORIENTATION

Let's begin orientation with the foundation of real estate: compliance. Think of orientation as an act of self-compliance, your own version of self-care for the real estate process. By engaging in a careful review, properly investigating, and conducting a prudent inquiry, you'll gain a calm, confident presence that empowers you throughout the transaction. This proactive understanding before negotiations and during the transaction ensures you are prepared, informed, and in control, ultimately leading to a straightforward and more successful experience.

Compliance means obeying the laws, meeting licensing standards, and following ethical practices that govern real estate transactions at every level. Before strategy, negotiation, or even showing a property come into play, legal obligations are in place to protect everyone involved—especially you.

As a buyer or seller, knowing your broker and their firm operate within these standards ensures you're not just entering a transaction but a protected and professional relationship grounded in protocol, accountability, and trust.

Standards of Practice

Generally, when entering an agency agreement, federal, state, or local regulatory disclosure requirements provided from a real estate professional to a client typically explain adherence to fair housing/anti-discrimination laws and regulations, as well as specific hazards. Upon receipt of any disclosures, clients are prompted to initiate due diligence and take responsibility for reviewing and researching all relevant information to protect their interests. In addition to industry requirements, a firm and its DB must adhere to what's required in the local jurisdiction—with audits often conducted to verify the firm is in compliance with the law with proper broker licensure and supervision.

Auditors may require a firm to provide proof of a reliable system for reviewing agency agreements and closed purchase and/or sale contracts from newly licensed brokers and verify where/how all documents are maintained and if they meet the jurisdiction's minimum standards. In my experience holding a DB license and as a managing broker, the lack of a reliable system can lead to violations that aren't typically malicious but rather so subtle that the offending broker is simply unaware they are not in compliance.

These compliant safeguards are designed to ensure professionalism, minimize risks, and protect buyers and sellers throughout their real estate journey—providing peace of mind by ensuring their licensed professional is held to high standards, accountable, and working ethically to create a secure transaction.

Negotiations before consultations? No way! A consultation is an initial meeting with a broker, offered as a courtesy and without obligation to create a relationship—demonstrating their value, commitment, and professionalism—while providing an opportunity for you to explore agency options and professional representation.

Seller Consultations: A Mindful First Move

What if a buyer—or a buyer's broker—contacts you (an owner) directly about selling your property? Before allowing them to view the property or discussing price or terms, seek out a well-deserved seller consultation with a local brokerage that offers seller agency representation.

Even if you weren't actively planning to list, this no-obligation conversation provides clarity on your current market position, considering your location and property condition. It offers a thoughtful pricing strategy and insight into potential leverage. If the broker earns your trust by providing relevant guidance, legal competence, and a clear path forward, you'll walk away with more control over your decision to allow a viewing with offered terms and more confidence in how to proceed.

If you choose to hire representation because of the consultation, negotiating and signing a listing agreement (for seller agency representation) will protect your interests, outline expectations, and create a partnership to advocate on your behalf every step of the way. Without it, a buyer's broker may seek compensation directly from you (the owner) to represent their buyer to enter negotiations with you, creating either no agency for you or limited dual agency for both you and the buyer—removing representation in your best interest.

Buyer Consultations: Prepping Before You Pounce

What if you identify a prospective property in the absence of a buyer agency agreement? In this case, it is in your best interest to seek a buyer consultation with a local firm that offers buyer agency (not necessarily with the prospective property's firm) before entering into any negotiations with no agency or agreeing to limited dual agency with the seller's listing broker. A same-day consultation with most firms or one of their brokers can often be arranged as soon as a property sparks your curiosity.

This consultation makes a difference in that it gives you clarity into the prospective property and a taste of representation. You will walk away informed, empowered, and positioned to arrange your choice in agency. If the broker earns your trust by offering current market insight, negotiation strategies and contract guidance, you'll understand all your options including whether the property of interest is offering compensation to a buyer's broker.

If you choose to move forward with representation, be prepared to enter into a buyer agency agreement with confidence. This courtesy goes beyond a mere conversation; it offers a well informed alternative to navigating the process with limited dual agency or no agency at all.

Whether you're a buyer or seller, negotiating a real estate transaction without a consultation and an agency agreement in place creates vulnerability, and no professional advocacy, risking transparency and compliance. Protect your interests, gather information, preserve your options, and create space for yourself to make decisions with full understanding. Being compliant for yourself isn't a burden—it's a safeguard.

Your Journey in Two Phases

This mindful approach, *REcoding the Real Estate Experience,* is organized into two distinct and critical phases: *before* **mutual acceptance (#B4MA)** and *after* **mutual acceptance (#MA).** As the industry adapts to updated compliance protocols, real estate firms and their brokers remain steadfast in upholding the highest standards of fairness, integrity, and trust. It is essential that all parties—buyers, sellers, and professionals alike—embrace this structured framework of clear discussion and strategic planning. By framing every conversation in terms of these two phases, we set the stage for mutual understanding, shared responsibilities, and aligned expectations. This approach not only clarifies each party's role but also transforms the way real estate transactions are discussed, empowering everyone involved in a real estate experience to act decisively and confidently. Adopting this systemized language and methodology ensures transparency, builds trust, and leads to refined and more successful transactions, every time.

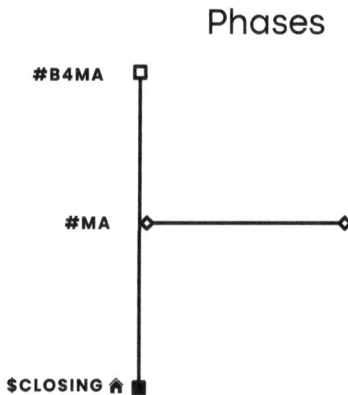

Phases

#B4MA

#MA

$CLOSING

Before mutual acceptance (#B4MA) is the window of opportunity for both parties to study how location and condition affect price, create a strategy to perform, initiate due diligence, negotiate agency terms to enter a representation partnership, and prepare for a future purchase and/or sale contract.

Mutual acceptance (#MA) is when both parties have consented and agreed to the same contractual terms, conditions, and obligations, binding them as principals to a purchase and/or sale contract.

Clear and concise. Different jurisdictions require the date and time to be recognizable and acknowledged from when the last accepted terms were delivered back by the **offeree** (the last party to whom the offer was made*)* and delivered to the last **offeror** (the party who made the last proposal): the principals of the transaction. Said acknowledgment by all parties of mutual acceptance is imperative and best when clearly documented as it concisely begins and triggers contractually specified timelines, contingencies, and obligations both parties are bound to. If an electronic signature platform is properly used, it typically provides an automated date and time stamp to ensure mutual acceptance is clearly recorded and trackable.

THE FIRST PHASE: #B4MA

To Acclimate is to be Responsible

What kind of market are you stepping into? Before entering an agency relationship, both buyers and sellers should take a proactive, unbiased approach to understanding real-time market activity. Price is directly influenced by location and condition, so it's essential to consider how these factors shape market value and opportunities. Understanding this dynamic helps set realistic expectations and positions you for a more informed, strategic approach to the transaction.

Acclimation is becoming aware of the market's pace: gaining general market knowledge, learning about its inventory without specific influence or emotional attachment, and developing a feel for market activity as it unfolds in a neutral, unbiased manner.

Be proactive and begin your acclimation process about three to six months before hiring a professional broker for representation. This early market awareness stabilizes you to make informed decisions when the time comes to buy or sell. A great way to start is by downloading a real estate app and setting broad search criteria—focusing on a location with a generous price range while avoiding restrictions on bedrooms, bathrooms, or square footage. This open-ended search, combined with viewing photos and virtual reality tours (when available), helps you observe market trends with an open mind.

MLS, NAR, and Apps, Oh My…

When choosing a real estate app, make sure it connects to a centralized database platform that promotes cooperation among brokerages and allows listings and their statuses to be shared openly. Keep in mind, not all property search engines provide the same level of access. Some apps pull data directly from an MLS, but not all MLSs allow brokers to share their listings universally. Some brokers may opt out of sharing their listings through IDX, making certain properties private and excluding them from your search. Furthermore, some apps (often backed by significant capital) create exclusive access to select MLSs or IDX systems and thus limit visibility to only a specific pool of inventory. This evolving landscape, compounded by changes in agency structures and class action lawsuits, adds complexity to property searches. For the purpose of acclimation avoid an app that limits your search to ensure you're seeing *all* "available" listings, verify the source of the app's data and understand the inventory it provides.

The outcome of the NAR lawsuit disappointed its membership by what many perceived as a lack of strong advocacy for its association's members and the integrity of the industry. As a result, some brokers who affiliate with an MLS that require a NAR membership are exploring alternative options— particularly those not affiliated with NAR or offering different approaches to enforcement, accountability, or a more centralized platform. These evolving MLSs are growing to syndication internationally, often promoting flexibility to advertise buyer broker fees and structure cooperating compensation in new ways.

It's important to recognize that each MLS is unique, with its own set of rules, standards, affiliations, and service models. Similarly, IDX content is designed to facilitate the sharing of listings and serve brokerages. The goal here is not to advocate for one type of MLS or IDX over another but rather to acknowledge that these shifts are prompting brokers to reassess their app affiliations. Some platforms focus on transparency and fairness, with the intent to build relationships, while others may capitalize on consumer naiveté, prioritizing shareholders at the expense of competitive integrity and the true needs of buyers and sellers.

Once you set up the criteria on your chosen real estate app, not only will you begin to witness market activity and become aware of its pace, but you can also track which properties buyers are making offers on and when. What is the market's current pace? Are buyers making offers in one day, two weeks, or three months? This acclimation period, whether you are a buyer or a seller, may create an opportunity to organize a list of potential broker candidates to interview and hire when you are ready for professional representation.

App Tracking

- Buyers–set your criteria to track properties you are attracted to and <u>might</u> qualify for.

- Sellers–set your criteria to track properties in the community or district your property <u>could</u> objectively compete with.

Such criteria should be broad and general for now; narrowing search criteria will likely come after you enter an agency agreement with a broker during a strategy session. The value of this acclimation period is to map a starting point for the acclimation experience, collect data, and (strangely enough) not engage desires nor competitive emotions but remain unbiased. Develop a personal system to note commonalities such as lot size, square footage, and room and bathroom count (beyond just bedrooms), and—most importantly—any common upgrades or enhancements offered in the market.

For those targeting luxury, waterfront, destination, or remote locations, you will want to collect data on how one accesses these properties (e.g., via a private or shared driveway, granted easement from a neighbor, etc.) and how much frontage or privacy each property offers. "Privacy" is a flexible term and varies by location and perspective. The earlier you acclimate, the earlier you can set aside personal biases and approach the market responsibly with realistic expectations and better preparation.

Assessing Acclimation

Assessing the market's pulse—by observing what current buyers and sellers are experiencing—gives you an advantage over your future competition. By **chunking the "available", "pending", and "sold" data into manageable units**, you can process it more thoroughly, identify patterns, and retain insights that inform your strategy. Repeating this review— maybe once a week—over time reinforces your understanding, so you clearly grasp what buyers expect from sellers and what sellers must do to attract buyers. The result is confidence: armed with these insights, you are free to strategize around price, location, and condition with clarity during future agency consultations, rather than feeling reactive or vulnerable.

The Unicorn

Every so often, a special property comes along that is not quantifiable: a unicorn, if you may, a property so unique that it skews the market data, the room count, and pricing for its location. If you carefully observe, track, and assess inventory, you can separate and identify such unicorns. Brokers who regularly analyze market activity and track which properties are absorbed will gain credibility with you if they can properly defend why these unicorns sell for a premium. In other words, just because a buyer is willing to pay a premium for a unicorn property does not mean a premium should apply to all future sales. When sellers fixate on an exceptional unicorn property and base their pricing on it rather than realistic market data, they risk losing valuable market time. As days on market add up, these sellers may need to adjust their price to attract a willing and able buyer: ultimately losing buyer momentum and delaying their goals.

Market Conditions: Inventory, Supply & Demand

Earlier, I asked: "What kind of market are you stepping into?" During the acclimation process, you track and assess market activity to prepare for how the relationship between location and condition affect pricing. Patterns will begin to emerge as the inventory status evolves from "available" to "pending" and finally "Sold." Here are some corresponding data points that impact strategy…

Available (Active) Inventory: Properties currently listed for sale that have not yet received an accepted offer.

Pending Sales: Properties that have reached mutual acceptance with a buyer and are under contract but have not yet closed.

Sold: Properties that have successfully closed and transferred to a new owner.

As inventory fluctuates and statuses evolve, your observation of these data points and their pace offers insight into which type of market you're entering:

Buyer's Market: This occurs when there's high supply, typically more than six months of inventory. Buyers have more choices, absorption slows, and sellers often need to lower prices or improve the condition to attract offers. Buyers generally hold more negotiating power in a buyer's market.

Balanced Market: This occurs when there is three to six months of inventory. Neither side holds a distinct advantage. Properties sell at a steady pace, prices remain relatively stable, and negotiations are often collaborative.

Seller's Market: This occurs when there's low supply, typically under three months of inventory. Buyers have fewer choices, properties sell quickly (sometimes with multiple offers), and sellers may have the upper hand. Buyers often need to act fast and may compromise on condition, price, or both in a seller's market.

Two Key Awareness Indicators: Months of Supply & Absorption Rate

To gauge pace and competitiveness, the industry tracks two important metrics: **months of supply** and **absorption rate**, two more terms to help you feel more informed as promised and shared for awareness purposes (not necessarily for you to incorporate into acclimation).

Months of supply and absorption rate typically use data that represents a snapshot in time, often measured in 30-day increments or on a month-by-month, quarter-by-quarter, or year-by-year basis: capturing the market's condition at that specific moment.

Let's say during acclimation, your search focuses on a zip code ("Universal Zip Code" for the purposes of this demonstration).

Universal Zip Code has 80 listings (properties) available for purchase.

In the last 30 days, 20 properties went pending (under contract) and 10 sold (closed).

Months of supply is a traditional statistic used to estimate how long it would take to sell *all* "available" listings at the current pace (assuming no new listings come on the market).

Months of supply formula:

Available Listings ÷ Sold Properties = Months of Supply

Months of supply Universal Zip Code example:

- 80 properties available
- 10 properties sold (in the last 30 days)

  → **80 ÷ 10 = 8 months of supply**

Over 6 months' supply indicates a **buyer's market** in Universal Zip Code.

Absorption rate is a pace indicator that shows how quickly properties are going under contract compared to other available listings.

An **absorption rate above 20%** typically indicates a **seller's market**, where inventory moves quickly and competition may drive prices up.

An **absorption rate below 15%** suggests a **buyer's market**, where listings may linger and buyers have more leverage to negotiate.

Anything in between may signal a **balanced market**, where conditions are relatively stable and both parties have negotiating power depending on the property and its pricing.

Absorption rate formula:

Pending Properties ÷ Available Listings = Absorption Rate

Absorption rate Universal Zip Code example:

- 20 properties pending (in the last 30 days)
- 80 properties available

  → **20 ÷ 80 = 25% absorption rate**

Above 20% signals a **seller's market** in Universal Zip Code.

What Happens When Important Metrics Conflict?

It's a red flag! The market is in transition.

In the aforementioned Universal Zip Code example:

- **8 months of supply** suggests a *buyer's market*
- **25% absorption rate** suggests a *seller's market*

Perspective Recap: this data's "snapshot in time" was the last 30 days. While "sold" data reflects 10 closed properties (which likely entered into a binding contract over 60 days ago since they just "closed" in the last 30 days), the pace of these "closed" buyers differs from current "pending" buyers who entered into a binding contract within the last 30 days. In other words, twice as many buyers (20) entered a binding contract last month as the month before that (indicating momentum is shifting in the seller's favor).

Why the transitioning shift in Universal Zip Code?

Perhaps the market is seasonal or interest rates have lowered—or something else altogether.

For **universal zip code buyer consultations**: A broker may warn buyers that inventory may not improve and urge them to act quickly with a strong offer. In this shifting market, waiting could mean losing out on options or paying more to compete in a multiple-offer situation.

For **universal zip code seller consultations**: A broker may encourage sellers to prepare now to list their property sooner rather than later to leverage rising buyer activity.

Brokers who understand market shifts don't use metrics and data to manipulate urgency during consultations—they use it to educate and empower clients. Translating trends into strategy, these professionals prepare buyers and sellers on how to move forward informed with intention, not coercion.

Consultation-Ready

Orientation through acclimation is just the beginning. Now comes the moment to decide: are you truly ready to perform? Being **"performance-able"** means more than simply saying yes to an agency agreement and buying or selling a property—it means being prepared to negotiate, perform due diligence, fulfill contractual obligations, and act with decisiveness.

A **buyer's consultation** should outline key performance-able factors required both *before* and *after* #MA. This includes understanding how purchase and/or sale contract language asserts the buyer has sufficient funds and will perform at closing once all contingencies and conditions are met, waived, or removed.

If your future offer is contingent on financing, the consultation should address the down payment source of funds (including gift funds or major deposits) and performance-able timing for an earnest money deposit. Confirm when payments for inspections and other buyer expenses—such as homeowner's insurance, lender fees, broker compensation (if applicable), and other common costs—are required. Clarifying these factors during a consultation prepares you to align your money now with your future timeline as a performance-able buyer, protecting your earnest money.

> *Gift funds and Estate Planning: Seek financial advice (from an industry partner) about receiving gift funds for a future property purchase that may offer tax benefits for both the giver and you? If you're a first-time buyer, it's a smart idea to explore the possibility of receiving a gift annually to set aside for a future down payment. The giver can take advantage of annual gift exclusions, and you, as the receiver, can benefit by using the funds to move forward with a future purchase. As property prices rise, this approach allows you to potentially get into a property sooner while offering tax advantages for everyone involved. Start the conversation with your family and their advisor about how gifting funds now can help you own in the future.*

A **seller's consultation** should clearly explain how the terms of a purchase and/or sale contract require the sellers to be performance-able, meaning they must have sufficient funds to fulfill compensation per the listing agreement, equity or funds to clear the title, and the ability to cover closing fees as outlined for execution once all obligations are met. Performance-able also includes a premeditated move-out plan, as a seller cannot "kinda" sell—once the property transfers ownership, you are required to execute all contractual terms, including vacating the property and giving possession to the new owner, unless otherwise negotiated. This plan may need adjustments for additional days or effort if repairs or replacements are necessary due to a mutually agreed-upon inspection requests or appraisal requirements.

A Disciplined Approach

Discipline is the foundation of being performance-able. It's not about perfection—it's about consistency.

A buyer's discipline lies in prioritizing needs over wants. If you're seeking financing, that means maintaining steady employment, minimizing debt, and avoiding new, non-essential purchases—especially large ones—until after closing. These actions not only support loan approval but also demonstrate your readiness to perform. Discipline is about aligning your behavior with your goal: securing a property. Save strategically, stay financially focused, and avoid anything that could compromise your ability to follow through when it matters most.

A seller's discipline begins with being realistic about the property's location, condition, and pricing. To position your property competitively, set the intention to offer the best possible product and thus outshine your competition: decluttering, deep cleaning, scheduling repairs, and/or staging if advised. This early preparation reflects your seriousness and sets the tone for how buyers will perceive your listing.

Once on the market, discipline means staying engaged: keeping the property show-ready, staying flexible with respect to showing schedules, and remaining open to feedback. If buyer responses consistently point to condition or price concerns, it takes discipline to pivot rather than take it personally. Markets shift, so your strategy must too.

Selling successfully requires more than a sign in the yard and a key box for access. It takes full disclosure, engaged effort, adaptability, and a mindset focused on collaboration with a willing and able buyer. The more disciplined your approach, the more empowered your outcome.

> *Disciplined Experience: I represented sellers during a progressive market downturn for a high-end property with a low-grade slope away from the home. The gentle slope entered a designated green space with wetlands and offered premium privacy but drew consistent feedback that buyers wished for a more level parcel. Before entering the market, the seller and I strategized how to price the "move-in ready" property with its unleveled backyard. Together, we viewed the competition (mostly with smaller lots with*

no privacy) and chose to undercut their prices by over 5% to outshine them. We were confident our price made up for the slope. The seller, meanwhile, stayed grounded in her "why"—a necessary move for her husband's job transfer—which gave her the discipline to stay focused even when pride and emotion tried to pull her off course. With a newborn baby, her spouse living away in a hotel where they were set to relocate, and two athletic, rugged dogs (removed for each showing), her determination to win over buyers was on overdrive; she was exhausted.

After about seven willing and able buyers went through and provided their feedback, we reevaluated the price in contrast to the current competition and agreed it was aligned with the location and condition—and thus did not adjust. Instead, the seller bet on herself and chose to level up what was in her control, pivoting to remind every new buyer not to dismiss the peaceful and beautiful setting. She thoughtfully staged the oversized back patio for each new showing to make it welcoming and entertaining with fluffy pillows and fuzzy throws; buyers could not help but sit down, loosen up, and enjoy the privacy. Depending on the time of day, she would get on her stepladder to pull the custom patio side curtains to create shade and even set out an appetizer with chilled tea or lemonade. One weekend later, this disciplined seller received multiple offers from buyers who sat, and imagined life on this special property.

Agency Agreement with Whom?

This experience underscores the importance of strategy and market understanding, qualities only cultivated through experience. For most buyers and sellers, the real estate process is something they encounter only a few times in their lifetime—which is why it's crucial to partner with professionals who have a deep, hands-on understanding of the market. Just as the aforementioned seller's disciplined approach was pivotal in turning her property's challenges into opportunities, working with an experienced broker who understands the full scope of market dynamics is key to navigating the complexities of any transaction. With buyers and sellers typically experiencing only three to four transactions over their lifetime, new agency law requirements emphasize the need to *REcode* the real estate experience—by ensuring professional relationships are founded on trust, transparency, and mutual respect. This Download section introduces a more empowering approach that can help you align with like minded professionals to create a more intentional and successful experience together. Remember, though, that not all brokers are alike. Experience matters, and the accumulation of transactions over time, or **saturation**, is what separates a seasoned broker from the rest.

Saturation Counts

Consider the following example…

Take three brokers, each with 10 years of experience. On paper, they seem equally seasoned, but experience isn't just measured in years—it's *saturated* by transactions.

- The first broker averages 12 transactions per year and closed around 120 properties.

- The second broker averages 24 transactions per year and closed roughly 240 properties.

- The third broker averages 36 transactions per year and closed approximately 360 properties.

The difference between 120 and 360 transactions is staggering: three times the strategy, negotiations, and problem-solving with exponentially more experience aligning pricing, managing inspections, and navigating appraisals.

Buyers and sellers should look beyond years in the business and listen carefully for how brokers advised their clients during shifting markets, leveled up their professional competence, sharpened their market expertise, and built a business based on referrals—all while leading their clients toward successful closings.

Practicing real estate consistently makes all the difference, especially for first- and second-time buyers navigating the pressure of today's competitive market. A broker with deep market and transactional knowledge and awareness brings not just skill but foresight; such insight is critical when buyers are weighing trade-offs, managing expectations, and making long-term decisions under short term stress.

More is better? Yes with respect to the quality of transactions but not always in years. Be mindful to fully understand a broker's experience and their level of market saturation, not just the number of years they've been in business but how effectively they've navigated unpredictable markets and difficult transactions to satisfy customers while developing a trusted client base.

Education, Not Manipulation

Buyers should focus on seeking a broker who takes a genuine interest in their needs, expertly shares their market knowledge, patiently explains contract law, and creates a tailored strategy to realistically prepare for the best possible outcome: centering the experience around the buyer!

Sellers should find a partner who will evaluate honestly whether the property meets buyers' *needs* and *wants* in the market, not just a broker who tells them what they want to hear. Sellers, please re-read that last sentence and let it be known, felt, and understood. If you objectively pay attention during acclimation to what sellers are experiencing, then nothing should surprise you here. If you are surprised, then you may be too attached to an outcome in a market you cannot control. Consultations provide a range of opinions and recommendations highlighting market expectations to prepare sellers and their property's location and condition for a willing and able buyer; sellers, in turn, must choose a broker who will align their capabilities, provide strategic options to help them reach their goals, and (together!) create a well-prepared synergistic plan.

Due Diligence

When to Inspect and What to Disclose.

As mentioned, real estate lawsuits generate changes, new laws, revised forms, updated best practices, and additional compliance. Since I started selling real estate back in 1990, the inspection contingency (a legal condition for buyers to back out based on inspection report findings) and associated negotiations to meet, remove, or waive the contingency have seen the most significant revisions.

For decades, buyers were expected to include an inspection contingency in their offer—which most sellers accepted as part of the process. That tradition continues today, especially in balanced or buyer-favored markets where inventory meets or exceeds demand. However, as the market has evolved, so too has the inspection strategy. In recent years, both buyers and sellers have increasingly opted for pre-inspections conducted before #MA—to reduce uncertainty, increase confidence, and set the tone for transparent negotiations.

Buyer's Pre-Inspection: In competitive, seller-favored markets, a buyer's pre-inspection can be a game-changer. It signals seriousness, demonstrates preparedness, and often provides a strategic edge in multiple-offer situations. By completing an inspection before submitting an offer (if the seller allows access), you gain valuable insight into the property's condition without delaying the offer timeline and streamline a path of collaboration with the seller. This allows you to make informed decisions about price, repairs, or waiving contingencies altogether so you can head into negotiations with eyes wide open: reducing uncertainty and strengthening your position, especially if you make time for due diligence. Keep in mind that while the pre-inspection offers valuable information, it does come at a financial cost. Be sure to seek your broker's advice to determine if this strategy aligns with your goals and helps maximize your negotiation potential.

Seller's Pre-Inspection: This provides the advantage of uncovering potential issues early on so the seller can correct any material findings before listing their property or otherwise disclose to potential buyers, demonstrating transparency by acknowledging issues upfront and thus showcasing good faith and a willingness to collaborate towards a successful closing. This proactive approach can attract a larger pool of buyers, justify an offered price (especially if corrections have been made), and prevent buyer inspection surprises such as a buyer legally cancelling the transaction (backing out) *after* #MA.

However, if you correct any findings reported in the pre-inspection and disclose or share in the listing, you should understand that a buyer may still want to perform an inspection for a second opinion or to complete their verification. A buyer's broker should encourage their buyer to seek their own inspection, if anything to verify the corrected findings are indeed completed properly. This can lead to additional findings or differing opinions, so be prepared for such possibilities. Your focus should stay on building trust to collaborate with potential buyers by reducing uncertainties, alleviating any buyer concerns, and offering clarity about the property's condition.

Seller Disclosure via Pre-Inspection

Sellers are legally obligated to disclose material facts and defects to the best of their knowledge. Most firms provide standardized forms for owners to fulfill this responsibility, but ultimately, disclosure must come from the seller.

If you hesitate to disclose something you discovered in the pre-inspection, it's often your intuition guiding you toward transparency. In such cases, it's wise to seek advice from your broker or legal counsel. While many sellers fear that sharing too much—especially when attaching a pre-inspection report to their listing—might deter buyers from making serious offers or create unrealistic expectations for repairs, transparency instead helps avoid potential legal pitfalls and ensures that both parties are operating on the same page. This approach encourages pricing the property according to its true condition and helps attract serious, qualified buyers who are aligned to proceed to closing with realistic and informed expectations. Case law shows that buyers who prove a seller knowingly withheld material information may be awarded damages. Disclosure isn't a risk; withholding is.

***Mindful Impact:** When sellers provide a pre-inspection report—especially for entry-level homes—this can give first-time buyers a clearer path to ownership. It helps these buyers begin due diligence early, stay informed, and prepare financially: reducing surprises or cancelled contracts after #MA. A seller's small step to prepare for market can make an impact in buyer assurance to prepare a confident offer and create transactional momentum towards a successful closing.*

Transparency isn't just about checking a box—it's about leading with integrity and setting your transaction up for success.

Buyers: Know Before You Own

Caveat emptor (meaning "buyer beware") tasks buyers with a personal responsibility to perform due diligence, conducting or verifying their research and performing inspections to ensure they make fully informed decisions. They can initiate this before ever stepping foot onto a property by researching city or county transfer of ownership requirements and/or suggested precautions for specific locations. Approach properties that have experienced rapid turnover or quickly 'flipped' with careful scrutiny. Sellers—often operating through LLCs or as contractors—may mark disclosures as 'unknown' or 'don't know,' citing their lack of residency, which can obscure critical information. While legally permissible, omissions can mask environmental hazards, concealed issues, or other problems that may have been overlooked or deliberately minimized. When viewing a property, buyers are encouraged to take notes to inspire additional research and seek advice (for example). Real estate and standards evolve, deferred maintenance happens, and regret always looms in the background; buyers, thus, shouldn't solely rely on others and must take action themselves to protect their best interests.

Author's Due Diligence Reflection: I've watched due diligence—once a vital and empowering act—get watered down to little more than a checklist. Buyers who ask the right questions or express concerns early on sometimes fail to dig deeper into the details, either because they feel rushed, overwhelmed, or don't see the relevance of exploring further. This erosion didn't happen all at once—the industry has diluted what encompasses due diligence and failed to prepare buyers before they begin negotiations—but sees buyers making compromises early on that cost them later. A skipped title report review. An HOA review skimmed, not studied. An inspection report "finding" never investigated. Due diligence isn't a box to check; it's your right, your leverage, and your protection.

Estate Sale Challenges

In most states, real estate disclosure laws provide specific exemptions for transfers made by a **personal representative,** also known as an **executor**: an individual appointed to administer an estate after someone passes away. This exemption means they are not required to complete standard disclosure forms. However, this does not absolve them of all responsibility. A personal representative has a legal obligation to disclose any known material defects they are aware of including environmental hazards or any future homeowners association (also known as HOA) assessments and predicted/proposed improvements not yet assessed. The estate has a duty to provide documentation pertaining to the property so the buyer can make an informed decision about whether they can manage potential compliance or financial obligations.

It's also common in estate transactions for the attorney or representative to draft language indicating the property is being sold *as-is*. This doesn't automatically mean something is wrong but simply a legal safeguard for an estate with limited historical knowledge of the property. Additionally, the buyer may be asked to accept a bargain and sale deed instead of a traditional warranty deed. While perfectly legal, the former type typically includes fewer assurances about the title.

> ***Estate Sale Due Diligence REminder:*** *Due diligence is not optional but a responsibility. A mindful buyer must prioritize verification, perform inspections, review HOA documentation carefully, and consult professionals as needed. This is your moment to investigate fully and not to assume, especially with estate sales. The deceased may have known the association had concerns and intended to seek estimates for future improvements, but the estate's representative may not. Therefore, make sure you hold the estate accountable to provide any and all up-to-date HOA documentation.*

Lean on your professional broker's experience and their trusted industry partners to strengthen your due diligence and disclosure processes. Brokers raise important questions, share industry insight, and draw on past experiences to guide their clients to be present, weigh options to strategize, and prepare for negotiations.

A Seller's Offering

When a seller "lists" their property for sale, they set the terms: price, condition, and compensation, giving the buyer (the offeror) permission to create an **offer** (a proposal made by one party to another party (the offeree)). If the seller (offeree) rejects the proposed terms but in return proposes changes to the original offer, they are now the offeror with a new proposal (AKA a **counter-offer**): a response designed as a new offer of terms to be accepted, rejected, or **negotiated** (a series of offers and counter-offers until both parties decide to walk away (agree to disagree) or reach an agreement and thus "exchange contracts." When both parties end negotiations and reach an agreement by "signing off" an "offer and acceptance," this acknowledges **mutual acceptance** (#MA) per an "executed contract" to create a "binding agreement" or "ratified contract." The choice of terminology reflects the legal real estate practices and contractual norms in a given area and signifies both parties have begun to navigate agreed-upon terms of the bounded contract.

Author Awareness REflection: I've represented many sellers who received multiple offers, often with a strong cash bid among them. Just like many other brokers years ago, I used to advise clients to go with those having cleaner terms—fewer contingencies, quicker closings, and perceived certainty—which made sense back then. As time has passed, however, I've become more aware of how some of those choices—especially when entry-level buyers are in the mix—contribute to gentrification. Every seller under the sun wishes for a "cash" buyer, but I've come to see how cash buyers (particularly for profit businesses) can remove opportunities for others seeking to secure homeownership and contribute as community members with the desire to build equity and grow personal wealth. For-profit investment funds and their managers build wealth for shareholders who don't think twice about removing opportunities for first- or second-time buyers nor intend to contribute to a community or cycle their income into it. I can't change those decisions, but I acknowledge them now with a clearer perspective. If I got the chance to do it all over again, I'd encourage sellers to consider more than just the path of least resistance: thinking about who's set to live there next and the lasting impact of that choice.

From #B4MA to #MA Terminology

Pending status begins once #MA is reached and the property is officially under contract and "in escrow". This phase allows both parties to fulfill or waive contingencies, perform agreed-upon obligations, and move the transaction toward a "firm" or "unconditional" sale.

Access is granted when the seller agrees to buyer contingencies, giving the buyer and chosen professionals permission to enter the property. This includes access for inspections, contractor evaluations, appraisals, and any other steps necessary to satisfy or waive buyer contingencies.

Contingencies are not loopholes but agreements. Each contingency in a binding contract whether for an inspection, financing, title, etc. It's a negotiated term that gives the buyer the contractual opportunity to perform and complete due diligence and move forward with confidence or otherwise exit the contract responsibly. For the seller, this period requires patience and trust in the process. Honoring the negotiated timeline gives the buyer space to fulfill their obligations and keeps the transaction compliant and on course. A mindful seller knows the most reliable closings happen when buyers feel informed, prepared, and supported (not rushed). When both sides respect the structure of contingencies, they protect the integrity of the transaction and increase the likelihood of a calm, successful closing.

Closing occurs once all terms are met, the point at which legal ownership transfers to the buyer, the seller receives their net proceed funds, and possession typically changes hands. Though it may feel like the finish line, closing is actually a critical transition point, reflecting (and celebrating) the culmination of all prior planning, negotiations, and collaboration to achieve this success.

SECOND PHASE: #MA

Contingencies & Obligations to Perform

Let me first refresh your memory with respect to #MA, meaning when both parties have consented and agreed to the same contractual terms, conditions, and obligations as a binding agreement. The first 10 days (depending on specific contractual timelines) *after* #MA typically focuses on the buyer and seller collaborating in good faith to remove the buyer's conditions before they exercise their right to terminate and cancel the contract.

Such conditions customarily include a verification period, a title contingency, an inspection (or feasibility) contingency, a finance contingency, and sometimes a contingency on the sale of the buyer's property (if the buyer needs the net proceed funds from a property to complete the purchase). Depending on buyer or property nuances, additional contingencies are sometimes encouraged. The buyer's experience during this fast-moving phase is best approached like an obstacle course— navigated with a clear plan that outlines best- and worst-case scenarios, grouped by contingency type with specialist (finance/lender, inspector, or advisor) support on standby for timely advice.

The Money Group

Earnest money is the buyer's initial act of good faith, a deposit (typically 1% to 3% of the purchase price) that signals serious intent and demonstrates the buyer's commitment to honor the negotiated contract terms. Delivered promptly—often within two business days—the buyer's earnest money is held in escrow (or per terms mutually agreed on) and later applied to the purchase price at closing. Once deposited, earnest money sets the rhythm of trust in the transaction: providing the seller with a degree of security and acting as compensation for taking the property off the market.

If the buyer fails to proceed to closing without lawful cause after the seller has fulfilled their obligations, the earnest money serves as the **remedy** for the seller and may be released to compensate for the failed closing. Since earnest money is typically the sole remedy, its delivery *after* #MA emphasizes the importance of respecting and adhering to the terms of the purchase and/or sale contract. A failure to do so may jeopardize one's right to claim the earnest money.

The loan application is one of the buyer's earliest and most essential performance steps. Once earnest money is delivered, the buyer should—if they haven't already—finalize their mortgage application using the property's address and promptly deliver a proof-of-application letter to the seller. Some agreements require this to be completed within the first few business days, reinforcing the buyer's commitment and the spirit of fulfilling contractual obligations.

Net proceeds funds from a sale means that if the buyer's purchase is *contingent* upon selling another property, the countdown begins with most contracts requiring the buyer's property to be listed within five days *and* under contract within

30; it's crucial to have a listing strategy and marketing plan in place!

Outside funds, such as securing gift funds, liquidating investments, drawing from retirement accounts, and/or paying down debt are additional financial responsibilities—each requiring timely discipline and intentional action to maintain momentum and satisfy contractual requirements.

The Due Diligence Group

Due diligence is about the discovery process, focusing on learning about an area or a property with the intent and effort to thoughtfully consider potential conditions and then identify how these can impact a purchase or sale. It's where you ascertain what might encumber the property such as any future community improvements that could lead to financial assessments, noise hazards, or construction disruptions. This is also an opportunity to gather documentation such as a homeowner association's (HOA) reserve study to clarify funds for future capital improvements (which may not currently be budgeted), financial statements to assess the HOA's current financial health, and covenants, codes, and restrictions (CCRs) to fully understand the property's regulations. Due diligence doesn't have to be intimidating; it's about approaching verification with curiosity and understanding that knowledge is power, helping you strategically prepare to make confident decisions.

Verification is the next step in this process. After gathering information during due diligence, buyers need to **verify** that everything, from the seller's disclosures to the HOA documents and the title report, is accurate and as represented. Common verifications include confirming lot size, square footage, utility connections, easements, and encroachments. Additionally, it's important to verify the **HOA's financial health**, check for any ongoing litigation, and assess insurance costs. Depending on location and intended use, buyers may also need to research zoning, local ordinances, and potential hazards. Verification is the buyer's responsibility; it's not up to the broker or the firm to do the legwork. The broker's role is to support, prompt thoughtful questions, and guide the buyer through the process within contractual timeframes.

Consideration begins #B4MA and continues *after* #MA. Sellers, as mentioned, need to consider the ramifications if they do not gather all known information, complete (to the best of their ability) all required disclosures and provide these (per the advice of their broker) with the listing at the time they enter the market. The longer they take to disclose, the more days tick by for buyers to change their mind.

SWOT: Once a property feels like "the one," the buyer, together with their broker, should collaborate to identify any strengths, weaknesses, opportunities, or threats (via a SWOT analysis) that may require deeper investigation and assemble a team of **inspectors, industry partners, contractors,** and **specialists**—any professional whose insight could impact decisions made during due diligence.

Exhaust the documentation first before reaching out to your broker or the listing broker with questions, taking the time to thoroughly review the listing, all attachments, and disclosures and thus showing consideration for the brokers who have already taken the time to provide this information (ensuring your questions haven't already been addressed).

Schedule concentration means aiming to schedule and coordinate as many appointments as possible on the same day when strategizing to enter negotiations. This approach concentrates your efforts, streamlines the process, and demonstrates consideration and respect by minimizing disruption to the seller's time and property: setting the stage for continued collaboration to fulfill obligations and creating a civilized path to closing.

The **seller's mandated disclosure** must be completed as accurately as possible, detailing any known past or present defects. It is in the seller's best interest to provide their disclosure early in the process, setting the foundation for a proactive collaboration with the buyer and helping to avoid unnecessary delays.

In **seeking advice** from your listing broker, I recommend attaching your seller disclosures and any supporting documentation to the listing when entering the market. Commonly, a purchase and/or sale contract grants the buyer a conditional window to review seller disclosures (typically with the right to rescind or cancel the transaction if concerns arise). Sellers who omit or misrepresent material defects may be held liable for court-awarded damages, even if the omission was unintentional. While brokers aren't required to inspect the property, they must disclose any known or observed issues that could affect the transaction.

Present to discover isn't just about logistics, but each property visit with your broker should be intentional and insightful: using consistent language for mutual understanding to uncover, learn, negotiate, and set expectations for the final walk-through. The most effective due diligence happens when a buyer and their broker are both physically present to carefully observe, raise questions, and strategize in real time together.

While it's common for buyer-broker teams to share responsibilities, buyers deserve to know who will be present when it matters most. Before hiring representation, don't hesitate to request the presence of the same person during inspections and follow-up visits—or seek to understand the team's communication process. Does the team have a system that holds them accountable to properly communicate, identify, and negotiate terms from the buyer's due diligence?

It is not the responsibility of an inspector or industry partner to use the necessary language to achieve the buyer's expectations; it is the *broker's*. The language an inspector or advisor notes in a report or estimate (for negotiation purposes) must sometimes be explained in an addendum in order to produce the results the buyer expects at their final walk-through. You are in a partnership, but your broker cannot read your mind. Say what you want, verify that is how it is explained, and then sign the request.

Many DBs must take calls to rectify omissions or mistakes (unintentionally of course) due to lack of proper care or verbiage between the showing broker at the original viewing, the attending team broker at the inspection, and whoever attends the final walk-through. This is not to sway you from hiring teams for representation—most of whom do have proper systems in place—but simply insight for you to seek clarification and comfort in who will be in attendance so you're not surprised when it matters. Beyond opening the door, brokers should be hands-on, responsive, and fully invested in their buyers' best interests—#B4MA and *after* #MA.

Inspection Request Language Example: A buyer's inspection report noted in the inspector's remarks that the furnace was "nearing the end of its life" and (according to the sticker attached to the furnace) had not been "serviced" for several years. The inspector noted and recommended the furnace be serviced by a professional HVAC (Heating, Ventilation and Air Conditioning) contractor.

During the inspection, the buyer told the attending broker they wanted the furnace replaced. The attending broker (not the lead buyer's broker) failed to mention the buyer's stated request for replacement but instead relayed the "furnace was an issue" to the buyer's team lead—who went on to review the inspection report, prepare the appropriate addendum, and negotiate any inspection requests from the buyer to the seller.

The buyer's team lead did not specifically use language requesting the seller "replace" the furnace but only *referenced the inspection page itself (which recommended the furnace be serviced by a professional HVAC contractor) via an inspection response addendum. Thanks to technology, the busy relocating buyer (who was traveling back home) electronically signed the prepared request to begin negotiations on the "furnace": failing to double check to make sure their broker was beginning to negotiate a replacement instead of just servicing said furnace. This could have been avoided with a quick, personal consult with the buyer to confirm their expectations.*

The seller accepted the buyer's request (per the addendum that referenced the inspector's noted remarks), and their inspection contingency was removed. When it came time for the buyer's walk-through, the lead buyer's broker (rather than the one who had attended the inspection) accompanied the buyer to verify the property's condition and that the furnace work had been completed. When the buyer (fresh from the airport) noted the old furnace was still there, guess who had egg on their face and ended up paying for a new furnace? The lead buyer's broker. Yep, even though the buyer had signed the inspection request addendum, it was ultimately the buyer broker's responsibility to carry out the buyer's stated request—team or no team. This was an unfortunate, costly mistake that could have been avoided.

Sellers, be prepared for inconveniences, fears, and unknowns. The more gracious a seller is during the buyer's due diligence process and inspection contingency period, the less risk there is that the buyer will sue the seller and pursue damages in the future. Much depends on the preparation and strategy implemented before the property enters the market, with the buyer owing the seller no updates during this process.

In honoring due diligence, this is not the time for a buyer to be passive nor a seller to be aggressive—especially if disclosures or inspections reveal something unexpected. The buyer is entitled to use the full agreed-upon contingency period to complete their due diligence, including multiple property visits if needed, and the seller should exercise patience. When both parties honor timelines and respect the process (not abuse), this ultimately helps these principals collaborate and move forward with greater clarity and confidence.

Once the inspection contingency is met (either waived or removed), the seller is responsible for promptly completing any agreed-upon repairs and maintaining the property in the same or better condition as when the offer was accepted. Preparing for the buyer's final walk-through, the seller may need to complete additional responsibilities specified in the binding terms such as completing specific maintenance tasks or providing health-related certifications for systems (e.g., water and waste).

Contingencies are not just procedural checkpoints; they are key milestones highlighting shared responsibility between the buyer and seller. After the buyer has completed their due diligence, the focus shifts to fulfilling the remaining terms of the contract—particularly those linked to financing.

Homeowners insurance is not only a closing requirement but an integral part of both due diligence and financing. A buyer cannot remove their financing contingency without securing coverage, making this a critical joint checkpoint for both parties. While the buyer is responsible for obtaining quotes and confirming coverage, the property itself is also assessed. Insurance companies evaluate risk by analyzing the property's condition through marketing remarks, listing photos, aerial views, and nearby claims. If the property has been sold before, insurers may review prior photos and note any major updates, seeking clarification if required permits were obtained.

For sellers, this is a timely reminder that consistent maintenance isn't just about pride of ownership; it can directly impact the property's ability to close and your ability to collect proceeds, the whole point of selling in the first place! A well-maintained property helps minimize red flags, reduces last-minute obstacles, and supports a promising path to closing.

The Closing Group

Contingent Buyer's Property

If a contract is "contingent" upon the buyer selling their property and the buyer has not delivered "notice" to the seller that an offer has been accepted to fulfill this contingency, the seller faces critical decisions as the contingency period nears expiration. At this point, the seller and their broker must gather data to make an informed decision: Should they extend the buyer's contingency period and continue collaborating or otherwise let the contingency expire, cancel the agreement, and disburse the earnest money according to the terms of the contract?

To Extend or Not to Extend?

Seller's Evaluation: Is the property priced competitively to reflect its location and condition, making it attractive to prospective buyers? Has the buyer adjusted the price or made improvements to generate new interest since the seller accepted their *contingen*t offer? How many willing and able buyers have viewed the property with a buyer's broker beyond just open house "looky-loos"? What is the status of the *contingent* property's competing properties? Still active or under contract?

Contingency Check Point: If 7 to 10 willing and able buyers, accompanied by brokers, have toured the property, given feedback, and still no offer has been made, it may be time to reassess the strength of the *contingent* buyer's motivation.

Upon evaluation, if the seller and their broker discover the buyer's *contingent* property needs improvements or a price adjustment (or an offer to compensate a buyer's broker) to attract new interest and the buyer is unwilling to take reasonable action within their control, it may be time to reconsider granting a contingency extension.

Everything Good Comes at a Cost

If the buyer requests the benefit of an extension, it should come with a cost. After all, additional time on the market can cost the seller valuable momentum. A seller's broker might suggest negotiating additional earnest money or converting a portion of the existing earnest money to a non-refundable deposit, payable to the seller.

Ultimately, sellers must weigh the risk of continuing with a *contingent* buyer against the option of going *back on market* (BOMK) to find a new, more prepared buyer. Before making that decision, the seller and broker should evaluate the most recent competition, examine newly "pending" sales (and any seller concessions), and determine whether current conditions still support the original price.

The buyer may still be worth waiting for—especially if the market has cooled and if the buyer is actively making improvements and adjusting their price. A well-timed data-driven decision helps the seller stay in control of the transaction while minimizing lost time and financial uncertainty.

Subject to Multiple Closings

If the *contingent* buyer has accepted an offer and delivered notice to the seller within the contingency period, the transaction shifts to being "subject to the closing" of multiple contracts: requiring open communication with multiple brokers, multiple lenders (if financing is involved), multiple escrows, and/or law firms to coordinate simultaneous closings and fund disbursements per the terms of multiple contracts. Have no fear! This happens everywhere, every day. Buyers and sellers can rely on their professional team and industry partners to navigate the complexities of the transaction, especially when they are informed and introduced early to the other parties involved. Early intent to collaborate fosters graceful closings later on, allowing buyers and sellers to exercise patience and focus on coordinating simultaneous move-out and move-in schedules. Hire a representative who exhibits an open style of communication, and refer to the "Mindful Seller" section for a personal example (pg. 246) detailing my own experience navigating multiple (stacked) closings.

To Close or Not to Close?

Approximately a week before closing marks a critical checkpoint as both buyer and seller must fulfill their obligations to secure the earnest money should the transaction be terminated if the other principal fails to close or breaches with fault. Otherwise, if the buyer has satisfied all conditions and the seller has completed their obligations, the seller must then provide access for the buyer to complete their **final walk-through**: ensuring the property is in the agreed-upon condition and any negotiated repairs are complete. Just as the buyer's action of delivering the earnest money activates the rhythm and spirit to collaborate during "pending" status, the seller's decision to excuse themselves for the buyer's final walk-through cements good faith efforts for both parties to confidently proceed to closing.

Final Flow with Escrow

As closing approaches, escrow will instruct the buyer to deposit the remaining funds and notify all parties once the lender's balance is received. At this stage, the seller must fulfill final responsibilities: removing all personal property (except items included in the contract), disposing of any trash or debris, and ensuring the property is clean for the buyer's possession. Escrow will also assist the seller in settling any outstanding liens or mortgages unless the buyer is assuming these as part of the transaction. Additionally, escrow will facilitate the accounting settlement of all contractual closing costs including broker compensation, prorated and transfer taxes, title insurance, lender fees, escrow fees, insurance, HOA transfers or negotiated assessments, and any agreed-upon expenses such as a home warranty. This pivotal stage marks both an exciting milestone and relief for both sides of the transaction.

When it comes to the transfer, a truly satisfying real estate experience will resonate long after the property changes hands. It's not merely about closing a transaction; it's about celebrating strategies crafted with integrity, honoring the contract terms, and respecting established timelines. These foundational principles, once the hallmark of a successful closing, are often overlooked in today's industry vocabulary. When both buyer and seller fulfill their obligations with care, then the seller is more likely to leave the property better than expected, funds are deposited and available on time, keys and final instructions are handed over to the buyer with pride, and the seller receives their expected net proceed funds. Everyone walks away feeling pleased and secure, with these moments marking more than the end of complex negotiations; they reflect a *REcoded* real estate experience that provides the lasting impression of a transaction done right.

This **mindful approach** to the transaction process does not diminish a broker's competitive drive to negotiate or their determination to navigate impending challenges with a "win," nor the nervous adrenaline spikes buyers and sellers experience before, during, and after the sale. Instead, it channels that energy into a framework that values strategy, adaptability, and aligned intent: ultimately leading to a stronger, more rewarding outcome for everyone involved.

RELATIONSHIPS

Real Estate Firm Sets the Foundation for Real Estate Relationships

Tried and True. A real estate firm is not just a place for brokers to hang a license but indeed a true nucleus of influence within the community. The most respected firms serve as both launchpads and polestars for their brokers, offering a place to practice real estate while nurturing growth through mentorship, support, and a commitment to integrity. These firms do more than simply facilitate complex property transactions for clients; they shape brokers into determined professionals who elevate the real estate experience and contribute to their community—often in behind-the-scenes ways. Many of these firms and their brokers are unsung heroes who support local teams, the arts, businesses, and charitable initiatives without seeking recognition. Their influence is felt far beyond the closing table, as they become trusted pillars in the effort to help communities build wealth and lasting connections.

Generous. A committed firm shares its wisdom, reinforces integrity by teaching contract fluency, and nourishes relationships with trusted local industry partners. These firms create a network of expertise by forming alliances with attorneys, title companies, lenders, inspectors, stagers, and escrow professionals—each contributing to a satisfying real estate experience. These industry partners not only support the success of every client they serve but also ensure the firm's commitment to assist the community in building long-term wealth together.

Established. Firms are deeply vested in their communities, work tirelessly to build a strong reputation, and proudly cultivate connections to provide reliable resources to those they serve. With this foundation, their brokers are empowered to focus on advocating while sharing these resources with buyers and sellers. Industry relationships often go unnoticed, but they are what set the best brokers apart from their less experienced peers: differentiating professionals who provide true value from those who simply act as app-assigned licensees. Anyone can search the web for a lender or plumber, but when a vendor is deeply invested in a long-term relationship with a firm or broker, they share a commitment to the client's long-term success. This partnership increases the likelihood of receiving timely, dependable service and ensures the fulfillment of contractual obligations. It's this network of trusted professionals that forms the backbone of a quality real estate experience.

Broker-Client Relationships

In the past, the "agent" model was not designed as a partnership but instead to simply broker an owner's property with a buyer for a fee: leveraging a licensed agent's personality, strengths, and ties to the community to fulfill a transaction. Necessary agency disclosures were provided, with broker-client relationships typically acknowledged after services began via a purchase and/or sale contract.

Is there a difference now? Absolutely. Today, buyers and sellers each enter into short-term partnerships with their respective brokers through a negotiated agency agreement, with transparent compensation outlined before any services are performed. Each broker, in turn, is committed to acting in their client's best interest. This may sound repetitive, but there's a purpose. Hang in there…

No matter what, expect procedure. To ensure compliance, real estate firms use systems to stay organized, transparent, and accountable. During your consultation, it's not unusual for a broker to present documents (e.g., disclosures or disclaimers) before a formal representation agreement is signed. These might include pamphlets outlining agency disclosures, fair housing, wire fraud, and environmental hazards (to name but a few), each part of a formality designed to inform, prepare, and protect your experience. While these documents are separate from a negotiated *agency agreement,* they signal that both the firm and broker are committed to professionalism, transparency, and protecting your interests before any services are agreed upon.

Not obliged. Receiving these documents does not obligate you to formal representation, which only occurs once a written agency agreement is in place—but how they're delivered *does* demonstrate how the broker will communicate, prepare, and prioritize a client's needs. While a delivery completed with preparation and care can signal quality service in the future, one without explanation and dismissed as routine formality can possibly prophesize a lack of attention to detail when it comes time to negotiate. With this protocol calling for skill and competency, pay attention during any presentation prior to hiring a broker.

Real estate professionals can operate under two key sets of legal obligations: **Statutory** duties imposed by state law and/or **fiduciary** duties that prioritize the client's interests above their own, act with loyalty, integrity, and good faith, maintain confidentiality, and avoid conflicts of interest. Upholding these responsibilities isn't just a matter of ethics but a structured commitment.

Broker-to-Broker Relationships

Despite one's best efforts, **positive and forward-moving energy** can get lost in the negotiation phases often due to opposing desires and a lack of collaboration toward a common goal. Let's be clear, though: negotiations need not mimic reality TV with cryptic confrontation, microaggressions, or drama. During the hiring process, it is difficult to know how a broker will operate during future negotiations as the consultation is typically focused on your *needs* and *wants*, current market activity, and how to achieve your desired goal.

> *Earnest Hint: It's often not the loudest voice in the room that protects your best interests. A grounded broker doesn't need to grandstand, chase recognition over results, or dominate the conversation: behaviors that tend to center the broker, not your experience. Instead, competent professionals lead with humility, stay composed, and remain fully tuned into your outcome—not their ego. Not every polished pitch equals a meaningful partnership, so stay mindful of those chasing signatures more so than shared success.*

Respect and diplomacy are how successful brokers approach negotiations. They use strategy, not ego, and treat the process as a collaborative problem-solving exercise. For both buyers and sellers, the key to feeling empowered and not held hostage is preparation. Take time with your broker to strategize more than one negotiation approach. This flexibility allows you to pivot with confidence, leaving emotional reactions behind as new information or shifting circumstances arise.

Negotiation challenges can be overcome when both parties **use cognitive empathy**—viewing the situation through another's perspective—and **practice active listening**, giving full attention without interruption. These techniques are not new, but some have dismissed them as signs of weakness or inefficiency while mistaking emotional intelligence for a lack of agency. In truth, they are the mark of a skilled broker. Brokers who remain open-minded and demonstrate understanding by asking clarifying questions and providing thoughtful responses elevate the negotiation process and lead their clients to satisfying outcomes more quickly and with greater trust.

With **emails and texts** documenting the real estate experience, parties to a transaction should not begin with **personal biases and assumptions**. Instead, approach written exchanges with **a neutral attitude** to avoid preconceived notions or opinions, and focus on the **actual words and facts** presented. This is difficult without practice, as life decisions are not made every day, and it is convenient to fall prey to emotions or past beliefs and not trust the process. Implement **objective reading** by pausing to evaluate the information based on evidence and logic.

By **eliminating an assumed tone** when reading a text or email, especially during negotiations, you can avoid misunderstandings that distract from facts and delay *REsolutions*. This is where an **agency partnership proves invaluable**, your broker guiding you through standardized contracts and forms (written and approved by attorneys) and helping you navigate offers and counteroffers with calm, clarity, and intention.

There's **no need to gamify** your real estate journey with ambiguous messaging, reactive tendencies, or performative behavior. Instead, hire a broker who leads with *REspect*, consideration, and professional technique. A trusted partner offers the flexibility to adapt as needed without making you feel like a hostage to the process or opposing party. The sooner both sides reach #MA with clarity and collaboration, the more committed they'll be to honoring the agreement—and the more likely everyone arrives at closing feeling respected and satisfied.

Caution: Don't REpeat past buying or selling mistakes or REvert to past belief systems (e.g., if the negotiation was "too easy," that must mean the broker "didn't negotiate in your best interest" and therefore "didn't earn their commission"). If negotiations were efficient, then take the experience for what it was; both parties entered negotiations well informed, created a plan accordingly, prepared alternative strategies, and collaborated with the intent of reaching mutual acceptance. Drop the mic—it can be that satisfying. **Negotiations don't need to be a battle when the upfront work is done thoughtfully.**

Trusting Relationships

Trust is mutual and, when extended thoughtfully, is earned through consistent, intentional actions. After entering a partnership with an agency agreement but #B4MA, if communication is rushed or lacking, it's common to feel anxious and lose confidence. This can undermine the foundation needed for a productive, trusting collaboration during negotiations.

> ***Two-way Trust REminder:*** *A trusting real estate relationship begins with a two-way consultation where the broker shares market insights and contract knowledge so you gain understanding while strategizing and planning your desired transaction experience together. This consultation builds trust to support your why, prioritize your needs, clarify your wants, and verify if the timing works to forge an authentic agency partnership in your best interest. Be curious, be open, and be honest.*

Maintaining trust involves respecting healthy boundaries, communicating efficiently, being present during negotiations, and collaborating through contingency periods with the shared intent to fulfill obligations, meet deadlines, and close successfully. Choose a broker who is not only saturated with competence and knowledge but whose business is built on referrals and repeat clients: a reflection of consistent advocacy, proven results, and a reputation earned through trust.

ETIQUETTE

Real estate has its own set of unspoken and/or often-overlooked rules; understanding and respecting them can make a difference during your journey. Whether you're buying or selling, these subtle etiquette tips are designed to help you avoid any embarrassment and instead cultivate a sense of confidence and control so you can navigate your experience like a pro.

Give yourself time. Acclimation is a form of etiquette, an intentional pause (before entering the market) stabilizing you to observe without attachment, evaluate without pressure, and resist the urge to act on desire or competitive emotion. It's how you respect your own process: unbiased, informed, and free from outside influence.

Due Diligence Etiquette #B4MA

Impress yourself by choosing the right broker. As you acclimate to the market—an essential part of your due diligence—be proactive in reviewing listing details, marketing remarks, and social media posts. Local brokers (during consultations, open houses or on their social media pages) may share knowledge regarding common environmental factors, trends, and area specific customs that can influence your future experience. Any hint should prompt curiosity, so ask questions to learn customs and processes about newfound factors while taking steps towards due diligence.

When compiling your list of brokers to interview, prioritize those who not only share their knowledge but also contribute meaningfully to their community (e.g., via fundraising, community clean-ups, food drives, and other local initiatives). Don't assume that a strong social media presence automatically means a broker is the right fit for your personal journey. Instead, focus on brokers who genuinely contribute by educating, sharing market updates objectively (not just good news), and celebrating others—signs they are true advocates. This due diligence etiquette helps you make informed, thoughtful decisions based on genuine insights rather than superficial impressions.

Partner with purpose. A common frustration among buyers and sellers is the perception that brokers care more about compensation than their clients. In truth, the best brokers are deeply invested in their clients' success and work tirelessly to guide them through every step of the journey. Real estate professionals navigate constant challenges: managing expectations, analyzing market activity, handling rejected offers, negotiating repairs, and balancing their clients' emotions with their own. While compensation is a part of the equation, it is not the driving force for the most dedicated brokers—who view this as a natural result of their commitment to delivering value and achieving the best possible outcome for their clients. A strong broker makes time to set the foundation for your experience early on by preparing you for out-of-pocket expenses, difficult or rapid decisions, and reality—with truth, not dismissal—demonstrating competence as they help you weigh your options throughout the journey.

Strategize and compensate. Regardless of how you find your broker—whether online or through referral—ensure they invest real time in outlining your path ahead rather than rushing straight to presenting agency paperwork focused solely on their compensation. While all brokers are required to present an agency agreement (as previously mentioned), this should not dominate the conversation. Your time should be spent learning a strategy that feels clear, intentional, and aligned with your goals before committing to agency representation. The best etiquette is to respect time, knowing this step should not take hours if you acclimated. Be transparent about your intentions, commit to the process, and ensure the consultation remains focused on a balanced discussion of strategy and agency representation.

Remember consultation etiquette. This involves not assuming brokers know you are "shopping" candidates. If you are interviewing more than one, it's common courtesy to inform each broker that you are seeking options to find the best match for your experience. Time cannot be returned, so do not hesitate to exercise transparency in fear of disappointment; brokers will respect this as they are accustomed to competing and will heed accordingly to earn your business. This openness will extract their best methodology during your consultation, helping you discern if they will invest in your journey. The more prepared you are for consultations, the more quickly you can absorb their level of competence: displacing any vulnerability and staying in control of the "hiring" process.

Referral etiquette is involved as well. As a courtesy, if you're interviewing a broker referred to you by a confidant, consultation etiquette needs to apply during your first conversation if you intend to interview other brokers. Your confidant may have referred and introduced you to a broker they trust, who in turn may unintentionally streamline the process and skip customary steps usually reserved for new clients due to the direct connection. This isn't a reflection of deficient professionalism; rather, it stems from the shared rapport that comes with a trusted *REferral*. Brokers appreciate transparency as they juggle their time between new prospects, existing business, and personal obligations. While they're not afraid of competition, upfront transparency from prospective clients helps lay a foundation of mutual respect for time and fosters straightforward communication to move forward into an aligned partnership.

Agency Agreement Etiquette

REcoding the real estate experience starts within the industry, reinforcing client agency and extending respect for existing agency relationships. Brokers are tasked with asking prospects if they've already entered into agreements with other brokers to ensure compliance and uphold ethical business practices, a transparent process to honor agency agreement etiquette.

Standardized agreement language in both types of representation agreements—buyer agency and listing (seller) agreements—designate you as the principal and identify the firm and individual broker providing services, outlining the duration of the agreement, compensation terms owed to the firm and broker, and when and how this compensation is paid.

Most agreements also request you consent to or decline limited dual agency, allowing your broker to represent both you and the opposing party in the same transaction.

Proper etiquette is for the broker to fully explain limited dual agency (and no agency) and not pass off these options as routine.

For buyers, the most effective brokers mindfully elevate the experience by not fixating on loopholes in another firm's agency agreements or strategizing how to override them (which is poor etiquette). Instead, they focus on enhancing their own market expertise, demonstrating their competence in contract law, and offer exceptional service: positioning themselves as the obvious, trusted choice during a consultation. Top brokers don't need to persuade a prospective buyer to abandon an existing agreement but instead show up so prepared, competent, and aligned with the client's goals that the decision is effortless. This can be easier said than done, as timing is everything with buyer agency agreement, and some clients are unknowingly committed to undesired representation.

For sellers, the most effective brokers mindfully elevate the experience by providing what the current competition is offering to compensate a buyer's broker in that market. A listing agreement will include an option for the seller to offer compensation to a buyer's broker with clear terms for how that fee is structured and when it applies. Sellers deserve to have current data to make an informed decision in their best interest. With this knowledge, sellers can then strategize and negotiate their listing agreement to best position their property to compete and outshine their competition.

Buyer Agency Etiquette #B4MA

A **non-exclusive agency agreement is like** *casual dating*; buyers keep their options open and see multiple people (brokers) to find the right match in the absence of a firm commitment. However, because there's no exclusivity, no single broker is fully invested in your success and may prioritize other clients who have exclusively committed to them. Yes, you can explore different approaches, but there's no guarantee of loyalty or priority from any one broker since a *non-exclusive agency agreement* may imply you are working with others.

When it comes to a **multiple non-exclusive agreement**, etiquette is to verify if you can simultaneously enter this and clarify the consequences if terms overlap to avoid owing multiple brokers compensation.

Non-exclusive buyer etiquette is to disclose to each broker that you have entered into other agreements and are therefore working with multiple brokers. Brokers should not project shame or guilt for this choice. Instead, they should aim to secure an *exclusive agency agreement* by providing value through market insights and contract knowledge and strategizing earnestly in your best interest. Do not take it personally if a broker does not choose to enter a *non-exclusive agency agreement* with you.

With respect to the length of non-exclusive agency agreements, I recommend a short-term arrangement—ideally one or two days and no more than 30—with clear parameters filtering for the broker most dedicated to your *why*, one who will set intentions to meet your needs and endeavor to connect with you and build a trusting relationship. Keep in mind some firms and brokers have a business model to only work with buyers who agree to a traditional *exclusive agreement*, ensuring they spend their time and advice on a committed partner.

What about combination agreements? Some MLSs or Real Estate Association forms give you the option to enter into a *non-exclusive agency agreement and an exclusive agency* agreement at the same time. Etiquette is to verify specified search terms of each agreement are distinctly unique and do not overlap (i.e., different cities, districts, zip codes, etc.) to protect you as the buyer from an unintentional financial obligation to more than one broker for overlapping consented terms.

An **exclusive agency agreement is like an official, committed relationship**; you've chosen one partner (broker) who will prioritize your goals, be your advocate, and fully invest their time and expertise into making your real estate experience a success.

In return, exclusive etiquette is rooted in transparent communication, mutual loyalty, and a collaborative approach that fosters strategic flexibility, all aimed at being offer-ready to achieve your optimal outcome.

Buyer Agency Etiquette: Key Takeaways

- Non-Exclusive = Brief Priority
- Make Aware, Don't Overshare
- Make Short-Term Trial a Best Practice
- Watch for Overlap Risks; They'll Cost You
- Not All Brokers Offer Non-Exclusive Agreements; It's Not Personal
- Exclusive = Full Commitment

Seller Agency Etiquette #B4MA

A **listing agreement** is a seller's agency agreement. In addition to the standardized agreement language already mentioned and transparent compensation, the agreement outlines responsibilities, marketing, and expectations.

Strategizing expectations is an essential part of seller etiquette, and it is appropriate to outline key expectancies. For sellers, this includes preparing the property for market according to a pre determined strategy and completing all required disclosures with honesty and transparency. It should also extend to specific expectancies regarding decluttering, deep cleaning, and necessary repairs to improve the property's condition—along with a possible financial commitment for professional staging, photography, and a virtual tour.

Agreement anticipations outline how and when buyer brokers may access the property (e.g., through a key box system) and authorize the listing firm to market the property through the

MLS, social media, signage, and other promotional efforts. Proper etiquette is to create a showing plan you can realistically accommodate, while still allowing for meaningful exposure. Once listed, the property becomes public knowledge— reinforcing the importance of anticipating likely negotiation requests in advance so you can remain grounded, strategic, and performance-able. Entering the market with clear expectations and prepared responses positions you to receive the most amount of money in the least amount of time with confidence and control.

Misrepresentation or omission etiquette is much like the Golden Rule ("Do unto others as you would have them do unto you"). This emphasizes treating others with the same fairness and respect you would want for yourself. Disclose what you know!

A well-prepared listing broker thoroughly verifies every detail— disclosures, title report, supporting documents, and HOA packets—demonstrating good broker etiquette by showing respect for the listing process and ensuring buyers encounter transparency from the start. This level of careful attention is in the seller's best interest, reflecting professionalism and a commitment to attracting serious buyers.

Seller Agency Etiquette: Key Takeaways

- Know What's Expected of You (And When)
- Gather Property Info & Share to Disclose
- Be Realistic (Location/Condition) & Price to Sell

- Know Obligations to Perform and Close
- Prep for Public Knowledge & Broker Access
- Move-Out Plan = Ready to Execute

Real Estate Industry Etiquette

REgaining **public trust** and upholding ethical standards is crucial for preserving the integrity of the real estate profession. As real estate customs have become compromised with technology eroding face-to-face communication (good intentions meant to save time), Wall Street speculators and some venture capitalists (VCs) have created apps intended to bypass professional brokers and advocacy: preying on convenience and buyer/seller vulnerability. For the industry to thrive, competent professionals must regain trust by fully equipping you for your experience, foster collaborative synergy, correct misunderstandings, and work to resolve any conflicts to provide a level of service apps cannot match.

REvitalizing **industry etiquette** is to show respect for the competition, compete fairly, negotiate and advocate honestly, and work together productively to ensure the real estate profession remains utilized, transparent, indispensable, and valued. Buyers and sellers deserve dedicated, full-time professionals who provide principled client care—not impersonal apps that create the illusion of expert service while prioritizing shareholder profits over client interests.

REbuilding **advocacy:** Advocacy in real estate is not just about supporting clients; it's about competing with integrity, ensuring their best interests are always front and center. A broker who advocates for their clients does so by balancing fierce competition with professionalism, never compromising their ethical standards. When choosing a broker, ensure they have a seasoned track record of advocacy—one that speaks to both their competitive edge and commitment to trust, transparency, and service. Integrity, like decorum and etiquette, may often be invisible—silently radiating outward and expanding in all directions. Yet, it's precisely these same qualities that help build lasting success and attract strong, collaborative partnerships in a highly competitive industry.

Breaking Up is Hard to Do

Need to end the partnership? This is possible #B4MA, not after. Take accountability and apply "sooner rather than later" etiquette if the partnership is not aligned or circumstances have changed. It happens! You can become disenchanted with a broker, but not being the "professional" in the partnership is not an excuse to not properly address issues promptly. While it's in everyone's best interest to strive for a resolution that preserves the relationship, it's important to be brave and forthright and make a call if this isn't possible.

REdirecting you during your experience is in your best interest and a core part of your broker's role, even when it doesn't feel that way in the moment. At times, brokers may reflect market realities you'd rather not hear and ask you to pivot. **Their**

responsibility is to guide you with clarity, not always with comfort. This *Mindful Real Estate Guide* is designed to help minimize unnecessary emotion, but it's indeed natural to feel disappointment when the market offers more options that meet your wants rather than your true needs.

> ***REspectful REminder:*** *This is a professional relationship built on trust and service. If, after honest reflection, you feel the partnership is no longer the right fit, don't "break up" over text. Have the courage to call, express your concerns respectfully, and follow up in writing to formally terminate the agency agreement. Transparency, even in closure, is a sign of respect—and a practice worth carrying into your next real estate experience.*

It's About You: Final #B4MA Reminders

REflecting the principle of "**cause and effect,**" one's deeds eventually return to them—our behaviors and choices directly influencing the results we experience. Once you've selected a broker and signed an exclusive agency agreement, etiquette is to reach out to other brokers you consulted with to end the dating phase: letting them know you've made your choice and thanking them for sharing their time and expertise. This may seem obvious, but people avoid this step to prevent disappointment, guilt, or a possible confrontation. While it can sting for a broker to hear that a client has chosen someone else, clear communication ultimately allows everyone to refocus their energy.

After #MA: Contract Etiquette

Now that you have reached #MA, the rhythm of the transaction begins and triggers all the conditions agreed upon to commence. While many of the obligations are on the buyer to meet, a seller's broker instinctively aims to **compress the timelines** and apply undue pressure to have contract contingencies met, waived, or removed prior to already-granted specified timelines.

As previously mentioned, buyers (armed with the aforementioned SWOT strategy) should display good etiquette in making their best effort to schedule all visits requiring property access: inspectors, contractors, and specialists on the same day when possible. By doing so, they concentrate efforts and time, minimize disruption to the seller's routine and property, and show respect to the pending process. Naturally, this takes planning and is not always achievable; but most importantly, this consideration requires concentrated etiquette to stay focused.

Why is there pressure to compress? Once contingencies are removed, the buyer cannot exercise the right to terminate without losing their earnest money; this is in the seller's best interest.

Brokers offer valuable agency services and work hard on behalf of their clients, cooperating and navigating a transaction to work through obligations and perform in a timely way. Nothing is more frustrating to a buyer's broker—who is working diligently to guide the buyer toward making confident decisions—than receiving calls, texts, or emails from the seller's broker early in the contingency process, subtly micropressuring for a contingency response. This is an example of poor broker etiquette.

Contract terms clearly state when the buyer needs to respond. It is not unethical to inquire, but it does lack decorum and disrespects the process if done prematurely. Sellers and brokers can cross their fingers for the buyer to remove contingencies early but remain obliged to honor the defined contractual terms.

Buyer Etiquette After #MA: P.R.E.P.A.R.E. to Close

P: Promptly deliver earnest money to honor the agreement and initiate the transaction rhythm.

R: Review and verify documentation thoroughly, then reply to comply with conditional timelines.

E: Evaluate the property in one consolidated site visit with inspectors/advisors to focus efforts.

P: Pull details first, not overwhelming with scattered questions before cross-referencing documentation.

A: Apply for financing and deliver documentation per the terms of the contract.

R: Respect time, implement alternative strategies, and pivot to collaborate for contingency removal.

E: Execute the final steps: Complete the walk-through, transfer funds, and close with confidence.

Seller Etiquette After #MA: H.O.N.O.R. to Receive

H: **Honor** the contract. Respect the contingency periods per the terms of the contract.

O: **Offer** timely access and answers. Respond to inquiries without taking anything personally.

N: **Nurture** to collaborate by extending respect to maintain communication.

O: **Organize** supporting documents. Be ready to provide receipts, warranties, or service records.

R: **Ready** the property better than expected to receive net proceed funds. Hand off the property proudly by completing repairs, scheduling cleaning, and moving out on time, so closing is a celebration, not a scramble.

Trusted Resource Referral Etiquette

The foundation of a successful broker business is supplemented and maintained with personal **and** professional relationships, combining a blend of trusted networks.

Brokers proudly serve their clients before, during, and after the closing of a property and find joy in acting as a *REliable* resource for solid and dependable referrals. What they may not openly share is that they have invested a lot of time and effort in building trust with these silent partners who are instrumental to everyone's success in their community. With referral etiquette, please treat these precious resources and their time with respect.

1. **Do not assume** the referred resource will offer a discount.

2. **Be prepared to pay** a premium for expedient attention.

3. **Pay on time** the trusted referral invoice, especially if the dependable referral moved you to the top of the list so you could meet a contractual obligation.

4. **Provide constructive feedback** to create opportunities for improvement, adjustments, or removal from the broker's trusted resource list; they want to align referral resources with their business model.

As the saying goes: "What goes around comes around." Brokers, likewise, need their reliable referrals paid and not left hanging so they will *REciprocate* and continue to be devoted to the next client in need—just as they did for you.

Pay it Forward

***REfer* your broker.** If your broker served you well and provided a great experience, consider paying it forward by connecting them to friends, family, or colleagues who may need guidance. Don't overthink it—your role isn't to ensure a perfect outcome. It's up to the professional to deliver exceptional service and up to the prospect to engage seriously. A simple introduction can go a long way in connecting someone to the right expertise.

No matter how successful a broker is in building their business, the industry does have cycles, and brokers will experience a lull every so often (disappointing but true). Nothing uplifts a broker more than a referral from a client, especially knowing that actively promoting others does not come naturally for some folks. When a potential buyer or seller referral comes in, helping the broker build a referral base, it greatly boosts any professional's confidence—especially when it's challenging to create opportunities for new business.

Initiate the connection. As a client, referral etiquette means taking a moment to make a thoughtful introduction. A simple yet credible way to do this is by starting a group text or email when possible. This small effort creates valuable synergy, reinforcing trust between both parties.

Deeply grateful, genuinely thankful. Just know that any referral is deeply appreciated and brokers are always grateful when a satisfied client makes the connection. Be bold in promoting professionals who have served you well. Investing in them helps *REplenish* the community, connecting more people to quality service as everyone builds wealth together.

▼

This concludes the <u>Download</u> for buyers and sellers. Offering a refresher for some, new perspective for others, and a starter kit for those entering the real estate process, it aims to remove ignorance, give clarity, and empower you to take responsibility to be #stronger&smarter during your real estate experiences. With CORE establishing balance, stability, and overall strength during a transaction, buyers and sellers reduce the risk of dissatisfaction because they trust themselves. Real estate, which has customs, structure, systems, and processes, must pause to *REincorporate* **mindful** practices for its own well-being. If each party reads each section to prepare appropriately—leveling up with new enlightened perspectives in *REspect* to others—then fewer surprises will be had as part of a more satisfying experience. Remain open to *REceive*, stay grounded and engaged, use discipline and your voice, trust your heart, and consciously create a wise transactional experience. This is just the beginning of a holistic approach to your real estate wisdom.

THE BUYER'S MINDFUL APPROACH

*The buyer's inner compass:
a tool for gaining insight, eliminating
anxiety and doubt, and trusting intuition
throughout the buying journey
to align with their vision.*

Mindful Strategy

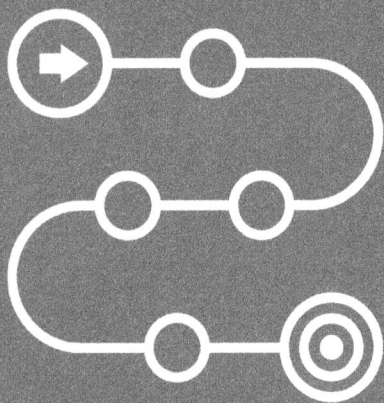

The Buyer's Journey

This mindful buyer section builds on the <u>Download</u> to help you *REcode* your approach to buying—creating control, clarity, and confidence by removing both practical and emotional barriers that can interfere with a satisfying real estate experience. Many people believe property ownership is reserved for the wealthy, which isn't true. Not everyone chooses to own, but for those who do, success begins within—with a willingness to learn, discipline, readiness, and strategy.

For some, the idea of owning property feels distant, maybe even unattainable. Whether shaped by generational programming, financial uncertainty, or self-worth doubts, these beliefs can quietly sabotage confidence before the process even begins. This section helps you recognize and release those barriers, transforming uncertainty into confidence and preparation into performance.

I've seen buyers at every stage prove the same truth: you *can* buy property, and you *do* deserve this.

Start by grounding yourself in your "why." *Why* do you want to buy? Perhaps to secure a property where your costs are predictable for the long-term, enjoy a stable and fulfilling lifestyle, or have greater access to health services, schools, and amenities that matter to you. Maybe you want to establish roots, engage more fully with a community, and/or create financial stability to leverage for future plans. Anchoring yourself in this deeper purpose provides clarity and resilience when the search process presents trade-offs, delays, or unexpected challenges.

Perhaps you're reading this guide because you've done a "rent vs. buy" analysis and are preparing for your first purchase to step onto the property ladder with plans to eventually sell and buy again. Or maybe you've bought before and had a less-than-ideal experience and are now ready to mindfully *REcode* your next one. Even if it's been a while since your last transaction, taking the time to refresh your knowledge and approach is a meaningful investment in yourself.

As you weigh your next move, consider the opportunity cost—not only in dollars but in what acting now could offer such as the chance to grow your financial foundation, diversify your investments, allocate resources toward what matters most, and deepen your connection to a community where you live, work, and belong. Sometimes the greatest cost isn't financial at all but instead the experiences, growth, relationships, and security possibly missed if you wait. Thoughtful, intentional action can transform a transaction into a stepping stone toward a richer, more fulfilling life.

Most buyers need some cash, whether saved or gifted; if you anticipate receiving help, it's wise to start those discussions early (especially to take advantage of gift tax rules that might apply). If you've been steadily employed, you may qualify for financing. While qualifying for a loan takes planning and preparation, there's no wrong time to start. Real estate industry partners such as local lenders, financial planners, or money coaches are skilled at guiding these uncomfortable conversations and can even offer tools to help you talk with family or friends about potential gift funds. The financial industry isn't just here for investors; it's built to support and serve real people like you who want to own a space rather than rent a moment.

As a buyer, you deserve clarity—not confusion—throughout your journey. This guide is your resource for making informed decisions without second-guessing. While market shifts and industry pressures continue to evolve, one thing remains unchanged in the process: your local real estate professionals are here to serve, advocate, and protect your best interests. Owning property is more than a transaction but a belief in your future. Motivation, discipline, strategy, vision, and a solid plan are what create the pathway to ownership—**and with it, the chance to build equity, stability, and long-term wealth.**

The Mindful Buyer

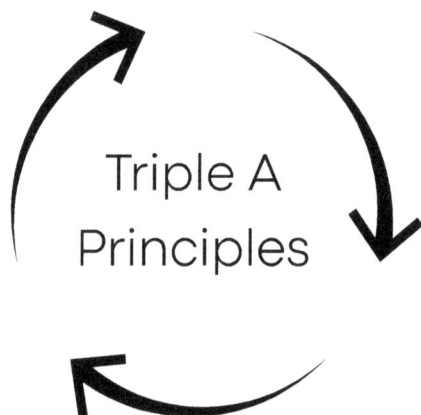

Triple A
Principles

The Triple A Principles: Acclimate, Agency, & Align

Buying a property involves more than just executing a plan around your *why*, with emotional elements often involved as well. Keeping an open mind, gaining knowledge, and staying positive throughout it all can help you develop trust with a real estate professional as you seek to learn market trends, comprehend contract expectations and consequences, and have the strength to navigate necessary decisions to achieve your purchasing goal.

As mentioned in the <u>Download</u> section, getting acclimated is a valuable step as you prepare to compete in the real estate market, enter an agency relationship, and align a strategy to negotiate and meet contractual obligations to ensure a successful purchase. The following Triple As—Acclimate, Agency, and Align—will benefit you and reduce stress so you can be faithful to your strategy and more confident in your decision-making pathway to achieve property ownership.

ACCLIMATE

Belief Matters. If you didn't purchase a property during the stabilization period that occurred after the Great Recession but before COVID-19, you may feel a sense of panic: this anxiety perhaps stemming from missing out on the appreciation and wealth security current property owners reap. When inventory becomes dangerously low, purchasing caters to buyers with a stable income who absorb any remaining inventory in a predatory manner thanks to the ever present fear of missing out (FOMO).

Restoring Access to Ownership. Many aspiring buyers face an uphill battle—not just from rising prices or interest rates but from a growing share of properties held by institutional investors such as real estate investment trusts (REITs). These entities, backed by shareholders, often acquire and retain inventory to maximize portfolio value, boost dividends, and deliver returns—primarily to wealthier investors.

This approach converts once-accessible properties into long-term rentals, limiting inventory available to owner-occupants and deepening wealth disparities by removing affordable entry points into homeownership. Awareness is the first step, though, so don't be discouraged—be determined! You deserve the opportunity to own property and build equity, which can indeed become a reality with strategy, support, and preparation.

I envision a future where REITs and portfolio managers **leverage their scale and influence to create measurable impact**, returning portions of their rental portfolios to the open market in ways that empower first-time and move-up buyers.

By doing so, they not only strengthen communities and enable wealth-building but also demonstrate that forward-thinking stewardship and profitability are not mutually exclusive— innovation and impact can go hand in hand. Solutions like lease-to-own programs for their renters or internal financing options can help bridge the ownership gap, preserving investor returns while restoring pathways to ownership for those ready to take that step.

Inventory lacking in your desired locale right now? Don't shrug off the prospect of owning at some point in the future! There's still time to strategize your ownership path and build deserved wealth. This guide, likewise, mindfully lays a foundation of knowledge to bake confidence into your future purchase experience and remove any existing belief systems—such as that only the wealthy can own real estate!

Market Activity: Location, Condition, & Pricing

Committing to learning a new language, adopting vocabulary and navigating unfamiliar procedures—such as financial responsibility, contract law, and due diligence—requires consistent courage, especially for first-time buyers. *REcoding* the Real Estate Experience equips you to divide the journey into two key phases. The first phase, prior to mutual acceptance (#B4MA), is focused on understanding the complexities and preparing for successful negotiations.

Once mutual acceptance (#MA) is reached, the second phase begins with the focus shifting to fulfilling contractual obligations, addressing contingencies, and ensuring a smooth path to closing. This phase is where all the groundwork laid in the first phase influences the outcome, allowing you to confidently traverse the final steps toward ownership.

The <u>Download</u> section prepares you to track the market's pulse and initiate due diligence, but now—as you move forward in your buying journey—it's time to gain sharper insight and clearer intention to position yourself as willing, able, and armed with deliberate knowledge.

Refine Your Eye During Acclimation. Acclimation isn't just about waiting for listings to enter the market simply to observe them shift into "pending" status; it's about training your eye to identify patterns, evaluate marketing claims, and interpret presentations beyond face value. Studying the market's pulse gives you a strategic edge as a buyer. By chunking "available", "pending", and "sold" listings into manageable units (e.g., by zip code, district, or price) and reviewing them consistently (perhaps weekly), you can detect trends, retain critical insights, and anticipate how sellers price their location and condition to attract buyers. Equipped with this knowledge—especially if sellers are offering compensation to a buyer broker—you can enter the market prepared to negotiate, make timely decisions, and fulfill obligations with clarity and confidence, acting strategically rather than reactively.

When listing remarks say "recently updated," ask yourself: Does that mean surface cosmetics or meaningful improvements like updated systems and remodeled upgrades? Pause to match marketing language with listing photos, virtual tours, and floor plans to discern how price aligns with location and condition. Then follow up on properties after they close to learn from real outcomes: Did the buyer successfully negotiate on the price or receive paid closing costs? Were any repairs completed? Did features such as parking or other unique attributes live up to expectations? These observations sharpen your judgment and help you anticipate what to expect when it's your turn to buy.

Acclimation is not yet about your personal *needs* and *wants*—which will come when you meet with your buyer broker—but instead focusing on condition and value alignment with your price parameters. Begin to notice what buyers accept, which inventory is moving quickly, and which brokers are consistently listing properties that sell efficiently: patterns revealing not just market rhythms but brokers who are guiding their sellers with skill and integrity in the location where you desire to own property.

Observe Broker Advocacy. As you acclimate, take note of brokers who proudly support local businesses and community initiatives. This consistency reveals their faith, loyalty, and credibility in a community, not just in real estate but in how they support others to build wealth *together*. Brokers who regularly share market insights and empower their community via education demonstrate they're invested in supporting both their clients and the neighborhoods they live or work in.

These professionals tend to reinvest their earnings into the communities they serve, building trust and credibility over time. When you see their listings move effortlessly or their names consistently associated with strong representation, this isn't by accident—it's earned. These are the brokers worth considering when you're ready for professional representation and to team up with a partner who'll help you craft your real estate success story.

Pay Attention to Market Movement. Acclimation provides an opportunity to pay attention to how properties move from "available" to "pending" as well as their condition. Are properties selling quickly even when they need remodeling, or do specific improvements truly accelerate sales? Do buyers pass on properties lacking fresh paint or with older roofs or unkept yards— and if so, would *you*? Are buyers indulging in updated kitchens, modernized bathrooms, and/or "smart" features? Pay attention to how much more buyers are willing to spend for added rooms, flexible layouts, or pet-friendly spaces. If listings in your preferred location linger, it might signal pricing is not aligned with buyer expectations—hinting that the market is shifting in your favor. On the flip side, if properties sell quickly regardless of condition, is there a pattern in pricing or presentation?

By observing what other buyers reject or accept, you'll begin to clarify which trade-offs in location, condition, and price you're willing to tolerate with your *why* in mind. Acclimation allows you to track buyer behavior in real time, helping you feel less anxious and more empowered to compete when it's time to negotiate price and terms to secure the right property.

Back on Market (BOMK). When a property's status shifts from "pending" to (BOMK), this is a valuable cue to **think critically.** Common causes include buyer's remorse, issues uncovered during the due diligence phase, or maybe a new listing prompting the original buyer to walk away from the transaction. Often, it comes down to an inability on the part of the seller and buyer to collaborate on a resolution—sometimes due to inspection findings. The seller may be unable or unwilling to address concerns, for example, causing the transaction to fall apart.

During acclimation, pay close attention to these scenarios, track patterns, and compile questions to bring into future consultations—especially for properties that interest you. This builds critical awareness of how buyers are navigating the market and gives you newfound wisdom as you prepare for strategy sessions. How a broker responds to such questions during a buyer agency consultation can reveal how they'll prepare and support you in your future transaction.

Listen closely: Do they offer insight into potential situations like BOMK? Can they speculate why a property went BOMK or what could have happened differently to prepare that buyer to avoid a failed experience? A broker's ability to prepare negotiation strategies with you, not just react to transaction challenges, is key to reducing your risk and elevating your real estate experience.

AGENCY

Benefits. One of the greatest benefits of working with a buyer broker is having a partner by your side who can help refine your *why* and compare to the current market conditions and then align "available" inventory with your *needs* and *wants* accordingly. They don't dismiss your emotions; they absorb them, helping you stay focused and grounded throughout your search. Your broker gives you the necessary perspective to prepare for due diligence, proposes strategies to meet obligations, and bestows context around contract law so you're ready when it's time to negotiate.

Beyond their own expertise, exceptional brokers gladly connect you with trusted industry partners—lenders, inspectors, and escrow officers—to form your team. These collaborative professionals are more than names on a list; they're invested in your outcome and dedicated to your success.

From Referral to Relationship. Finding the right buyer broker for representation can align in several ways. The most direct route? Going through a personal referral from friends, family, or colleagues, often trusted and *REliable* sources. Otherwise, those who responsibly acclimate by app and track the market can take note and start a list of who's consistently active in their target location and price range.

Fact Check: Don't be misled by paid ads in real estate apps. Brokers featured next to listings are often paying for placement and don't necessarily represent or are familiar with the specific property, nor are they necessarily local experts vested in your desired community. The listing broker and their firm are always disclosed as part of the property details.

Don't Skip and Click. If you're feeling anxious about a specific property before you have hired representation, pause before rushing to "click" and schedule a spontaneous showing. Brokers are required to secure an agency agreement before providing services (e.g., property tours) as a matter of compliance. Instead, stay firm and request a consultation to understand their buyer agency services. You're entitled to a consultation without committing to an agency agreement and can use that time to gather information and evaluate whether their approach aligns with your needs. Whether in a professional setting or via video, consultations are meant to build trust—not pressure to be hired.

Once you've simplified your potential representation list, you've likely followed these brokers' market activity and maybe even checked out their online presence. Now, it's time to interview them and find out if they're a fit with your personality and will match your motivation, share knowledge, and communicate with you in a sincere way during a consultation.

Face to Face. Some buyers prefer to meet a broker casually at an open house to get a sense of their personality, gauging chemistry before committing. Others take a more intentional route and schedule a buyer consultation in their firm's office, observing how they work and their process firsthand before committing.

Business Model & Boundaries. Most firms and brokers have a consultation protocol and operate with a defined compensation model. Brokers are required to ask if you are bound to an existing exclusive buyer agency agreement; if you're not, it's their chance to earn your business by focusing on your goals, demonstrating market insight, and sharing strategy. If the conversation addresses fees, and they respectfully remain committed to their business model, do not take it personally if they choose not to negotiate their compensation—it's a reflection of their professional clarity, not a personal rejection.

Representation That Honors Access, Not Privilege. Most buyer brokers can view all "available" inventory, yet some firms hold select listings in-house and thus not ensuring fair and equal access to all buyers in the market. These firms may entice buyers with "confidential showings" to their "off-market properties" or "exclusive listings" only accessible to buyers who have signed an exclusive agency agreement with the firm, which promises access to these non-cooperative listings— excluding buyers not signed with their firm.

While this may seem like a supposed benefit at first glance— fewer buyers to compete with—it's important to recognize that these exclusive listings are often priced at a premium (or above market value) since the firm's business model revolves around offering exclusive access to a limited pool of buyers. As a result, buyers may end up viewing properties whose location and condition are overpriced compared to similar, fully accessible listings that are truly testing the market and competing for buyers. These agency agreements may also confine full market access, restricting you from seeing all "available" properties. Be sure to verify during the consultation that you are entering into a true buyer agency agreement, not consenting to limited dual agency or no agency without fully understanding all the compromises.

Urgency, Not Advocacy. When full market access is limited, the pressure to act fast on what you are restricted to—and pay more—rises. Such firms often prioritize speed and sales volume over mindful representation, relying on buyer *urgency* rather than buyer *advocacy*. Inexperienced buyers may not be encouraged to conduct thorough due diligence, may face limited negotiation power and contingencies, or have their concerns brushed aside under the guise of privileged convenience. Don't compromise your advocacy without full approval, as the firm may have competing interests in selling those exclusive listings at a premium within a limited time frame: creating urgency for their benefit, not yours.

Exclusivity—Are You the Beneficiary? True representation isn't about limiting you or fast tracking you to a contract, it's about prioritizing your comprehension and ensuring you're aligned to access all "available" inventory, strategize favorable contractual terms, and empowered (not rushed) to make decisions for yourself rather than the seller or firm. Some of these firms are backed by investors or venture capitalists

(VCs) pressuring return on investment (ROI) and profit, not your protection. Transparency matters. When the process is open and clear—not in the fine print—and not limited to confidential insiders or restricted access, it fosters accountable compliance. Firms driven by outside investment often employ systems designed to close transactions quickly (not carefully), sometimes at the expense of integrity and professional standards. Choose representation that informs, empowers, and walks beside you—not just ahead of you.

> *Author Perspective: Even off-market or discreet listings can serve a purpose when done with full transparency and mutual consent. I've walked that line, closing deals quietly with both parties understanding the trade-offs and benefits. These cases, though, were always honest, intentional, and strategic—not marketing gimmicks dressed up as an exclusive advantage.*
>
> *While these "proven models" are often promoted as a competitive edge, it's important to recognize that these opportunities—though marketed for privacy and security—may not always serve your best interests. While exclusivity may appear to limit competition, it can also inflate prices. Incentives should be transparent and beneficial to both you and the seller.*

The FSBO Challenge: Why Buyer Representation Matters

Buying a "For Sale by Owner" (FSBO) property might seem appealing; maybe the price is right or the location and condition checks your *needs* and *wants* boxes. Without a buyer broker by your side to advise, advocate, and ensure compliance, this path can come with unnecessary risks.

Some buyers may hesitate to work with a broker due to concerns about the financial commitment required in an agency agreement, especially if the seller is not offering buyer broker compensation. Buyers often worry about affordability or feel unsure about how to negotiate a broker's fee within a future offer. However, choosing to focus solely on FSBOs limits your options and may lead you to compromise on important factors like location, condition, and price. FSBOs don't always reflect the true market value as they lack the competitive pressure that comes with broader buyer exposure. A FSBO receives fewer showings and limited feedback, which are crucial for gauging market demand and offering a realistic price. This allows the seller to remain in their bubble, waiting for someone unaware of other choices and without representation.

While the cost of working with a buyer's broker might initially seem like a concern, you forfeit access to their expertise, market knowledge, and access to a full range of properties in not doing so. This also extends to pre-approved and trusted industry partners—such as inspectors, appraisers, and other professionals—who will help you conduct thorough due diligence. Their involvement ensures you make informed decisions, negotiate favorable terms, and ultimately avoid overpaying, saving you time and money in the long run.

Touring FSBO homes also presents unique challenges. Often, the owner insists on personally guiding the tour (at their pace), sharing sentimental stories while making it difficult for you to take in and really feel the space to prepare a SWOT (strengths, weaknesses, opportunities, and threats) analysis. Without a broker to buffer, protect your pace, and guide the process, you may feel pressure to rush or avoid asking curious questions for fear of "offending" the seller. This tampers with due diligence.

Who ensures the FSBO seller meets all their legal obligations, including required disclosures and access? Who guarantees you have an uncompromised inspection period and appraisal and access to meet contractual timelines, tracks negotiated repairs, and reviews receipts and warranties? Who verifies the seller's move-out plan and oversees the final walk-through process? Without a buyer's broker, you take on these responsibilities— and the potential consequences—on your own, with no one to hold the seller accountable or protect your best interests.

Hiring a skilled buyer's broker will reduce your risks and:

- Hold the seller accountable and to industry standards to meet compliance.

- Offer guidance and strategies using market data to position your terms favorably.

- Negotiate concessions, repairs, or replacements.

- Coordinate timelines, appraisals, and closing requirements
- Ensure your rights are protected during the final walkthrough
- Establish the seller has left the property per the terms of the contract and you receive keys and take possession on time.

In the absence of professional advocacy, emotionally attached owners are known to derail negotiations, ignore compliance requirements, not respect time or contractual obligations and dismiss buyer concerns. If you opt for no agency representation—leaving yourself without a dedicated advocate—consider hiring a real estate attorney to review FSBO contracts and protect your interests. I've worked with many excellent attorneys over the years, and while they provide invaluable legal insight, most are not deeply familiar with local contingencies, MLS rule changes, or the nuances of revised contracts and their addendums. Attorneys typically focus on drafting, reviewing, and counseling on documents and contracts while a professional broker advocates for you and manages the entire transaction process: ensuring compliance and guiding the transaction every step of the way. Costly missteps are made when a competent professional doesn't oversee a FSBO seller's responsibilities. Your financial security and peace of mind shouldn't be left to chance.

***Wisecrack Warning: Be FSBO Careful.** Some sellers see real estate professionals—especially brokers—as commission-hungry intruders. These high-risk owners believe they know more than the experts, treat guidance as manipulation, and view disclosures as optional. They'll smile while sidestepping required forms and insist you're "getting a deal" so long as no one else gets paid. These sellers prey on buyer naiveté. Don't take on risk without professional advocacy.*

One FSBO exception? Current licensed real estate brokers who choose to sell their own properties. Unlike unlicensed FSBOs, professional brokers are held to a higher standard: their license requires them to follow state disclosure laws, grant access, and comply with contract obligations. It's in their best interest to accommodate, collaborate, and ensure compliance with a buyer and their broker.

If a FSBO property is your top choice, schedule a buyer consultation and hire a local experienced buyer's broker for representation and their competency.

The Buyer Consultation Process (#Needs&Wants, #Strategy&Success)

Plan a 30-minute consultation to personally explore each broker's take on market conditions, learn their buying strategy, and ascertain their competence with buyer agency agreements and purchase and/or sale contracts. If a buyer agency agreement is the first thing they present even before learning about your *why*, they may not be the right fit for you.

Feel out a potential partnership. Arrive ready to experience a broker's professionalism and gauge if they're eager to strategize and create a plan based on your *needs* and *wants* at your pace—not theirs. Are they actively listening? Listen to your intuition.

> *Some people may be turned off by the idea of brokers as salespeople, but the truth is, you want an advocate who is attentive, engaged, #needs&wants and motivated to win on your behalf. It's time to* **REcode any past biases** *you may have about salespeople—people who profit from your decisions do not automatically deserve your trust. Approach the consultation with an open mind, setting aside preconceived notions, and focus on assessing whether the broker's personality, communication style, and authenticity align with your needs. Their intent should be centered on #strategy&success, always with your best interests at heart.*

Pause and listen for broker confidence, objective perspective, and market knowledge as you present your compiled list of questions from the acclimation phase. Do they respond mindfully or dismiss your questions and simply push for you to sign an agency agreement with them? Pause and assess—does their approach align with how *you* process information? If not, thank them for their time and move on. If yes and you feel their energy compliments yours and you're ready to view properties, be prepared to enter into a buyer agency agreement.

Verify the Broker's Service Limitations. This relates to your search criteria, which must be identified in the agency agreement to fulfill your needs and wants tied to your tethered why. Understandably, you may have to surrender certain locations or conditions in order to align fully with your needs and wants in pursuit of your why—but this should not come as a surprise if you paid attention during the acclimation phase. A buyer agency agreement with the firm and its broker is a commitment to a timeline and a realistic search radius for properties the broker may present to you.

Local Market Insight: Just because the buyer broker is licensed to sell in that particular state or country doesn't mean they are the right fit to represent *you* in your desired location just because their license allows. If you are unfamiliar with an area or its services in your identified search, ask the broker to share their knowledge of local customs so you can properly prep and strategize for negotiations. For example: Where does the water come from? Where does the sewage go? Is there recommended testing? If so, when does that happen, and who customarily orders and pays for it?

Homeowner Association (HOA): If your criteria or radius will focus on locations or condominiums bound to an HOA, confirm whether the broker can decipher HOA documents into practical risk awareness when you initiate due diligence to learn if there are any unacceptable restrictions (#B4MA). You're not just buying real estate; you're joining a governing body with binding rules, shared financial responsibility, and collective decision-making. Those about to be bound to an HOA need someone contract-competent who will protect their interests—especially with respect to potential resale concerns when buying into a poorly managed HOA.

Beyond "Available": Verify how the broker collects and tracks aggregated "pending" and "sold" data within your desired radius for future negotiation strategies. Why is this important? It's easy to watch for "new" and "available" listings entering the market. Any broker can do this, but serious, professional brokers consistently track properties that are going "pending" and the "sold" details of those that actually close.

Why does this matter? A skilled broker tracks crucial details:

- **Concessions** on price or buyer closing costs
- **Repairs** or replacements and improvements
- **Compensation** offered or paid to buyer broker

This cumulative data takes diligence to collect, track, and apply, helping shape future strategy and negotiations for buyers and exposes their expertise.

***Anecdote; Data = Tools.** As a mentor and after earning my DB license, I was surprised to see how many brokers—even seasoned ones—failed to eliminate properties that clearly wouldn't meet underwriting guidelines (the how). Too often, a broker tries to make their client happy by forcing a square peg into a round hole, only to hit a dead end when no strategy exists to close the transaction. Everyone walks away frustrated and disheartened.*

*This illustrates the importance of distinguishing **needs from wants, and the how**. Buyers often get emotionally attached to properties that exceed their wants but don't fulfill their needs. Data, when diligently tracked, becomes an invaluable tool to guide those emotions. A broker who uses data to redirect a buyer back to their needs is truly working in the client's best interest—and helps prevent regret down the road.*

***The Informed Pause Example:** If "closed" data shows sellers aren't conceding on price or closing costs but are making repairs, and "pending" data shows the market slowing, a skilled broker will recognize a shift. Up until now, their buyer was prepared to overpay and give up wants. But by reading the "pulse" (pending data) of the market, the broker can help the buyer pause, strategize, and negotiate more effectively. Without that guidance, the buyer may have overpaid, missed out on closing cost credits (needs), and failed to secure repairs (wants).*

Data plays a crucial role here. Buyers naturally get excited about properties but a skilled broker can redirect focus when emotional wants take over. You need (and deserve) a buyer broker who grasps the data and has the intent to manage the experience with you—someone who prepares you for due diligence, expenses, and obligations to prevent surprises or emotionally failed sales.

This *Mindful Guide* is about *REcoding* the real estate experience, and that means deep, sometimes uncomfortable, and always realistic broker-to-buyer conversations. Most buyers don't realize the value of a broker who can spot why a property came *back on market* (BOMK)—such as an appraisal requiring a roof replacement—or who knows how much seller concessions are actually being negotiated in their area. These are the types of collected details that matter when it's time to strategize, so you can prepare to either compete against another buyer or protect your time, energy, and earnest money.

Money talk. Each firm you consult with may have a different compensation model, and may offer more than one type of buyer agency agreement, but regardless, expect to commit to either an exclusive or non-exclusive agreement—the most common—as referenced in the <u>Download</u> section.

> **Compensation.** It's important to verify what sellers are offering as compensation for buyer brokers in your target market search. This can vary, so having knowledge of what's being offered—if anything—is powerful. During your consultation and review of the buyer agency agreement, avoid simply opting for

no agency to bypass a compensation arrangement. Instead, aim to understand the ratio of properties offering buyer agency compensation compared to those that do not. This information will empower you to make an informed decision and negotiate the best buyer broker compensation terms for your needs.

Until you've identified a property of interest, a broker can't confirm whether the property offers compensation that aligns with the terms of your buyer agency agreement. Depending on the market, the compensation offered by the seller may not fully cover the agreed-upon compensation in your agreement. If there's a shortfall, you as the buyer will be responsible for covering the difference or negotiate with the seller in additional terms. However, once a property is listed and on the market, compensation information can be easily verified and shared by your broker to clarify your financial responsibilities (if any).

Depending on the language of the agency agreement, buyers may have the option to specify that the broker only presents listings that align with the agreed-upon compensation. However, if you limit your viewings based on compensation alone, you risk missing out on properties that may not offer a buyer broker compensation fee. While this approach can help avoid additional costs, it also limits your access to a broader range of properties that may better meet your needs, wants, and long-term goals.

Know your options and that compensation discussions can stir an emotional response such as a sense of vulnerability or overwhelm. As mentioned, unless you are in a trusted relationship or fortunate to have a reliable referral with a proven performance history, I recommend consulting with more than one broker to get acclimated to the compensation discussion; you can then compare which fees they consider customary and which dedicated services they offer.

Commit when It feels like a partnership. Sign your representation agreement when you've found a broker who feels like a true partner—someone who aligns with your goals, communicates with transparency, and has earned your trust. A real partnership is more than sending you listings to view and filling out forms on your behalf; it's about hiring a dedicated and skilled professional who lives and breathes real estate, takes pride in satisfied clients, and demonstrates care, mindfulness, and competence.

Buyer Agency isn't just a formality—it's a professional agreement backed by law. Buyer brokers do more than open doors and collect a fee at closing; they are bound by legal standards designed to protect you. These laws ensure your real estate journey is based on mutual respect, transparency, and accountability, not assumptions.

While brokers are licensed professionals, they are not attorneys. In many states, however, brokers are granted limited authority because of their license to complete standardized real estate forms such as a buyer agency agreement or a purchase and/or sale contract—forms that have been reviewed and approved by legal counsel. This enables brokers to assist with contract preparation without stepping into the practice of law.

Clear boundaries exist, however. If legal questions arise beyond what's covered in standard forms, brokers cannot draft custom language or offer legal advice unless they also hold a law license, like an attorney. In such cases, they will consult with their designated broker or refer you to a qualified real estate attorney. This system is designed to protect your best interests and ensure compliance with the law, providing you with not just practical guidance but peace of mind.

Exclusive agency agreement. The word "exclusive" in an agency agreement is used to protect the broker's time and ensure you are fully committed to working exclusively with them. This should not be confused with "exclusivity," which would limit the listings you can view. Rather, it establishes a reciprocal arrangement that defines how you and the broker will work together, for how long, and outlines the responsibility for how and when your broker will be compensated for their professional representation.

Non-exclusive agreements, while providing more flexibility, allow a buyer to enter into other agreements and therefore offer very little protection or motivation for the broker. As mentioned in the Download section, either type of agreement (exclusive or non-exclusive) is needed before services may begin—non-exclusive agreements sometimes useful for short-term service or trial relationships. If you enter multiple buyer agency agreements, it is up to you to make sure the radius and other search criteria do not overlap: thus avoiding the risk of owing multiple buyer broker compensations.

A **tail provision** is commonly included in a buyer agency agreement. This clause protects the buyer broker's compensation for a specified period following the expiration or termination of the agency agreement. It ensures that if you purchase property that was introduced by the buyer broker—without their direct involvement during the tail period—the broker is still entitled to compensation for the transaction within the agreed upon time frame. In this way, clients cannot circumvent broker compensation by waiting for the agency agreement to expire before finalizing the sale of a property the broker had already found and introduced. Ensure you're comfortable with the number of days (or expiration date) noted in the tail provision terms.

An uncommon incentive option (not to confuse but *inform* you) can be added and outlined in the buyer agency agreement regarding the difference your buyer broker negotiates from ("off") the list price. If you as the buyer intend to significantly negotiate and challenge a seller's price ("lowball"), you may want to introduce the "achievement incentive" to your buyer broker to sustain the challenge—often useful in high-stakes negotiations for luxury price points when hundreds of thousands or millions of dollars are challenged. This incentive, when relevant to high-value properties, ensures your buyer broker is highly motivated to achieve the best-possible price concession and terms for you.

Uncommon Incentive Example: imagine you are interested in and qualified for a property listed at $5 million. Both you and your buyer broker value the property at the asking price and agree it is not overpriced. If your broker successfully negotiates the price down to $4.5 million, you will pay them the additional percentage incentive for the negotiated $500,000 difference as specified in your buyer agency agreement.

Incentives can prove invaluable, especially when buyers complicate negotiations with requests for items never intended to convey—like furniture, art, or a yard sculpture. Sellers, sometimes clouded by sentiment, may lose sight of creative solutions to reach their selling goal, while buyers may fixate on these non-conveyed items and add unnecessary friction. Such distractions can derail progress and fatigue even seasoned brokers, who must remain focused on their client's goals while guiding negotiations toward #MA. In these situations, a financial incentive to achieve serves as recognition of the broker's dedication—acknowledging the extra effort it takes to manage unreasonable requests while keeping the negotiations on track. This incentive is a rare addition to a buyer agency agreement, added here to keep my commitment to sharing what I know.

Limited dual agency, a unique occurrence, is addressed in buyer agency agreements, asking if—under specific circumstances when the broker also represents a seller—you would consent to the broker representing both you and the seller in the same transaction. This arrangement requires the informed consent of both principals, you and the seller as the parties to the transaction, which must be documented in your separate agreements and acknowledged together in the purchase and/or sale contract. If a broker claims to consent to limited dual agency "all the time," *run*. On multiple occasions, I have mentioned it takes a high-caliber, experienced broker willing to commit to this as doing so opens them up to doubling their risk. This should not be common practice but instead considered on a **case-by-case** basis.

Before making an offer, always confirm if the seller is offering buyer broker compensation or if your offer must negotiate how and when your buyer's broker will be paid. The seller's broker may offer to "facilitate" the transaction—a workable solution—legally side-stepping dual agency and staying committed to representing the seller only per their listing agreement; if the seller's broker proposes this (designating you as a no agency buyer) *and* you have confirmed their seller <u>is</u> offering buyer broker compensation, it is in your best interest to find a buyer broker and <u>not</u> choose no agency. Don't have a relationship with a broker? The seller's broker or their firm's DB will refer a recommendation (or two) for you to consult and choose. Referrals within a firm are not uncommon, and legal. More importantly, having buyer agency options for strategy, guidance, and advocacy is always in your best interest.

If **no compensation is offered** within a listing, this does not mean the seller is not willing to negotiate buyer broker compensation. When reviewing the buyer agency agreement, ask the buyer broker to explain a negotiation strategy if you choose a property not offering buyer broker compensation or otherwise less than what's outlined in your negotiated buyer agency agreement fee. Ultimately, the buyer agency agreement ensures you are prepared to compensate for the professional services your buyer broker performs through closing.

Never choose "**no agency,**" remembering that the law requires an agreement for real estate services; don't give up and choose a no agency agreement due to fears regarding buyer agency compensation. Representing yourself is rarely in your best interest and not your only option!

True representation means working with a broker who not only connects you with the right properties but also has a proven history of guiding buyers to successful closings. When the relationship feels in sync—balanced between trust, advocacy, and results—that's when the real momentum begins.

ALIGN

Before Mutual Acceptance (#B4MA)

Expectations and Strategy. Now that you've committed to a *RElationship* with a buyer broker and entered a buyer agency agreement with a radius and search criteria plan incorporating your *why, needs,* and *wants*, it's time to add the *how*.

Unless you've already secured financing, you'll need to interview recommended local mortgage lenders to compare, commit, and apply for a mortgage: such effort demonstrating your commitment to the *how* process as the buyer broker will need to "sell" your "able-ness" to the seller's broker and their client—especially if you are purchasing during a seller's market that favors cash buyers.

Choose local, rather than an E-lender. Big brand lenders operate primarily online, often through a website or app, and assign your file to a facilitator not a dedicated lending partner. Despite their promises to streamline the lending process, these websites prioritize their profit over your interests and time: each call involves frustrating protocols and delays with a different person every time. Since these companies have no stake in helping you or your community build wealth, you're just a file to collect fees and pad their corporate pockets.

As "**matchmakers**," local lenders actively broker and rework programs to provide opportunities for all buyers and often have access to big brand money. The real benefit of working with a local lender? They are personally vested in your circumstances and the community. They also understand the unique needs of your local market and will match you with relevant financial opportunities, including down payment assistance programs when available. By personalizing your experience, they help you secure the best loan options because *their* success is tied to yours. More importantly, these local lenders live and reinvest their earnings into your community, supporting its growth and working diligently to help you and others achieve ownership while fostering wealth-building opportunities for all—rather than just benefitting distant shareholders.

A good mortgage lender is also a **coach** shaping your strategic plan for a successful loan application. They know the necessary steps and will enable you with a strategy to receive loan approval while guiding you on budgeting and maintaining ownership. Choose to overcome any fear of rejection, and then follow a lender's recommended disciplinary steps: maintaining employment, paying off debt, and (just as importantly) not incurring new debt. Focus on your strategic goals and shift your debt-to-income ratio in your favor for loan approval. If you match the lender's effort, you can own property. This process can feel overwhelming for some, but just know you are not alone. Staying disciplined and doing whatever it takes to accomplish your goals—perhaps driving a Mazda instead of a Mercedes, for example—is a beautiful arc to witness. Nothing makes a mortgage lender prouder than coaching a buyer to achieve loan approval for ownership.

Going from acclimation to focus (unless your buying parameters are highly restricted) is the ideal time to remain open-minded, explore fresh ideas, and gain valuable insights from your buyer broker and mortgage lender to focus and fulfill your *needs*. A team approach, paired with expert, current insights into market dynamics (e.g., inventory trends, inflation, Treasury yields, and shifts in monetary policy) can help buyers better understand how these factors influence financing options and interest rates. Keep your strategy adaptive and responsive to factors beyond your control. In ever-changing markets, your team will monitor conditions, keep you informed, and prepare to negotiate both the property and financing terms best aligning with your goals.

Now the fun begins (kidding). Warning, it can hurt the brain! Your buyer broker and lender will conduct multiple searches and provide you with multiple market updates (new listings and rates or loan options) to keep you informed—either steadily, in waves, or in full-blown blasts.

Remember: they're just doing their job. Some buyers love the service of personalized property searches with anecdotes from their broker, really feeling representation at work in the process. Others must adjust to the realization that their new partner is not pressuring them to buy but simply sharing real-time insights. Believe that your buyer broker is filtering to eliminate properties that do not meet your *why*, *needs*, *wants*, and *hows*. At the same time, they're monitoring which inventory has accepted offers and comparing recent "pending" and "sold" properties for location, condition, accepted terms, and any concessions. This data collection is to assess, remove ignorance, and set you up with realistic expectations.

You should expect communication from your team when market conditions and interest rates change, especially if they're not in your favor. This awareness is valuable to your mental journey, this assortment of information coming at you like jumping Double Dutch: you gotta get in there and absorb the facts to find your rhythm and not take changes personally.

Location over condition is a decision to weigh. If location and building wealth are strong *whys* for your purchase, a strategic rule says to buy the smallest property you can live with on the block (or one in poor condition). It's great if an opportunity hits the market to enter a desirable neighborhood with pride of ownership, where properties are well-maintained, modernized, or even over-improved. By purchasing a property in poor-to-average condition, this offers an affordable entry point into a high-value community, but may come with risks you will need to uncover with due diligence. The choice depends on the market, your willingness/capability/skills, and financing/funds (the *how)*. With the potential to improve a less attractive property or add square footage to significantly increase its value, the odds will lead to a favorable return on investment.

Consider becoming a community shareholder if the purchase is long-term, investing in an underappreciated location—one where potential for growth or amenities may be overlooked—merge and become a shareholder by contributing to the well-being, progress, and stability of a neighborhood or local community. Support nearby businesses, participate in local initiatives, engage in neighborhood associations, volunteer at local schools, and collaborate with neighbors to create a vibrant, safe, and prosperous community. You can bring fresh inspiration to improve or uplift proud but tired and ignored locations. Pride of ownership attracts additional funds and attention to boost local businesses and renew motivation to existing members of the community. The goal is for properties to appreciate over time, so why not be an accelerator and invest yourself in a community and its schools—generating momentum and wealth appreciation as a whole.

Set realistic expectations when committing to a search radius meeting your *needs* and *wants* tethered to your *why* and identifying properties to view. By the time you visit a property, you'd have studied it on an app; now the goal is to rule it in or out. Photos do a good job of capturing the essence but not always the condition or the neighborhood, not every property holding up as the image conveys and thus perhaps not meeting your *how*. Ultimately, it's about you receiving loan approval to complete your purchase experience. If your offer is contingent upon receiving financing, it is not too much to expect your buyer broker—your partner in this journey—to filter and show properties that meet your *how*. This may take a few showings and test your tolerance, but this is a partnership. Your buyer broker cannot read your mind and is not required to read your body language; be honest in your feedback so they are better equipped to identify a good fit. As inventory sells, know you may need to adjust your expectations. Some sellers markets do not offer enough time for brokers to filter or preview new listing conditions, meaning they need to schedule a showing and risk disappointing you in the process. Breathe into your intuition, reminding yourself your buyer broker cannot control the inventory available and is doing their best to not waste your time nor theirs. Trust the process you and your team outlined.

Five-Year Perspective

Consider the length of time you plan to hold the property, based on its location and current economic climate. The average length for first-time owners is 5 to 7 years; this duration varies based on circumstances, market conditions, and life changes such as job relocation, growth, turnover in occupants, or financial adjustments. Economic factors like rising property values or interest rates can also influence the timing of a sale. For second or third-time owners, the average length of time to remain with a property is about 7 to 10 years—this longer duration is sometimes impacted by a bigger financial investment, greater sense of stability, and community connection.

If you plan to own the property for **less than five years**, consider the potential ramifications of selling including transaction costs, fees, and other selling-related expenses. As with any investment, there are inherent risks so it's important to position yourself for the best-possible return. Five years or less shifts the focus to locations known for appreciation and quicker sales—such as condos in popular neighborhoods or single-family in desirable school districts or small commercial properties—for market liquidity to accommodate your exit strategy as you target a positive ROI.

To compromise or not to compromise, that is the question. Don't overthink but prepare to compromise on condition in order to purchase in a location associated with appreciation unless you can afford to make improvements as an owner. Otherwise, seek high-demand communities in urban centers close to major employers, or consider neighborhoods with historically high appreciation (e.g., near universities) to improve the chance of renting quickly, making a profit, or breaking even to cover fees associated with selling.

Know the potential investment. If the property is part of an HOA and you plan to occupy it for the first few years before eventually converting it into a rental property, initiate due diligence to clarify if the association has a rental policy before making an offer. Some associations may limit the number of properties that can be rented out at any given time and/or have a waiting list for approval. Additionally, clarify any planned improvements that could result in further financial commitments as well as construction projects that could disrupt and limit the pool of renters willing to accommodate without a discount—increasing the risk you won't be able to cover your mortgage, taxes, and insurance plus the HOA fee.

Pay a premium for less. Don't have the time and money to afford renovations and make repairs or the skills to create "sweat equity?" Focus on low maintenance, knowing "move-in condition" properties may need minimal repairs and updates and—as with new construction—minimize unexpected repair costs during your short-term investment. Everything good comes at a cost, though, which in this case is likely a compromise to accept less square footage and fewer rooms. "Turnkey" properties cost a premium but typically offer modern systems and warranties while avoiding significant maintenance costs, making them convenient for you to attract future buyers or renters.

If you plan to own the property **for more than five years**, prioritize lifestyle factors to enhance long-term livability (or leaseability), stability, comfort, and a potential growth in value. Focus on areas with strong community shareholders—residents who take pride in their neighborhood and actively vote to maintain or improve local schools, parks, and essential infrastructure like bridges, emergency medical services, and telecommunications. These communities are loyal to local businesses and tend to reinvest in their districts, ultimately increasing property values and building wealth collectively.

In tailoring your focus to the length of your intended ownership, you mindfully strategize how to best secure your initial investment and cover selling expenses while potentially realizing a profit.

Per #buyeretiquette, there are dos and don'ts when **viewing properties** that vary depending on whether the listing is residential, tenant-occupied, or commercial. For residential and tenant occupied properties, rely on your buyer broker to provide specific viewing instructions. Respect common viewing courtesies such as refraining from using the bathroom and bringing along drinks, pets, and (ideally) young children. If children are present, keep them close and respectful of the space to avoid mishaps. Viewing a property is a sensory experience: see, smell, listen, and feel as you imagine the property as yours. Always ask for permission before taking photos or videos, and avoid unnecessary snooping. During open houses, keep opinions discreet to avoid the ears of the competition, seller, and seller's representative.

Perform an assessment midway through visiting properties, typically after seven to ten visits, to examine your partnership with your buyer's broker and the market. Are they still committed to your goals, showing you properties that align as planned? Or are they pushing anything and everything available to make a quick sale? Their services should prioritize your *needs* over *wants* while keeping your *why* and *how* at the forefront. This integrity safeguards your success but can be challenging in low-inventory markets no matter how talented the buyer broker is. Keep communications open and honest, and make necessary changes sooner rather than later.

Be cautious, knowing it's not unusual to untether your *why* and test the boundaries when something new and shiny enters the market that appeals to your *wants* but distracts from your *needs*. For instance, a stunning new kitchen or bath may tempt you to overlook critical needs such as the number of bedrooms or baths. When viewing properties with the intent to have an additional occupant (to help with the mortgage payment), keep in mind they may leave; this purchase is an investment in yourself. Do not let their *wants* override your *needs*, and choose a property that serves you and your financial goals first and foremost.

The Process of Elimination: Saying Yes to the Right Property

Perform a SWOT analysis. The purchase experience is a dynamic process and requires clear intrateam communication to be satisfying. Openly express your thoughts and any concerns to refine the approach en route to your goal. Staying organized helps, and applying a consistent method such as a SWOT analysis (strengths, weaknesses, opportunities, and threats) after each showing provides valuable clarity in the absence of emotion: saving time at the next property. Make notes to compare properties objectively and thus ease any hesitation when you find a property to make an offer on, your SWOT discussions strengthening your offer strategy by assisting your buyer broker in negotiations (highlighting strengths or threats that justify your offer or additional terms) to reach #MA.

Filter "Back on Market" (BOMK) properties. During your search and every so often, a property status might change from "pending" to "available" or "BOMK" status. An exciting opportunity? Sure! It can also signal potential issues, however. Ask these questions before scheduling a BOMK viewing: Do the listing remarks (property details) explain why the property is back on the market (e.g., did the sale fall through due to buyer financing or an inspection)? Can the buyer broker learn if the seller was unable to make repairs (or perhaps uncooperative)? Your broker can inquire but may not get the answers you seek. Also expect them to try to determine if there's an "issue" that could interfere with your financing or appraisal in order to save time and a possible emotional letdown. **This new information allows your team to filter and strategize a plan** and assess options for possible negotiations. Ideally, these questions are addressed before scheduling a viewing. An answer may also be available if the seller updates the disclosure to inform potential buyers of any new material defects. Observing buyer behavior and market trends gives you a competitive edge and confidence; it takes time to understand BOMK situations to avoid related pitfalls.

Prep for rapid decisions. After touring properties with your buyer broker, you'll start to recognize each other's learning and communication styles and feel anxious to find "the one." Thoughtful dialogue isn't wasted time; it's an investment. Together, you'll track location, condition, and price, especially in relation to recently "pending" and "sold" properties. A buyer broker cannot always anticipate which features or issues matter most to you in each property. Reviewing conversations and previous SWOTs helps you assess "what ifs," explore trade-offs, and sharpen your ability to make confident decisions when the right property appears.

Pivot and protect. On the flip side, during your journey in this #B4MA phase, you may come to unexpected realizations and choose to pivot to an alternative location or change the level of condition you're willing to accept. This is a reminder to review and amend (if necessary) your buyer agency agreement(s) to protect and verify your commitments. However, as your partner, your broker is committed to setting you up for success and should likewise proactively share any concerns that come to light when you are excited about a property and decide to make a move.

There's risk and reward in all this. Your broker may reference past or current market activity to support—or caution against—a rapid decision. That's their job. Try not to misinterpret this guidance as pressure; it's designed to help you navigate risk, whether that's the risk of losing out or overpaying. On the other hand, if your broker's response to each property is simply "Do you want to write it up?" without deeper discussion or a strategy for reward, that could be a red flag. Rely on your past conversations and SWOTs and listen to your intuition.

Time is of the Essence: Preparing an Offer

If you haven't already, begin due diligence, verify **listing details**, and review the **preliminary title report** containing the property's boundaries, easements, encroachments, dedications, delineated matters, and any agreements or restrictions affecting its use or value. Some of this information is buried in hyperlinks within the title report. Rest assured, the escrow officer assigned *after* #MA will review and is instructed to "clear" the title of any noted liens and encumbrances prior to closing. Each report will include the name and contact information of the person (likely a "title officer") who ran, researched, and personally reviewed the report. Some title officers may take your call directly to clarify any questions regarding the preliminary title report, but only take these calls if your broker and title representative cannot direct you to the answer first.

Finalize your pre-approval and block time. If you haven't selected your local lender yet, now is the time to complete your application, strategize closing costs, and lock in your rate. Leverage your broker's industry partners to assemble and align your due diligence team—inspectors, contractors, etc.—and coordinate a future date and time. You've prepared for this moment, and while there will be many rapid decisions to make, finalizing your team sooner rather than later will reduce stress, streamline the process, and position you for stronger negotiating power.

Starter Kits for an Offer Strategy Discussion

The "no-fuss" approach: You just want to make a "clean offer" to the seller, get it accepted, and close. If you are receiving financing, you will want a clear understanding that your offer reflects little to no intentions to negotiate concessions off the price, towards your closing costs, or for buyer broker compensation.

The "let's just ask" approach: You want to try and negotiate off the seller's price, your closing costs, and/or compensation for your buyer broker if they're not offering. You have the capability and are prepared to pay these, but the market has exposed a margin of negotiation in your favor. In other words, properties are not selling for full price and/or sellers are closing with buyer concessions: creating an opportunity for you to negotiate terms.

The "must ask" approach: You have enough for your due diligence and down payment, but to close on a property, you must negotiate and request the seller pay your closing costs and compensate your broker (if their listing does not offer this). The buyer broker will assist with this ask after determining how the market is receiving such offers. In other words, if inventory is low and you have competition and thus find yourself in a multiple-offer situation, the offer may need to be structured above full price to compensate: cushioning the impact to the seller. The expectation can be adjusted if the buyer agency agreement has pre-determined the buyer broker is willing to credit a portion of the compensation fee towards your closing costs to sweeten the deal for the seller.

Details Matter

Strategy details begin to dominate the conversation and come into play as you begin the transition out of the #B4MA phase and into #MA. But first, the negotiations. You've done every responsible thing in preparation for making an offer: acclimating to market conditions, entering an agency relationship (with a competitive and competent professional), viewing multiple properties, initiating due diligence, and (when a loan is needed) aligning your expectations with a local lender.

Real estate markets evolve day by day, with subtle shifts most buyers never notice. Apps try to keep pace—tracking new listings, pending sales, expired listings, and closed transactions—but even the best platforms out there only tell part of the story. They reveal list and "sold" prices but may omit vital context: Did the seller offer buyer concessions? Were funds applied toward repairs or closing costs? Have buyers negotiated buyer broker compensation that influenced the final price? It is time to mindfully apply this tracked available data to your negotiation strategy.

In getting the "how" ready, your team will have gathered and interpreted this data to the best of their ability. Together, you'll craft a comprehensive offer strategy focused on details that set the tone for a successful negotiation: offer price, earnest money, closing and possession dates, and any contingencies needed to protect your interests.

Stay curious. If you feel any hesitation or anxiety in preparing to negotiate, this is the time to express it. A satisfying real estate transaction is grounded in making informed decisions that position you as a willing and able buyer, prepared to meet the terms of a contract. Trust your team's confidence with your intuition to guide you in crafting a strong and balanced offer; they'll explain how contingencies for inspection or financing can protect your interests while also preparing you for how these terms might impact your leverage in a competitive market. Armed with this knowledge, you'll be ready to negotiate.

Negotiation is not just about winning or losing; it's about securing your position while staying adaptable. Accepting the seller's terms isn't a loss—reaching *#MA* is a win worth celebrating. Stay confident, stay focused, and embrace the excitement of moving forward toward ownership!

Traditionally as part of an offer, contingencies, conditions, or clauses are added to the contract to preserve buyer due diligence. These contingencies are often outlined in separate addendums that modify or add new terms to the existing agreement, overriding standard contract language to address specific requirements or circumstances. Think of each contingency like an obstacle course to navigate simultaneously during the contract's timeframe and strategize in your best interest. Each contingency must be met, waived, or removed for the agreement to become legally binding. To recap, contingencies are typically designed to benefit the buyer, ensuring that specific conditions are satisfied before the transaction proceeds and the buyer commits to closing. If a contingency is not met, waived, or removed, the buyer may have the right to terminate the contract but could forfeit their earnest money (EM) as a penalty depending on the agreed-upon terms.

Get "contingency nitty-gritty" before making an offer, doubling down on understanding the ins and outs of potential contingencies you may request therein.

Add a "net proceeds" contingency if you need to sell a property for its net proceeds to purchase another. This requires prioritizing a plan to prepare the current property for market before considering preparing an offer—so if and when your offer is accepted, you and the property are prepared to perform the terms of this contingency obligation. Typically, the contingency terms to sell another property will specify when the contingency property will enter and be available to the market (e.g., within 5 days of mutual acceptance).

The inspection contingency, if you include in your offer, commands a lot of planning. Typically, there are multiple unique layered time frames dictating preparation and rapid decisions.

Note: After the inspection is conducted, it is on you to inform the seller of your contingent response. You'll likely have three choices in this respect, depending on the inspection contingency terms:

Caveat: If you fail to notify the seller with a formal response (accept, request, or reject) within the specified inspection contingency time frame, depending on the specific language of your inspection contingency, you may be obligated to move forward to closing. Failing to respond within the agreed timeline may be treated as acceptance of the inspection results. In other words, a "no response" could be interpreted as an automatic waiver of your inspection contingency, moving you forward to the next phase or toward closing. To protect your earnest money and maintain control of your options, always provide a formal written response within the required timeframe.

Here is an example with three choices and multiple layers:

A) **Accept** the inspection —> indicating inspection has been met and waived and you are choosing to proceed to the next contingency or closing.

B) **Request** repair(s), replacement(s), concessions, or a combination for said inspection findings.

—>Round One; if you formally make a "request" properly within the specified contingency response time, this initiates a fresh specified time frame (new layer) per the contingency terms. At this point, it is on the seller to either accept or reject your request or propose an alternative solution.

—>Round Two; if the seller rejects your request and/or proposes an alternative solution (bumping the responsibility back to you the buyer), then a fresh specified time frame (possible last layer) per the contingency terms begins.

—>Lastly; if the seller bumps a formal response back to you for another round of inspection contingency negotiations, your intrateam communication must be on point and focused. This "round two" time frame may be your last round and opportunity to reject and legally back out (exercise your right to terminate) to protect your earnest money—or your last chance to accept the seller's last proposal (as long as your formal response is within that last protected time frame/layer) and proceed to closing.

C) **Reject** the inspection —> exercising the right to terminate, with the earnest money distributed per the terms of the contract and both parties going their separate ways.

The inspection contingency negotiation process has evolved over decades, with each form and its terms shaped by regional differences, association guidelines, and MLS rules. It's essential to confer with your broker and team to establish a clear understanding and specifics with respect to your contingencies, their time frames (and layers, if any), and how to navigate them (think obstacle course) to either protect your intentions (and earnest money) or fulfill your contractual obligations.

Consider a finance contingency if you need a loan. This contingency takes time, typically 15 to 30 days to receive loan approval, and your team will advise per your needs. The loan process is three-sided, each side required to come together for the contingency to be met and eventually waived.

First, the underwriter needs supporting documentation to confirm your ability to repay the loan. This is in your control, so respond in a timely manner and forward any requested documentation to fulfill any lender requirements.

Second, the lender will send a neutral third-party appraiser to evaluate the property's condition and value. This step protects the lender by ensuring the property meets the required standards, securing their investment in case of loan default and potential foreclosure. Lenders are not in the business of acquiring foreclosed properties—they are in the business of lending money, with foreclosure being an unfortunate risk they must account for in their business models. Mortgage lenders do not lend expecting foreclosure—they rely on timely mortgage payments to sustain operations, reinvest funds into new loans, and ultimately generate profit.

Third, you will acquire a homeowners insurance policy. This binder is a necessary step to protect the lender's investment in the property and ensures the property will be financially protected against potential risks (such as fire or natural disasters) during the life of the loan. Once the underwriter has reviewed your ability to repay the loan and the appraisal and received the binder, they can issue final loan approval: signaling financing is secure and the contingency can be waived.

Be mindful when strategizing contingencies in a multiple-offer scenario. Sellers prioritize offers with fewer contingencies that in turn limit a buyer's ability to back out, with their brokers naturally advocating for the strongest, cleanest terms to protect their client's best interest. One exception? A cash buyer (with proof of funds) may still request an inspection contingency.

> *For example: If a seller has received two offers and is weighing…*
>
> *a) a cash offer **with** an inspection contingency, vs.*
>
> *b) a financed offer **without** an inspection contingency*
>
> *… they'll often favor the cash offer with an inspection contingency. Why? Because an inspection contingency will wrap up quickly (approx. 10 days) while the financing contingency introduces longer-term (15-to 30-day) risk tied to the buyer performing to receive their three-sided loan, as described above. In short, cash usually wins— even with an inspection contingency.*

Compete to win. Some buyers opt to perform a pre-inspection before submitting an offer, with the intent to waive the inspection contingency with confidence or otherwise negotiate repairs in their offer. This is discussed in the <u>Download</u> section. Other strategies to demonstrate serious intent include:

- Offering above asking price.

- Providing a clause to escalate the price in an attempt to outbid competitors.

- Waiving inspection (not including an inspection contingency) with a willingness to take on potential unknown issues unconditionally (WARNING: rarely should a broker ever want, encourage, or require a buyer to waive a high-risk strategy to win, especially on a "flip" property).

- Waiving financing (not including a finance contingency), betting on yourself and the property to get a loan.

- Offering the earnest money—or part of it—as non-refundable, giving the seller an immediate financial incentive.

- Being willing to take on any disclosed financial responsibilities for known future assessments.

- Delaying taking possession, giving the seller additional time to vacate the property with their net proceeds in their pocket.

These are just some of the calculated strategies used successfully and should not be taken lightly; buyers must understand financial risks and emotional impacts if they change their mind after committing.

It's important to understand the distinction between a non-contingent offer and a contingent one. A non-contingent offer typically refers to the buyer not needing to sell another property to proceed with the purchase. If you use strategies to submit an offer without contingencies, it's crucial to remember that the seller's broker cannot assume your offer is truly non-contingent until they verify there are no additional addendums or clauses. This does not include statutory rights, such as the buyer's right to verify conditions or the seller's disclosure acceptance, which remain separate from these considerations.

Delaying occupancy can be a strategic consideration for a buyer in a multiple-offer situation, offering the seller a genuine convenience. Traditionally, a buyer is entitled to take possession upon closing. However, offering to delay possession is a strategy the buyer can offer to provide flexibility to the seller. This extended occupancy allows the seller to not have to pack, clean, and be out the same day the property transfers ownership while still ensuring they receive their net proceed funds. When the property is occupied, assume your competition will offer the seller extended occupancy and that you'll need to structure your possession date to win. Do you charge the seller per-diem rent (temporary leaseback) or offer free rent, and for how long? The bottom line is to strategize the earliest closing date and the latest possession date to provide the greatest benefit to the seller.

Keep your eye on the prize when formulating your offer, understanding your strategy is to have your offer accepted into first position (not "kinda" buy a property)—which means no game playing nor wasting time. In a multiple-offer market, write a competitive offer to win.

Your professional team will guide and advise you on making a competitive offer and counteroffer and should be able to defend the options provided to you. If you feel supported, continue finalizing key terms. Before presenting your offer, they will set you up (and even schedule) to make rapid decisions to complete necessary obligations in a timely manner; now is the time for your buyer broker to advocate and negotiate on your behalf to secure the best possible price and terms.

> ***Rapid Decision Example:*** *Your buyer broker has prepared you from the start: tracking market shifts, reviewing and informing you of pending and sold activity, and analyzing multiple SWOT notes with you. Now, in a low-inventory market and when the right property surfaces, you're not just ready but committed to reach mutual acceptance even though your current lease isn't up for another 2 months. If the property is owner occupied and offers compensation to a buyer broker but has an older furnace compared to others you've seen (for example), you're already prepared to make rapid decisions grounded in strategy and aligned with a trusted plan.*

Rapid decisions span…

- **Offer Price:** Instead of negotiating a lower price, you may offer above asking to stand out—or, if notified of multiple offers, include an escalation clause that automatically increases your offer above competing bids up to a capped amount.

- **Earnest Money:** Instead of the traditional 1-3%, you may increase your good faith deposit to show you're serious and committed.

- **Inspection:** If you do not have time or access for a pre-inspection, one option is to shorten the default contingency period. Block half a day for your pre-scheduled inspection and pair it with a furnace evaluation plus any relevant local inspections (e.g., a sewer scope) so you can comfortably honor the shortened period.

- **Financing:** Don't wait until after #MA to select your lender, lock in a local lender and rate, and complete a full loan application for pre-approval.

- **Concessions:** The good news is the seller is offering buyer broker compensation, but you are forced to weigh your other wants (paid closing costs or furnace replacement, for example) against seller benefits so your offer can ideally reach first-position status.

- **Closing & Possession:** Because your lease still has 2 months remaining, you may have an option the competing buyers don't. First, you can offer to close in 30 days (committing you to paying the overlapping rent and mortgage for a month). Second, you can offer to delay taking possession until 30 days after closing (2 months from now) and thus offer the seller post-closing occupancy to appeal to their convenience.

Your broker may reference past and current trends to help support or caution against these strategies. That's not pressure; it's their job to provide you with as much information as possible so you understand your choices and can make the best decision for you and your situation. Rapid decisions aren't reckless but focused, informed, and made with intention for the right property.

Friend & Family Opinions

During negotiations, your willpower and self-discipline will help when sustained effort is required. All of your preparation has prepared you to make thoughtful and reasoned decisions to reach your long-term goal, but your confidence may be challenged when friends and family share their experiences or project their worries and insecurities onto your decision to purchase a property. Unless they are involved in your financing, have viewed every property, and contributed to each SWOT analysis, you must rely on your own intuition and strength to regulate your emotions and maintain focus on reaching #MA with the seller.

Last-Minute Due Diligence

If you haven't already initiated due diligence and researched, it's good to be aware of potential environmental hazards or concerns such as flood zones, soil contamination, or proximity to industrial sites and future development plans that may boost or hinder future value.

The location, year built, and condition may all require preparation for specialized pest, mold, asbestos, and lead inspections. When you interview professional inspectors, they will clarify if these are within their scope to perform.

Most licensed inspectors evaluate a property's condition, identify any structural issues or potential repairs, and assess overall safety: ensuring essential utilities (water, electricity, gas, and sewage) are properly connected and in good working order.

Real-World Example: A DB or firm manager receives a call from a past buyer—now a homeowner—who recently began to repair or replace something, or started a remodel project. During the prep work, they uncover something that appears to have been hidden or covered up by the previous owner. Understandably, they're concerned and want to know: Why wasn't this disclosed?

It's a common question, but unfortunately one a broker or manager cannot answer. While they cannot offer legal advice, they can try to help the new owner understand their options moving forward and guide them toward making informed decisions.

The new owner may choose to:

a) Hire a professional to test or evaluate the material and pursue remediation if necessary.

b) Consult legal counsel to determine whether the issue warrants action against the previous owner.

c) Do nothing, which is (frankly) not uncommon.

The bottom line? **Every purchase carries some level of risk.** As a future property owner, it's important to address any issues upfront and resolve them before they become bigger concerns. If a problem remains unresolved, you'll need to disclose it when you sell. That's why brokers often advise clients to document findings, hire specialists when needed, and consult legal counsel to ensure they're fully informed and protected.

Sometimes, defects are genuinely unknown or undiscoverable during due diligence—even with all precautions taken. Still, this underscores why buyers must take due diligence seriously: reviewing disclosures, investigating common findings for the property's location and age, and asking questions (especially if you plan on making improvements to the property).

Any due diligence is better than none. Buyers often associate due diligence with a professional inspection, but it's far more comprehensive than that. From the moment a property sparks your interest, your responsibility is to research as any smart investor would. Learn what's typical for that property's age, design, and location and ask: Were any building materials used during that era recalled or involved in class-action lawsuits? Are any common defects tied to this style of construction? Your broker may not be an expert on material defects, but they can help frame the right questions and forward them to the seller. What's under that carpet? What's behind those boxes in the basement? I'm not saying this to discourage buyers from purchasing older properties; it's simply about empowering you to make confident decisions. Do your best to accumulate estimates (or at least guestimates) to prepare for future improvements during due diligence. When due diligence is applied, it will help you prepare for short-and long-term planning to nurture your investment. Keep asking, keep digging, and don't settle for surface level information.

No #MA—Now What?

Back up might be best. If your offer isn't accepted and the seller chooses another buyer, you can—with your buyer broker's guidance—request to collaborate to reach #MA with the seller to seek the *back-up* position. This means entering a formal contract as a *back-up* buyer and taking second position; if the first buyer's contract falls through, you automatically shift into first position. One major benefit in doing so is flexibility; you can typically terminate the back-up contract any time prior to receiving notification that the first contract was canceled.

***Experience Anecdote:** Buyers often reluctantly accept moving into second position, sincerely believing there's no way they will shift into first position. Yet sure enough, they do! The odds are slim, maybe 1 in 5, but you never know the first-position buyer's situation. Are they prepared to make rapid decisions to meet obligations? Do they have their financing in place? In multiple-offer situations, many buyers get wrapped up in the competition and do not follow established strategies to protect themselves. They win at all costs, then remorse kicks in and they back-out. If you become second best, don't be afraid to occupy the back-up position.*

Keep searching. While in the *back-up* position, you're free to continue your property search—and should! If you find an alternate property to pursue, you'll need to give formal notice to the seller to withdraw from the *back-up* contract before making an offer: preventing you from accidentally being under contract for two properties, legally obligating you to perform on both. Many back-up contracts require only the buyer's written notice to terminate without needing seller confirmation, making it easy to move on to the next.

Until you give notice to the seller removing yourself from second position, you'll automatically **shift into first position** upon receiving formal notice from the seller when the first buyer's contract falls through—whether due to a change of heart, inspection disappointment, or failure to secure funding. Shifting into first position allows you to avoid another potential multiple-offer situation (for the same property) with new competition and spares the seller from the stigma of going *back on the market:* a win-win!

Occupying the back-up position is a smart strategy when the property aligns with your top priorities and goals. Many transactions fall apart before closing, so don't hesitate to negotiate for second position if the property truly meets your *why*, *needs*, and *wants* (working with your buyer broker to plan how and when to notify the seller if you find another opportunity during this time).

Mutual Acceptance—Congratulations!

Whether your offer was accepted or you shifted from back-up position to first, both you and the seller have consented and agreed to the same contractual terms, conditions, and obligations: binding you both as principals to a purchase and/or sale contract and putting you in escrow. Now that you have #MA, it's time to move forward, lean into your pre-determined strategies, take action with clarity, and focus on making regret-free decisions at a rapid pace while fulfilling the terms of your contract.

Coordination and rhythm guide the transaction, with your team bringing invaluable expertise to this phase and preparing for any contingencies. Escrow will be opened, earnest money deposited, and paperwork finalized to ensure compliance and pave the way for a successful closing. The contract serves as a course of action for all parties, identifying obligations, timelines, and consequences. Much like navigating a contingency obstacle course, when intent aligns with action, the path to closing becomes both efficient and rewarding. Your buyer broker will be there every step of the way, helping you navigate each turn and transforming your contract into a foundation for building equity, stability, and long-term wealth.

After Mutual Acceptance (#MA)

In the coming weeks, comprehensive conditions, contingencies, and obligations will shape your journey. You're more than ready to navigate this obstacle course following so much preparation; you've got this! With your buyer broker as your partner, they'll assist in coordinating trusted industry partners to assist you to perform and meet your obligations. You're more than ready to navigate this obstacle course and make informed decisions to get one more step closer to ownership.

If the seller accepted your net-proceeds contingency to **sell a contingent property**, it's time to implement the plan you and your buyer broker created and get it on the market.

Now, actualize your **inspection contingency** and commence to finalize your due diligence obligations. Verify the listing and seller-provided documentation, complete your inspection(s) and visits, successfully negotiate, or terminate within the specified time frame.

As for your **finance contingency**, get started on applying for homeowners insurance, provide proper loan-application proof to the seller, and get the appraisal ordered: the last part of the contingency obstacle course unless you still need to sell a property. When the lender's underwriter is satisfied you can repay the loan and the property meets their standards, also verifying the insurance binder as proof of homeowners insurance, they'll complete their process and give final loan-approval notice.

Perform with intent to satisfy all the contingencies properly to protect your earnest money so you can proceed to closing.

When **scheduling the move**, confirm closing and possession terms and dates beforehand—especially if a deposit for moving services is required. If your scheduled move is planned for a major holiday weekend, it's best to risk a deposit and book in advance as these are popular times to move in and move out.

Proceed with final actions to complete the second phase of your real estate journey. The contract may provide you with an opportunity to walk through to verify the property is in the same or better condition than when you made your offer. This is the chance to verify the seller has satisfied your negotiated repairs and/or replacements and learn the protocol for transferring utilities.

The closing day is here. Title is updated, the lender's funds have been wired, and the moment has arrived to review the settlement statement. The escrow or law firm holding the earnest money is preparing to receive your final down payment, to settle the seller's obligations, and record the new deed—officially transferring ownership and turning your plans into reality.

Clarity Gained

Understandably, buyers rarely have the bandwidth to deconstruct the transaction experience after closing. However, deep introspection may reveal how they lacked a plan to navigate the experience and its timelines or how specific decisions (or a lack of proactive engagement to collaborate) contributed to an unsatisfactory outcome.

Buyers sometimes hesitate to fully trust their buyer broker during the transaction, unconsciously projecting their concerns and expecting the broker to handle all aspects of due diligence without fully engaging in the process themselves. When strategizing an offer, anxiety can lead to missed opportunities such as failing to request additional information or explore contingency options and potential consequences. As time passes, embarrassment over not asking key questions can turn into regret or frustration: manifesting as blame toward the buyer broker who earned compensation from the transaction.

Some buyers enter the experience assuming they will be taken advantage of—reinforcing a passive approach or claiming naiveté when things do not go as hoped—and exit it just as cynical. This mindset is neither necessary nor productive!

My hope is that this mindful real estate guide helps you engage, feel informed, and approach/ execute the buying process with intent: the insights you've gained *REcoding* the experience and empowering you to approach choices with clarity, confidence, and a deeper understanding of how preparation for due diligence, rapid decisions, and collaboration work together.

Those who've read *both* the Buyer and Seller sections have hopefully released outdated beliefs, adopted a holistic view, and can facilitate new information supporting competent strategy: leading to a more satisfying, grounded real estate journey for everyone involved. A bonus section on **industry partners** awaits, designed to wrap up your mindful real estate journey and further empower your buying experience.

.

THE SELLER'S MINDFUL APPROACH

A seller's flow to embrace objectivity, channel creativity, and navigate the selling process with trust and emotional balance.

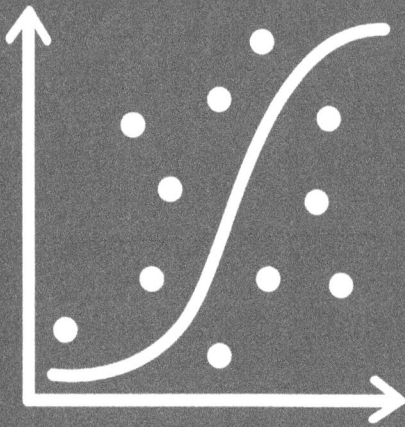

This mindful seller section builds on the <u>Download</u> to transform what you already know into something sharper, more intentional, and more rewarding. Whether this is your first sale or your fifth, it's designed to help you see the process through a *REcoded* lens—one that elevates awareness, confidence, and control at every step.

Curious about the new agency laws and how they affect you? Confused about your seller obligations or whether you still need to pay a buyer's broker fee? Unsure about who to hire for agency representation? Whether it's your first time selling or you simply want to *REcode* a previous real estate experience, you're not alone—and I'm glad you're here.

Selling a property is more than a transaction; it's an experience that often marks a major life transition. Given that you're tethered to *why* you are selling—whether you're making space for growth, navigating a loss or divorce, responding to a lifestyle change, or simply ready for a new chapter—emotions often accompany the logistics (and, in turn, can drive the experience from behind the scenes). This guide is designed for property owners who may feel uncertain or skeptical about the process. It offers an efficient approach that provides clarity and support, empowering you to lead with intention, take control, and actively navigate the selling process rather than simply react to it.

You'll gain insight into market activity, learn how to prepare purposefully, and understand how to choose an advocate who's focused on your best interests. We'll also explore how your property's location and condition affect your goals, how compensation impacts your negotiations, and how to leverage industry relationships to make informed decisions.

Having read this section, you'll set yourself and your property up to outshine the competition and be aligned for a successful transaction with a trusted agency partner committed to putting money in your pocket—not just a sign in your yard. Let's get started.

The Mindful Seller

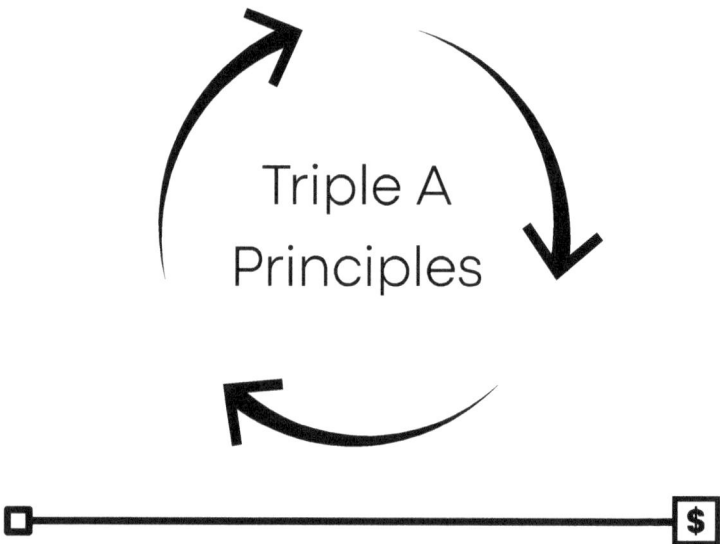

Triple A
Principles

The Triple A Principles: Acclimate, Agency, & Align

Selling a property isn't just a financial exchange; it involves navigating emotional challenges and making rapid decisions. While many apps might lead you to believe the process is simple and streamlined, the reality is far more complex and requires a commitment to integrity and transparency. By staying objective about the market you're about to enter, preparing thoughtfully, understanding buyer expectations, and gaining perspective, you as a seller should choose representation that advocates for your best interests while safeguarding against potential legal risks. This mindful approach ensures a smoother path to keep sellers centered throughout the journey.

As mentioned in the Download section, acclimating to the market is a gift you can give yourself—preparing you to align with a strong agency partner to create strategies to meet marketing and transaction obligations and thus presenting a check to you at closing. When sellers invest time and effort into the Triple As—Acclimate, Agency, and Align—before entering the market, they know what to expect, have more patience, and enjoy more control over their transactional experience because they trust both themselves and their professional team.

ACCLIMATE

As a seller, it is not on you to track every shift in the market. This *REsponsibility* belongs to local experts, brokers, and firms as the nucleus of your community. *Your* role is to acclimate to the current pulse so you are not surprised when you consult and interview local brokers and learn their interpretation of the market you are entering. Acclimating involves understanding the current pace and recent activity sellers are facing in seeking to attract willing and able buyers who will follow through to closing: preparing you for the reality ahead. This process can either validate your belief that the market favors you or otherwise reveal that your property value isn't what you had hoped. Ultimately, a property is only worth what a buyer is willing to pay and close on.

Market Activity: Location, Condition, & Pricing

Location is widely accepted as the most important factor when making a property purchase decision and often a solid way to build wealth, a consideration always at the forefront for buyers. When viewed from a "bird's eye" perspective, it's easy to understand why land is a precious commodity— making this scarce resource a valuable asset that can appreciate over time, particularly in areas with growing populations, economic development, and urban centers. Buyers seek conveniences, value community, and want their equity to grow and supplement their long-term portfolio. Location, meanwhile, is heavily influenced by proximity to utilities, amenities, schools, transportation, and financial hubs: all of which drive desirability, raise prices, and create high demand. As someone who knows your location better than anyone else and if you haven't already, now is the time to become aware of the community's effort (or lack thereof) to improve property values and understand what businesses are investing to be there and serve your community.

The key to optimizing your sale is timing. Consider aligning your listing with community projects, whether that means selling before construction begins to avoid disruptions or waiting until after a project is complete and the area has fully realized its enhanced value. Be proactive in soliciting and supporting new businesses to help them not only survive but thrive, contributing to the ongoing growth and prosperity of your community. Just as real estate investment trusts (REITs) shareholders rarely reinvest in or make direct contributions to communities where they hold properties, it's now more important than ever to cycle your wealth into your own community and support others to succeed. In nurturing the local economy, you'll create opportunities for everyone to build wealth *together* while also attracting the best buyers to your property when it eventually hits the market.

Condition. Acclimation for you as an owner is about observing the experiences of other sellers and collecting behavioral data. Be careful not to slip into direct comparisons against your own property, which happens later on when you align your location and condition with a price. After downloading your preferred real estate app and as mentioned in the Download section, monitor activity in your location and track properties *your* property would likely compete with in the same community/ district. This acclimation phase allows you to observe how buyers respond in a specific location, which property conditions they prioritize, and which features command top dollar as they enter the market. For example, buyers in one area may not hesitate to make an offer on a home with a small, dated kitchen lacking an island, if it offers an outdoor covered built-in grilling station with an adjoining entertaining space.

Sit back and observe. Are properties in your locale offering major interior improvements to attract buyers such as newer kitchens or baths or updated electrical and plumbing? What are sellers offering exterior-wise? A new roof, new siding, or fresh paint? Are there any patterns? Also note how many rooms or showers other properties offer. Does the floor plan accommodate aging family members? How flexible is the outdoor space, and is the home pet-friendly? This acclimation exercise is not about comparing/contrasting but instead becoming aware of your competition's enhancements, perhaps inspiring you to consider necessary improvements or accommodations (for an aging population or pet-conscious buyers, for example) to prepare for a strategy consultation with a local broker.

Quick Transition Note: I do lean into enhancements, improvements. and updates throughout this mindful guide, but during acclimation, you may find the collected data of buyer behavior points to pending and closed properties that offered little to no improvements. No matter the condition, this indicates a hot market and provides relief to owners who in turn will not be expected to make upfront investments in improvements to prepare to sell. Beware, though: If the market only recently transitioned into a seller's market, buyers may still have expectations for the inspection and appraisal to carve out opportunities to negotiate such requests.

If the market transitioned from a seller's market to a neutral or buyer's market, on the other hand, you'll need to be prepared for more competitive pricing strategies. During this transition, buyers may have more negotiating power and expect a higher degree of flexibility with respect to price, repairs, and/or contingencies. While improvements are perhaps optional in a seller's market, they can become necessary to attract the right buyer in a more competitive environment; it's crucial to have the ability to pivot your pricing and preparation strategies accordingly. Let acclimation help you prepare responsibly. By staying informed and maintaining control over your pricing and positioning, you ensure you're always ready to move forward with confidence no matter the direction the market takes.

Be curious. It can be difficult to feel out a property, but do your best to identify the lifestyle it offers when marketed properly. Which features does it provide to meet buyers' #needs&wants? A preferred, convenient, or waterfront location? Meticulous landscaping or a unique lot? Thoughtful design to showcase a view or provide privacy? Handy amenities? Buyers will accept inferior conditions for superior land or conveniences—or simply the property's potential—especially if surrounding properties are of higher value or neighbors are making improvements and thus building wealth appreciation collectively.

Buyer hesitation = time to pivot. As you acclimate to the market, you'll start to notice which properties attract ready buyers and thus quickly transition from "available" to "pending" status. When buyers hesitate, it typically signals that the property doesn't meet their needs or wants in terms of location, condition, or price. This is a clear cue for the seller to pivot their strategy to better align with the market. Leaving a property listed as "available" for too long a duration sends a passive signal that the seller is perhaps unwilling to acknowledge necessary price adjustments or improvements— implying they may be in denial or not prepared to collaborate. Pay attention to how brokers react when their listings are rejected. Do they enhance marketing to highlight key features and/or advise the seller to make necessary improvements or adjust the price? The bottom line: **Price is the ultimate equalizer for location and condition.** Overpriced properties do not go unnoticed; they simply go unsold. If you're planning to sell, take note. Observing others' attempts to test the market reveals what *not* to do: overprice based on location, condition, or both.

Smart marketing. As you prepare to sell, take time to study how the current inventory is presented: reviewing listing photos and hyper focusing on how marketing remarks are crafted to highlight key features. Professional staging serves multiple purposes, showcasing a room's potential, complementing property architecture, and subtly distracting from any imperfections. Smart marketing can tempt buyers to prioritize a *want* over a *need*, sometimes even leading them to pay a premium for it.

Smart Marketing Example: A buyer may <u>need two bathrooms</u>, but a property hits the market with <u>one</u> stunning bathroom featuring a double vanity and luxurious shower. Despite the lack of a second bathroom, these appealing features could trigger an emotional *want* and thus cause the buyer to prioritize this over their original *need* for a second bathroom.

Capitalize on property strengths when "pending". If your property has standout features but lacks what buyers in the market *need* or falls short compared to the competition, a well negotiated earnest money deposit can serve as a key leverage point. Buyers can be fickle; if reality doesn't align with their needs *after* mutual acceptance (#MA) and during due diligence, they may experience buyer's remorse and back out of the contract—unless they fear losing their earnest money, that is. While improvements can add value, sellers should be mindful of the risk of *over*-improving (investing more than necessary for the neighborhood or market). This can lead to a mismatch between what the property is worth and what buyers are willing to pay. Keep a close eye on "pending" listings to see which properties actually close ("sold") and thus successfully balanced strategic marketing with improvements aligning with market challenges and buyer *needs*.

Back On Market (BOMK). Pay attention to properties that move from "pending" status to "BOMK" status, indicating the buyer backed out *after* #MA. It's difficult to know exactly why this happened, and the seller sometimes never learns why. **Every seller assumes some risk with every buyer**—there is always the possibility that a buyer may choose to cancel the contract.

Beware of new competition. Aside from discovering something unacceptable during due diligence, an unexpected detail from the seller's disclosure, or a surprise in the inspection report, buyers sometimes realize the market shifted in their favor and want to move on to a better option now available. Depending on #MA terms, they may choose to exercise their right to rescind the first contract; this happens! In other words, if you accept an offer but a flood of new inventory for buyers to choose from suddenly hits the market, you must do your best to keep your buyer in contract during their due diligence. Aim to collaborate and remove their inspection contingency to avoid going BOMK and being forced to compete with new listings that may be priced lower or offer superior improvements.

Watch for patterns and shifts in market activity, noting how BOMK properties adjust their marketing to recapture buyers. These subtle yet important nuances can impact your future experience. The more curiosity and effort you invest during this acclimation phase, the better prepared you'll be to collaborate with your broker on a successful strategy—helping you avoid potential BOMK pitfalls.

Closed (sold) properties. When your app of choice reveals your tracked properties have "sold", if possible, make an effort to unveil if sellers

1. Consented to a lower price,

2. Made any improvements after the sale went "pending",

3. Paid any of the buyer's closing costs,

4. Paid any of the buyer broker compensation.

This closed data reflects the market and how sellers are negotiating with buyers to remove their contingencies, perform, and close: ultimately putting net proceed funds in seller pockets. The acclimation phase is like a science project whereby you observe how other properties test, fail, or succeed in the market; witness how other sellers get it done in real time by observing how they finalize contract terms per their location and conditions to meet buyer demands. Get to know what it takes to reap the most money in the least amount of (marketing) time while simultaneously creating a satisfying selling experience.

Comparing Brokers

As you acclimate, pay attention to local brokers in your community who consistently close sales, *especially* those with a high "list-to-sell ratio": an indicator of how well a property's final sale price aligns with its original listing price. These brokers work closely and partner with their sellers to price properties appropriately for their location and condition while leveraging strategic marketing to highlight key property features; this often involves honest (and perhaps tough) conversations with their sellers to encourage necessary (and perhaps inconvenient) improvements to attract the most buyers and maximize value.

A high list-to-sell ratio is an underappreciated metric that reflects a broker's ability to effectively position a property in the market. As you track "closed" properties, add these brokers to your list to interview—particularly those with a proven record of closing above, at, or near the original listed price. They've earned another seller's trust!

I'm getting a little ahead of myself here—as I want you to focus on acclimation—but let's lean into agency for a moment to truly appreciate this metric. When interviewing to hire seller representation, you will know whether a broker is truly invested in your success: the right one not just telling you what you want to hear and diluting facts but providing honest insights about how your property will compete. Their BPO (broker price opinion) will reflect your location and condition to match market conditions and include recommendations to attract serious, qualified, and able buyers.

If you receive multiple BPOs from your consultations and one is lower with burdensome suggestions compared to a higher BPO with little to no suggestions, it might be a red flag. These discussions can be difficult for owners—as it's easy to adopt a passive stance and believe the lower BPO broker only wants a quick sale and thus dismiss their strategic advice—when they in fact could set you up for a swift and smart sale with a high "list-to-sell ratio".

Too many times, I've lost listings to brokers who "bought" them by offering a higher BPO. I'd see a property come on the market with little to no preparation—just a sign in the yard—then sure enough, a price reduction or two would occur a few weeks or months later before it finally went under contract. It's frustrating and, frankly, fails to serve the seller's best interest when a good property suffers "days on market" (DOM) and becomes a "stale" listing because the broker didn't act with competence. While the seller may believe the higher BPO is in their best interest, it often leads to frustration—lots of showings and no offers along with inspection-driven repair requests. They may lose faith in the real estate industry altogether and miss an opportunity to work with a good broker, one who makes the time and effort necessary to create a thoughtful market preparation list: setting the owner and property up to attract the right buyer and achieve a successful sale in less time at the right price.

List-to-Sell Example: An owner ("John") had owned a property that featured a large open kitchen with an island, living there happily for several years. I was personally recommended to him for real estate representation when he retired and decided to relocate out of state. During our walk-through, I instantly remembered the property when it was on the market years before (due to its unmistakable bright-blue Formica countertops) and advised him to replace the dated countertops with neutral-colored granite or quartz. The property was in a fantastic location and in good condition overall yet still had not updated the original single-pane windows, which the competition had, something else I remarked and noted in my BPO. John was stubborn, almost defiant, and took the countertop recommendation personally. He loved the kitchen, and it was one of the main selling points back when he'd purchased the home.

Although he received a quote for new countertops, John was dead set against going through the "hassle" and expense but liked my suggested BPO and requested I get the property on the market. I politely declined, as my BPO stood only if he upgraded the kitchen counters, and we found ourselves at a standstill.

We toured competing properties the next day, and after just one afternoon of viewing, he realized the competition's offerings were better (and pouted all the way home). We then reviewed "pending" and "sold" comparables, after which John reluctantly agreed that updating the countertops was in his best interest to attract buyers—and avoid being known as "the blue countertop house" (with outdated windows). I assured him he would receive top dollar if he acted immediately to take advantage of his late-spring partial water view—something few of his competitors offered—but reminded him that we were at peak season so time was of the essence. John decided to trust my guidance despite his hesitations and invest in new countertops.

We listed the property the week the countertops were updated. To John's good fortune, he accepted a full-price cash offer in less than two weeks—much faster and better terms than his competition. At closing, he revealed he'd interviewed other brokers and received several BPOs at a lower list price with no recommendation to update the countertops—only to replace the windows—and hadn't believed that going through the hassle and expense to make any improvement would put more money in his pocket than what the other BPOs had stated. As a thank you, John surprised me with a bouquet of flowers and a hug (two things I love!).

This experience reinforces the value of remaining open to professional advice, even when it challenges preconceived notions. As sellers, staying mindful of both emotional and practical factors impacting a sale—paired with thoughtful upgrades and attention paid to time the market—can make a significant difference in securing a successful, profitable transaction.

Shifting market curiosity. Most sellers don't take enough time to acclimate, let alone track recent seller journeys *before* mutual acceptance (#B4MA) or understand what those sellers ultimately consented to *after* #MA in order to successfully close. Without investing time and effort to acclimate, BPOs that don't match an owner's outlook can create a margin of misunderstanding and unrealistic expectancies. During broker consultations, be inquisitive and learn what recent sellers did to succeed—actually close and receive their funds. Did they need to incorporate a price adjustment (or two), and if so, after how many days? Was it due to overpricing or a shift in the market? Did they negotiate and collaborate on improvements to satisfy the buyer (inspection contingency) or buyer's lender (appraisal)? Not every broker has full insight or a relationship with other brokers to uncover all the particulars, but they *can* make qualified guesses based on their own closing experiences and hints from MLS listing history or closing details. Avoid naïveté, be proactive in your curiosity, ask questions, gather specifics, and mindfully prep multiple strategies to prepare for market.

Search for thriving brokers who don't dwell on the challenges of a shifting market but navigate it with confidence, leveraging their experience and data to guide their clients through strategic choices and knowing how and when to adjust to market changes. Since the average property owner sells three to four times in their lifetime, it can be difficult to distinguish between a broker's genuine confidence and perceived arrogance. At the same time, avoid brokers with a negative or defeatist attitude; this energy is not welcomed when entering the market and during negotiations. Seek pragmatism, not pessimism. Stay focused on finding a broker who aligns with your goals, has the competence to outline strategies, and is committed to helping you attract the right buyer—even in a shifting market.

REturning to the Earlier List-to-Sell Example:
Because I was actively previewing new listings at the time and had a comprehensive understanding of all "available" inventory (along with a consistent closing record spanning almost 20 years at the time), my confidence was unwavering. I also knew the partial

water-view property had to capitalize on the spring season and leverage its open kitchen (with, hopefully, brand-new countertops) to win a buyer's heart despite the original windows. As John continued to contemplate, I noticed his strongest competition had gone "pending"—the market introducing little new inventory. Timing was crucial, and he had a small window of opportunity in his favor. Once I explained the data and how it aligned with my spring marketing strategy, he decided to move forward and schedule the work immediately. Not only did John earn his "countertop investment" back, but he received a higher price than the other brokers BPOs stated he would receive—making it all worth the effort!

Interview Etiquette

As a paying client, you deserve to hire the best broker to represent your interests. Loyalty matters, so if you're considering working again with the broker who helped you purchase the property you now want to sell—but want to interview others—be transparent about your intentions. Let your previous broker know you're exploring your options. While they shouldn't assume they'll automatically represent you, they'll likely hope for the opportunity—especially if they served you well during a challenging purchase.

If that broker has proven their value, it's worth starting the consultation process with them first to see if the chemistry and fit remain strong for your current goals. *Mindful Real Estate* was written to empower you to #strategize&bewise, giving you the confidence to make deliberate decisions—whether you stay with a trusted partner or explore new options.

Non-solicitor. Once you've decided who to partner with, you are under no obligation to meet with another broker seeking a chance to discuss your upcoming sale. Be polite, but don't waste your time—or theirs. If a broker pushes aggressively, pressures you, or tries to shame or personalize the conversation—perhaps due to a past connection, shared affiliation, or sense of entitlement—they are revealing their true character. They are acting in their own best interest, not yours. This happens more often than you'd think. Be clear and honest in your communication, and choose a broker who demonstrates integrity, respect, and support for your process.

The trust formula. How brokers conduct consultations provides valuable insight into how they will manage your future transactions. To earn your trust and display competence, they should begin by implementing a regimen to ensure compliance with local laws and regulations so you can focus on your future responsibilities (e.g., disclosure and contractual obligations to achieve your selling goal). To identify a results-driven professional, seek out those who provide accurate information (in their BPO), proactively address potential challenges (e.g., a potential market shift), and demonstrate a proven record of selling and serving their community. Accomplished brokers leverage their relationships, industry partners, and experience to set their clients up for success. Above all, they uphold the highest standards, ensuring transparency and rooting every interaction in sincerity to earn your business. A client-focused broker practices with a commitment to ethical conduct, calculated to minimize your risk while earning compensation through market expertise, conscientiousness, and advocacy.

Value-driven guidance. Sellers often experience anxiety and fear of judgment, especially when their property has deferred maintenance or lacks updates. These concerns can trigger feelings of inadequacy, hesitation, or even defensiveness about entering the market. It's important to recognize that these emotions are natural and that every broker has worked to guide other sellers who've felt similarly. Committed listing brokers work with the intent to earn their compensation because they care about what they do and aren't there to judge but instead provide valuable services to help you push past any worries and reach your desired outcome.

Mutual consent. There's nothing wrong with hiring a success-driven broker with substantial goals so long as they remain committed to your best interests. I've personally worked alongside and managed equally successful brokers with contrasting winning styles. Some are direct and calculated, delivering matter-of-fact opinions that many owners find reassuring to provide a clear and confident path forward. Other owners, however, perceive this approach as overly assertive or dismissive of their unique selling situation: feeling the consultation is more about the broker's ego than their future success. Let me assure you this is not always the case.

Then there are the brokers who take a more diplomatic and collaborative approach, thoughtfully guiding sellers through market data and gently easing them into the market reality at a slower pace. Their empathetic approach complements a side-by-side cooperation that encourages the client to reach their own pricing realization. While this can morph into an attentive partnership, some may perceive it as lacking assertiveness—which is not always true.

Neither style is inherently better than the other as both can lead to successful results. The key is to compare brokers during the consultation process to identify who aligns with your *why,* timeline, and communication preferences while also ensuring the right chemistry for a working relationship. Finding a respectful broker you connect with on a personal level can make all the difference during the collaboration phases #B4MA and *after* #MA. Together, you can enjoy a trusting real estate partnership built on mutual consent, clear expectations, and respect in order to create your satisfying real estate experience.

Hiring representation provides numerous advantages. Entering into a short-term relationship with a professional broker is a critical decision in the selling process. As a seller, your acclimation to the market has created a list or pointed you to a competent broker offering market insight, a proactive approach, and the skills to navigate legalities and negotiations. Brokers with deep ties to local communities are committed to upholding the highest standards of ethics, integrity, and transparency and will always prioritize your interests and avoid conflicts of interest. Following your seller consultations, you'll have multiple BPOs in hand to help you align your location and condition with the right price along with a tailored strategy—one that includes alternatives to pivot if necessary, depending on shifting market conditions. The advantages of professional representation include access to up-to-date market data and trends, a plan to secure the best possible terms, contract law guidance to meet obligations and avoid costly pitfalls, and an essential marketing strategy that highlights your property's strengths to attract serious qualified buyers. These advantages are crucial for ensuring your property outshines the competition and can successfully close in a competitive market.

Unlike app-based platforms driven primarily by algorithms or corporate incentives, a dedicated local broker is committed to your goals—not just transaction volume. By choosing representation from an established firm that prioritizes transparency, high ethical standards, and a focus on agency, you gain a trusted advocate who is fully invested in protecting your interests. They serve as your partner, guiding you through local selling customs and providing a well-informed, satisfying real estate experience. This approach helps you build long-term wealth rather than benefit corporate stakeholders.

AGENCY

Hiring an Agency Partner

Top brokers are in demand and operate with a level of professionalism that prioritizes efficiency and results. They bring consistency, strategic foresight, and a deep understanding of market dynamics to every transaction. The most effective brokers are strong listeners who maintain balance, avoid burnout, and stay sharp under pressure—their calculated advice and performance-driven approach providing clients with the clarity needed to move forward in the market with confidence.

In acclimating responsibly—tracking inventory activity to feel the pulse of the location your property will compete in (zip code or district)—you make the consulting and interview process that much more efficient, jumping straight into market data to strategize your location and condition and ultimately target a competitive price point. As I mentioned before, the opinions brokers share regarding what your property needs to prepare for the market should not come as a surprise since you've already observed what other sellers have done to attract buyers (adding a new roof, updating bathrooms, slapping on a fresh coat of paint, etc.).

Consultation (#Needs&Wants, #Strategy&Success)

Schedule a 30-minute consultation with each potential listing broker to assess their market expertise, pricing strategy, transaction philosophy, and competence with listing agreements and purchase and/or sale contracts. As you explore their selling record, you'll uncover how they define success—through measurable stats like DOM and "list-to-sell ratio," as well as testimonials that reveal their ability to deliver a satisfying client experience.

Be mindful during each consultation to differentiate a broker who truly listens and collaborates versus one who simply tells you what you want to hear. Competitiveness is valuable, but blind appeasement is a warning sign. You deserve an advisor who provides honest, fact-based insights on positioning your property and defends their recommendations with diplomacy and clarity. If a broker's first move is handing you an agency or listing agreement before understanding your why and the specifics of your property, they are not the right match. Their time is offered as a courtesy to earn your business, and the agency discussion should follow once you've both confirmed you're a good match for this listing partnership.

To collaborate is to work together toward a shared goal. In the past, property owners often sought out a "shark" to negotiate aggressively and with little regard for collaboration or a mutually beneficial outcome. That approach is far less effective today and considered weak and unsophisticated— the mark of a broker more interested in domination than in doing meaningful representation or building a reputable business. When choosing a quality listing broker, you'll instead want to focus on their reputation, ability to build strong, loyal relationships, and strategic mindset to achieve satisfying results: all signs of a collaborator. This sophisticated combination will identify a broker who's driven by client success and will advocate in your best interest.

Time is money: Prepare, prepare, prepare. Many capable sellers overlook the value of strategic pre-market investments, dismissing time- and cost-intensive recommendations. As days on the market accumulate, reluctant price reductions often become necessary to attract qualified buyers just to meet a need or want. Once under contract, additional negotiations can further disrupt the *after* #MA flow, often leading to frustrating last-minute repairs—tasks that should have been completed when first advised. The result is a "pending" phase that feels unprepared and unsatisfying—all while juggling the logistics of a move.

Strategic brokers can confidently advocate for tried-and-true methods to invest time and money upfront in order to address deferred maintenance, make smart updates, and present a market ready property—or defend a suggested price to make up for the condition while striving to meet buyer demands. While it's difficult to quantify the future dollar value of such efforts, reducing market time can minimize risk, refine negotiations, and potentially attract multiple buyers willing to meet or exceed original expectations.

Challenge brokers with curiosity if they don't recommend improvements *or* if they do. Either which way, you'll receive their market perspectives so you can weigh your risk accordingly. How they reply or deflect can build a stronger connection or otherwise eliminate them from your hiring list. If recommendations are in fact made, this is an opportunity to seek professional opinions and cost estimates to either apply immediately or as deliberate choices in preparation for potential negotiations with buyers—especially if a few key updates could help an incoming buyer secure financing. It's how you mindfully prepare for future showings, inspections, or appraisal obstacles, controlling your experience because you're informed of the required time and costs to correct conditions #B4MA or during negotiations to reach #MA.

A BPO is often reported in a comparative market analysis (CMA) or by letter, providing recent data to speculate on your future sale and comparing/contrasting your location and condition with market data to find a ready buyer—unlike some app-based algorithms. If the BPO value does not align with your acclimated belief, this could signal a shifting market or your own personal skepticism towards commission-compensated salespeople. The misnomer is that a broker's lower price opinion may be grounded in gaining an "easy sale." Common disconnects like these are perhaps related to ignoring reality, your unawareness of recent sellers' necessary actions integral to meeting market demands, your unwillingness to respect recommended improvements, or simply the fact that unexpected price opinions are in your best interest. Please take this last sentence seriously, choosing to invest time and effort to acclimate and thus understand the realities of the market.

To expand your reach and attract as many buyers as possible, strive to appeal to **owner occupant buyers**—those who want to live in and be part of the community. It's worth considering how a few thoughtful repairs can make a real difference here, these buyers often using **conventional, first-time, or VA (Veterans Affairs) buyer loan programs** that require the property's condition to be safe, functional, and free of major defects.

Updates that support lending and ownership include, but not limited to:

- Repairing roof and gutter leaks
- Fixing exposed wiring or other safety issues
- Replacing broken windows
- Correcting cracked or damaged tile grout
- Caulking the floor around the toilet and tub
- Ensuring the heating system is in working order
- Addressing peeling paint or signs of water intrusion

Taking care of these items isn't just a transaction strategy—it's an **act of stewardship** reflecting pride in what you've owned and contributing to a more accessible path to ownership for prospective buyers.

Anyone can sell a property as-is, but sellers who choose to make their property loan-able for the next generation of buyers support the kind of ownership that strengthens communities and narrows wealth gaps. A few thoughtful steps can help someone start their journey toward stability, equity, and generational wealth—and that's an outcome to be proud of.

Representation or Restriction? Know the Difference.

Some firms are quietly redefining the word "*strategy*"—not through better preparation or deeper market expertise, but by restricting exposure under the guise of "exclusivity." Polished marketing can enlist sellers to withhold listings from the open market, making available only to a limited internal pool of buyers. On the surface, it sounds tailored; in practice, it's a restriction disguised as service.

Achieving the highest value for your property in the least amount of time is your goal. That means attracting all the best buyers—those who are qualified, ready, and able to commit to closing. Be discerning. Grasp how firms market properties using sophisticated "exclusive" promotions to funnel sellers and buyers into a limited internal pool, creating the illusion of upscale service. What may seem strategic can actually limit exposure, obscure true market value, and misrepresent demand. Hire a service-oriented broker whose competence, experience, and sound guidance—not buyer feedback or phased price adjustments—drive the process. With transparent, data-driven insight, they ensure your property reaches the right buyers and achieves the best possible outcome.

Don't mistake exclusivity for strategy. Stay curious and ask the tough questions:

- How will I get the most money given fewer buyers within the confines of an exclusive marketing strategy?

- Does real market data back my premium price?

- What percentage of your exclusive listings reduce their price after receiving buyer feedback?

- How prepared are your buyers to fulfill the contract and actually close?

- What is your firm's sale fail rate?

- Are you actively analyzing current market activity or just waiting for buyers to react?

- From the original private list price to the final "closed" price, what is your "list-to-sell ratio"? (The broker may loop in the company's average to skew their own.)

When listings aren't restricted and made visible to all, agency is held to the highest standard: ensuring professional representation is accountable to ethics. The entire market benefits, and everyone has an opportunity to build wealth. High-caliber brokers affiliated with these firms prioritize inclusivity over selective or preferential service levels, and remain committed to professional ethics. Transactions become more satisfying when buyers are fully informed, and sellers gain true value rather than manufactured momentum. Inclusive practices are not a weakness but the foundation of a stronger, more trusted profession and the reason clients return and hire professional advocacy—loyal, educated, and confident they were fully represented.

Motivation: Truth

Are you selling to meet a deadline? If so, you'll need to price the property competitively to beat the market as there may not be time to make marketable improvements. Scrutinize the current "available" inventory buyers have already picked through to compare and contrast your property with the intent to undercut others' pricing and/or gauge their price-adjustment strategy. Remember: You need to find the buyer before *they* do.

While you may lose some buyers willing to pay more for upgrades or in need of improvements to meet their loan requirements, your priority is to partner with the right broker who can help you find the pricing sweet spot and accommodate your deadline—someone with the availability and focus to give your listing the attention it deserves. Ask your broker if they recommend a pre inspection, and weigh the risks: Will it save market time? Will it be convenient for buyers? In situations like yours, if your property is in "loan-able" condition, then a pre-inspection could be in your best interest to take the necessary steps to meet the deadline smoothly.

When time is of the essence, it is not appropriate to attempt the "spit-wad" approach, meaning "Let's just see what happens." I've witnessed many sellers who—torn by FOMO (fear of missing out)—attempt to chase a higher price only to face difficult negotiations to reach #MA. Added stress during the inspection contingency follows, leading to an unnecessarily challenging transaction that could've been avoided. The deadline is your *why*, and you lack the luxury of time. Stay grounded and choose the lowest-risk path to move forward to your next chapter.

Being prepared means being loan-able. Too often, sellers unknowingly cut themselves off from a large, qualified buyer pool simply because the property doesn't meet basic lending standards. Here's the truth: some of your most motivated buyers out there are veterans, first time owners, or people using down-payment loans. They're emotionally invested, financially qualified, performance-able to close, and want to become committed members of the community—but can only do this if the property passes appraisal and meets loan guidelines. Think of it as preparation with a purpose: the more loan-able your property is, the more eyes you attract, the more offers you invite, and the more leverage you have when it's time to negotiate.

You don't want to leave your sale up to chance or chase one elusive cash buyer. You want *options*. The best way to increase them is to ensure your property qualifies for *all* types of financing. This is especially important when you consider your competition, how many properties are actively for sale in your area (months of supply), and how fast they're going under contract (absorption rate). Mindful sellers don't just list their property; they proactively position themselves for a successful closing. Being loan-able is a smart, strategic move that gives you—and your future buyer—the best possible outcome.

Are you selling because you need more space, additional rooms, or better amenities? Is your property an ideal alternative for a condo buyer or first-time owner? If so, it's likely in high demand—not just among owner-occupied buyers but also large-scale investors such as REITs and other cash investors. As a seller, you can steward your community by marketing to attract buyers who want to own so they may contribute to its growth and vitality, rather than serving outside investors or REITs who prioritize shareholders and do not concern themselves with the long-term well-being of the neighborhood or the people who live there.

While a cash offer can be appealing for its convenience, remember that you were once a first time buyer too. Selling to large investors may feel easy, but it's important to weigh the long-term impact. Large investor portfolios can displace future homeowners and alter the character of a community, while local investors often support neighborhood sustainability. Partner with a knowledgeable local representative who can assess your property's eligibility for FHA, VA, or down-payment assistance programs and guide you on improvements that make the home more "loan-able". Selling to a new homeowner allows them to build equity, appreciation, and generational wealth— strengthening your community in the process.

Jumbo buyers. Understanding if your property will likely attract buyers who plan to apply for a jumbo loan is crucial, directly impacting your expectations and selling experience. If your property falls into a luxury price point, it may attract high-net-worth buyers—some of whom may obtain a jumbo loan to finance their purchase. Jumbo loans, often for amounts above conventional loan limits (which vary by location and are subject to change), typically involve more stringent underwriting and extended processing, which can lead to appraisal delays. Sellers should be prepared for these potential delays and understand that financing may take longer since jumbo loans carry greater risk for the lender. Clarifying the type of financing associated with an offer helps anticipate timelines for the purchase and/or sale contract, supporting a smoother transaction.

Selling on behalf of an "estate?" As an assigned executor, you might have to oblige or be mindful of heirs in how you spend money and prepare the property only to divide the net proceeds later. This can be tricky and depend on how the estate is set up, beneficiary dynamics, or both—everyone who stands to benefit seemingly knows someone who "sells real estate." Handling an estate, likewise, is often a complex and emotionally charged process. As the executor, you must hire a broker who respects these circumstances and—as your partner—will collaborate with the estate's attorney to ensure all legal requirements are met. If you are not obligated to confer with those who benefit, neither is your broker. The attorney will manage communications, navigate any potential legal issues, and ensure all necessary documentation is properly filed: ultimately safeguarding the interests of all beneficiaries involved. You and your broker, in turn, can strategize and perform all necessary duties to set the estate up for success to meet market conditions so final funds can be distributed per the deceased's wishes.

Selling a destination property? If your property relies on seasons or is a retreat/second home, your plan must be calculated. The season during which your property is most attractive to buyers is probably no secret, so be sure to choose a broker who's in tune with seasonal activity—or a lack thereof—over the past 12 months. Your goal is to optimize when buyers traditionally make serious offers.

If you value privacy and your destination-style property is in a close-kit community, be cautious about who you share your intent to sell with; you may not be the only owner strategizing a future sale. If you're interviewing multiple brokers, make it clear that the consultation must be kept confidential. You have the right to request an NDA (non-disclosure agreement) with restrictions regarding whom on the team the broker can discuss your file with.

Need to sell in the off-season? A calculated approach to outshine the competition includes perhaps hiring a photographer and videographer to shoot the property and showcase its lifestyle features during the destination's peak season: controlling the narrative and marketing to achieve top dollar, no matter the time of year. The goal is to surprise your future competition when you eventually hit the market, leaving them no time to prepare and outshine your listing.

How to Strategize an Offering Price

By now, you've familiarized yourself with the market, received consultations, and discussed strategies to opt for. Local brokers spent time to provide consultations and prepare CMAs with their BPOs as a complimentary courtesy to earn your trust and be hired to facilitate a sale. If you haven't already, it's time to choose a broker for a short-term partnership with a listing agreement, set expectations, and commit to a compensation plan.

With your acclimation experience, current analysis of the market, and suggested price opinions, you know approximately the price range your property will compete in. Now it's time to strategize your offering price—including conversations around your price margins and future price adjustments. *That doesn't make sense*, you might think. Actually, it does. Let me explain…

Because the BPOs you received disclose what sellers of recently "closed" properties consented to (justifying their location and condition) to not only attract buyers, but keep them under contract, and eventually close, you now have the same data buyer brokers (and appraisers) have access to. This information, when studied, can predict the endgame with respect to upcoming new inventory. Will prices and/or terms remain flexible? Will prices come down or otherwise rise?

So how do you get the most money in the least amount of time? By looking beyond closed ("sold") sales data, you and your broker can compare side-by-side "available" and "pending" inventory to anticipate the competition's next move and position your strategies to succeed.

- Available inventory is the current competition who, at the present time, are "testing" their price against location and condition while waiting for a ready buyer.

- Pending inventory reflects the pulse of the market, revealing what inventory recent buyers have committed to (*after* #MA) in the last 30 days.

Collect the data by printing "available" and "pending" search lists. Start with a broad price margin to flank each side of the suggested value from your recent BPOs. Before printing, ideally, sort or filter the price column to be shown in descending order. Additional columns, if offered (bedrooms, bathrooms, square footage, lot size, days on market, and buyer-broker compensation) provide valuable data to include as well. Once both lists are printed, the contrasting breakdown will uncover differences: exposing how the market is or is not responding to buyers' expectations.

> _Example:_ If recent BPOs reveal your property's **suggested price** is around $450,000 but you were **hoping** for $500,000, let's test a "hopothesis" and prove the BPOs are wrong (Get it? Hypothesis but with a little "hope." Sorry, I couldn't help myself.).

> In this case, the margin will flank $50,000 on **each side of the BPOs' suggested price**, ultimately printing a range from $400,000 to $500,000 (not limiting other criteria such as square footage, etc. for the purposes of this example).

Exposing a broad range such as this may reveal a market shift, obvious or subtle, whether in your favor or otherwise. Are prices going up or coming down? Are properties going "pending" within days or taking months to accept an offer? Has the number of rooms (AKA "room count" all rooms, not only bedrooms), baths, or square footage shifted? Are sellers offering major improvements, or are buyers accepting conditions that need updating or perhaps less square footage? What can you predict from this collected data?

Example Pattern: If the majority of "pending" properties are under $460,000 and "available" inventory is holding steady above the $475,000 price margin, this tells us three things:

1. BPOs suggested $450,000 list price seem realistic to what buyers are making offers on;

2. Current competition above $475,000 will soon enact price reductions to correct the misalignment and generate new buyer attention;

3. You may need to adjust your "hope" mindset for a $500,000 buyer.

Breaking Down Price Ranges: On these printed lists (in descending price order), a reliable method is to draw a line to segregate listings into price range groups. In this case, on both the "available" and "pending" lists, draw three lines dividing the inventory into $25,000 ranges: $475,000, $450,000, and $425,000. Segregated price ranges are the same, but the number of listings within each one will vary.

Note: Ranges may vary depending on the price point (e.g., $10,000 margins for budget-conscious properties and $500,000+ for premium ones). Your local broker will suggest appropriate margins.

Feel the Pulse of the Market

"Pending" Competition Snapshot

Start by reviewing the segregated "pending" inventory list—properties reflecting recent buyer behavior and accepted offers—and each range to analyze pricing momentum. For example:

- **$500,000–$475,000:** 2 properties pending, average days on market is 45
- **$475,000–$450,000:** 5 properties pending, average days on market is 50
- **$450,000–$425,000:** 3 properties pending, average days on market is 31
- **$425,000–$400,000:** 8 properties pending, average days on market is 12

In this case, 18 sellers have negotiated, accepted offers, and are now "pending" between $400,000 and $500,000. This snapshot reveals buyer demand and gives you a real-time sense of the market's pulse.

Reading Between "Pending" Ranges

Two price ranges stand out within the data:

- **$425,000–$400,000**

  - 8 of 18 pending sales (44%)

  - Indicates strong buyer activity, taking less than two weeks to make offers. These buyers aren't too picky.

- **$475,000–$450,000**

  - 5 of 18 pending sales (27%)

  - Indicates a seller's market, taking four times longer to go under contract (yet still under 6 months). These sellers may have tested the market above $475,000 (maybe $499,999?) and adjusted the price before attracting ready buyers.

Together, these two price ranges account for over 70% of buyers who made offers yet are operating in two distinct ranges. This is where objectivity matters most. It's time to be curious, analytical, and open-minded. The data may not make it convenient, but it's revealing the market's truth. This is the nitty-gritty. It's easy to give up—Hang in there.

"Pending" Differences

With such a segregated divide between the **$400,000–$425,000** (44%) and **$450,000–$475,000** (27%) ranges, what's driving the difference beyond price? Likely contributors include:

- Room and bathroom count
- Square footage
- Location, lot size, or both
- Scope of improvements
- Whether the listing offers compensation to a buyer's broker or not
- Past price adjustments

Such factors should differ significantly to justify such a great divide. Can you spot the differences? Now, you and your broker know the market's pulse and can strategize to outshine the "available" competition—your hopeful heart setting aside emotion and staying objective to get the pricing right.

"Available" Competition Snapshot

Now, compare your property's location and condition to the list of "available" inventory priced from $400,000 to $500,000.

HOPE Price = $500,000

- **$500,000–$475,000:** 10 properties available, average days on market is 55

- **$475,000–$450,000:** 5 properties available, average days on market is 34

    —BPO (suggested) Value = $450,000 —

- **$450,000–$425,000:** 10 properties available, average days on market is 15

- **$425,000–$400,000:** 5 properties available, average days on market is 7

Here, 30 sellers are actively competing for a performance-able buyer. Competition is evenly split on each side of the BPO value, but average "days on market" is significantly distinct. With our hopothesis ($500,000 price) in mind, what is the highest price we can offer and outshine the competition? "Pending" data has already prepared you for the $475,000 to $450,000 range, meaning you can study your competition through this lens.

Understanding the Competitive Data

Above $450,000 BPO Value:

- **$500,000–$475,000**

    ○ 10 properties "available" and are competing in your "hope" price margin.

    ○ These properties have been sitting for nearly 2 months, likely strategizing price adjustments and an updated marketing plan to compete with future competition and attract a fresh set of buyers.

- I would really scrutinize their improvements, room count, and the lifestyle these properties offer in contrast to yours. Buyers have high expectations, and this inventory isn't meeting them.

- If I were these sellers' listing brokers, I would likely recommend to stop wasting precious market time and either make improvements based on feedback (if possible) or adjust their price to shift under the $475,000 line.

- **$475,000–$450,000**

  - 5 properties "available"; with 27% of current "pendings" in this range, this indicates active buyers like this price range a lot.

  - Moving three weeks faster than those competing above $475,000 (and with an average market time of just over a month, compared to "pendings" in this range averaging closer to 2 months), this indicates these buyers are hungry.

  - Dig a little deeper to verify if any of these properties have made price adjustments; if not and to strategize ahead, I would guess they will in about 3 weeks (as to not surpass "pendings" average days).

- In reviewing this range, I recommend having a calculated mindset to win the buyer these sellers will be aiming for after their price adjustment.

Strategy session: Pause and ask: What risks do I take if I price above the BPO value to get closer to the "hope" price? The data does not support competing above $475,000 as the $475,000 to $450,000 range offers less competition and fewer average days; this is where you and your broker collaborate and objectively review all data to build confidence in your final strategy and price.

Now let's turn to the other perspective.

Below $450,000 BPOs:

- **$450,000–$425,000**

  - 10 properties actively (available) listed

  - These properties are seeing stronger activity, averaging half the market time of the upper tier and pendings data to reflect a subtle shift in the seller's favor; buyers are eager, so sellers should hurry to take advantage.

- **$425,000–$400,000**

  - 5 properties actively (available) listed

  - Hmmm, this market time is super appealing— averaging one week with hardly any competition. With 44% of pendings in this range and your BPOs at $450,000, those who chose to undercut the competition and land within this range are almost guaranteed to receive multiple offers above asking price with fewer contingencies than offers made to sellers above $450,000.

Now what? Staying tethered to your why—ask yourself how long are you willing to wait for a buyer?

Remember, it's in your best interest to receive the **most money in the least amount of time**—which requires scrutinizing the competition's details within the price ranges and asking what sets your property apart. Convenient location? Superior condition? More rooms or bathrooms? Better updates? Peaceful lifestyle? Buyer broker compensation? It's time to filter the competition through a buyer's eyes to compare and contrast and thus best the competition.

Once you objectively discern what buyers are shopping, ask yourself: *Will you divide the competition and price the property right at $450,000 to try and attract buyers searching up to $500,000?* Or will you drop below it to compete with faster-moving inventory to try and capture highly motivated buyers offering stronger terms?

What might the "available" competition do next? It can be difficult to predict the current competition's strategy, but you know they're getting anxious. Depending on their average days and buyer feedback, they are likely considering making improvements or reducing their price—or both. It's rare for properties to go temporarily off market to make improvements, and this strategy is typically reserved for a buyer's market (when supply exceeds 6 months).

Final Thought: Outshine and Best the Competition. I know I've given you a lengthy exercise, but this example *REcodes* the approach to collaborate with your broker on pricing with less emotion and more control. The goal is to set your mindset for success, not to chase buyers. Remain objectively curious and competitive to reach your goal. You may even choose to make improvements along the way, but keep an eye on any shifts in the market (and new competition) as buyers evolve quickly.

Hopothesis Result: $500,000 is likely unrealistic. Sellers asking above $475,000 have already tested the market and will soon make price adjustments, so we want to position the property to capture the majority of buyers now and price as the data supports. Consider the following:

(A) If your room and bath count are equal to or greater than the competition

(B) If your square footage or lot size is superior

(C) If your property has minimal deferred maintenance

(D) If your property offers notable improvements or features

In this case, you can price under $475,000 to try and outshine the competition hovering between $475,000 and $500,000. If your property does not check these boxes, however, you may need to price closer to $450,000 to stand out.

Divorce or dramatic change? Divorce and major life transitions can bring out a range of emotions, everything from grief and fear to resentment and frustration. While some sellers are motivated by the need to move forward and turn the page, others may unconsciously hold on to the past and use the sale of the property and its net proceeds as a battleground. Spite can easily surface in passive-aggressive behaviors, especially when there's resistance to honoring commitments or an unrealistic attachment to the property's value. Instead of letting emotions block your path, focus on creating a clear, actionable plan that allows you to move forward with confidence.

Pricing not aligned with buyer behavior will only lead to unnecessary delays and added emotional strain. It's crucial to approach the transaction with intention to transform the sale into a step toward closure, empowering you to embrace the next chapter with clarity and purpose. Otherwise, buyers will pick up on unhappy energy as long days on the market fuel negativity—making it that much harder to move on and reach the goal, to close and collect the remaining net proceeds.

Based on the average days on market accompanying each price range, pricing your property above $425,000 is likely to result in 31 to 50 days on market. Rather than clinging to the "hope" price while trying to maximize equity (which will ultimately be divided), let go of emotional attachments and price to sell quickly. I recommend working with your consultation broker(s) to create a written strategy agreed upon #B4MA, adjusting the price after 30 days or after seven to ten willing and able buyers have viewed the property—whichever comes first—with the goal of reaching #MA before Day 60.

Remember: Buyers have access to the same data as you and will know if a listing is priced in line with its location and condition—or not!

Seller's Agency Agreement

Agree on a strategy and marketing expenses. When you're ready to sign a listing agreement with the chosen broker (AKA your new partner) take time to confirm and agree on a shared plan. This includes clear expectations for the broker's marketing campaign: what they'll do, when they'll do it, and how progress will be communicated. It's not uncommon for agreements to include clauses requiring sellers to reimburse the broker for marketing expenses if the listing is canceled before the expiration date or cover costs depending on the campaign and pricing. It's essential to establish a well-defined timeline outlining both the broker's responsibilities and your own commitments to ensure clarity #B4MA.

Seller commitments. I've found it helpful to translate seller commitments into weekends. For example, as the owner preparing the property, you commit to dedicating three weekends to decluttering, organizing, landscaping, cleaning out the garage, and making trips to the dump or a storage unit. Not only does this hold yourself accountable to manage your time in order to complete the necessary preparations but also to compete in the market you studied so hard to enter. No matter the timeline you need to prepare for market, this gives your broker the leeway to schedule industry partners to fulfill expectations and implement a marketing campaign that will outshine your competition's.

Strategy also includes adjustments or pivot plans. You might agree to reassess every two weekends… or in 30 days… or as mentioned, after seven to ten willing and able buyers have viewed your property and provided feedback. The objective is to pivot to meet buyer expectations with respect to condition, price, or terms you are offering. Sometimes it requires a bold price adjustment to drop down into a new range and thus reach a fresh pool of buyers. After acclimating to the market and consulting with your broker, these commitments shouldn't come as a surprise; they're simply the next step in moving from preparation to performance.

__Give and Take__. Sometimes you just have to try, right? The data clearly supports a realistic price range your property should compete in, but you feel like that's "giving in" and want to test the "hope" price. The broker's job is to provide all possible information for you to make a decision, risk and all, but that doesn't mean they have to support your choice to not make necessary improvements or list at an unrealistic price. Consider the broker's professional opinion and their marketing plan/commit to pivot to reach #MA; otherwise, they may decide to end the partnership with you. Every time I've agreed to work with an unreasonable and unrealistic seller (and their "spit-wad" price) without a pivot plan, I've regretted it. Times have changed: data is more accessible and easier to present than ever, so take the time to understand it.

Signing a listing agreement to sell a property means you are formally authorizing the broker and their real estate firm to represent you with the exclusive right to market and sell your property for a specified period of time. This exclusive agreement should not be confused with "exclusivity," which refers to limiting a property's exposure to a smaller, restricted pool of buyers. This agreement defines your commitment to the broker's compensation—typically a percentage of the sale price and sometimes a fixed rate, payable upon the successful closing of the property—and ensures all activities related to the sale comply with real estate laws and regulations. The agreement should also instruct their loyalty and confidentiality to you as the seller to disclose any conflicts of interest, perform the duty of good faith, and make a continuous effort on your behalf to find a buyer.

Limited authority to practice law. Depending on governing laws and regulations controlling real estate practices to ensure compliance with legal standards, when a broker selects and completes standardized real estate forms (e.g., a listing agreement), they are engaging with limited authority to practice law on forms approved by an attorney(s). Just like a buyer agency agreement, the listing agreement includes details on limited dual agency if the broker represents both you and the buyer in a transaction. This arrangement legally requires the informed consent of both you and the future buyer, which must be documented in their separate written buyer agency agreement and acknowledged by both parties in the purchase and/or sale contract. Brokers are advocates who must avoid providing legal advice or drafting custom legal documents unless they are also licensed attorneys. If legal questions arise outside their limited contract law knowledge or if a custom agreement is needed, brokers will consult with their firm's designated broker (DB) or refer their clients to a qualified real estate attorney. This routine helps ensure all legal aspects of the agreement are handled appropriately, in your best interest, and in compliance with regulations to provide the benefit of confidence and peace of mind.

Compensation. A listing broker's compensation—whether a percentage of the sale price or a fixed amount—goes beyond a simple transaction cost. It reflects the value of their advocacy and the risks they assume in protecting your interests throughout the selling process. From developing a marketing strategy, ensuring obligatory disclosures are completed, and preparing you for seller obligations, to navigating negotiations and guiding you through contingencies, your broker shoulders significant responsibility. The fee you agree to is, in essence, compensation for partnership—acknowledging the liability they take on, the expertise they apply, and the steady management of challenges from the first day of preparation through closing. Compensation earned is not just a line item; it represents the depth of agency, risk management, and professional guidance that helps you achieve a successful and satisfying conclusion.

This compensation conversation in the listing agreement naturally leads to the **buyer's broker fee** (your broker will disclose whether the current competition is offering this type of compensation and advise). In offering a buyer's broker fee, you're choosing to compensate the buyer's representative at the time of closing—often as a way to attract both the broker and their qualified buyers. It's important to stay informed about what the market is offering and what other sellers have committed to in order to remain competitive in the eyes of buyers.

Compensating a buyer's broker is sometimes a strategic move to attract the strongest buyers in the market. I personally advocate for this "pay-it-forward" model because it positions your property competitively both now and in the future. With new laws requiring buyers to have an agency agreement outlining broker compensation, it's essential to understand how your compensation agreement benefits you and impacts future buyer negotiations. Brokers and firms typically structure their models to align with market conditions; verify this to ensure you make an informed decision and thus create opportunities for an efficient sale.

FYI: It's natural to feel skeptical when someone profits from your decisions, but a quality broker earns trust through transparency (not persuasion) and is committed to ethical conduct focused on maximizing your opportunities with integrity. If you feel swayed by mistrust, *REcode* **your mindset** and focus on how they communicate a compensation strategy. Do they welcome tough questions and/or offer data-driven advice empowering your decision? Knowing your *why*, they're aiming to help you get you there as comfortably as possible.

No "Kinda" selling. Clarify with your broker—especially if you're offering buyer's broker compensation—whether you're perhaps still obligated to pay commission if you receive a full price, no-contingency offer and choose not to accept it. Some agreements carry compensation obligations even if you ultimately decide not to sell, so know that adopting a "let's just test the market" or "I don't have to sell" mindset could have financial implications if you reject a performance-able buyer who offers terms matching your listing.

Limited dual agency. Just a reminder that if your listing broker has a buyer agency agreement with a potential buyer for your property and suggests limited dual agency, it's important to understand what you stand to gain or lose by agreeing—as this significantly changes their responsibilities and loyalty, as previously mentioned. Here are some limited dual agency basics: your broker must avoid actions that harm your *and/or* the buyer's interests, promptly disclose any conflicts of interest, advise you and the buyer to seek expert advice for matters beyond their expertise, and keep all confidential information private unless required by law. Note that showing or listing other properties does not automatically harm you nor create a conflict of interest.

Possible gains include the possibility of having a highly motivated and well-prepared buyer willing to pay the asking price, purchase "as-is," and pay a portion of the broker's compensation (as an example). A possible loss is not testing current buyers in the marketplace who would otherwise compete with this buyer for your property to possibly obtain better terms or more money—it's impossible to know. If convenience aligns with your *why* and you are willing to accept the broker's limited responsibilities, loyalty, and the price and terms of this buyer, then limited dual agency deserves your strong consideration as the best option.

Granting limited dual agency must be taken seriously, calling on you to weigh the convenience of the buyer with the limited duties of the broker. It is a case-by-case scenario and truly takes a highly skilled, competent, and experienced broker to successfully execute limited representation. Each party— the buyer and the seller—must value the corresponding convenience and opportunity, knowing limited dual agency is often a great experience and can be successful if the seller thoughtfully discloses everything they can think of and the buyer is provided ample time and opportunity to perform due diligence, leaving both parties with no regrets.

An interested buyer? Your listing broker is not restricted to limited dual agency while working with a ready buyer who's interested in viewing your property but can suggest alternative agency options to them. One option is to show the property after the buyer agrees in writing to not be represented by your listing broker—thus choosing no agency and representing themselves, or the option to seek buyer representation. **No agency** allows your listing broker to facilitate the services of showing, handling paperwork, and conveying the buyer's offer (in the absence of advocacy) while ensuring buyer access during due diligence and their contingencies while performing agency duties in your best interest so the transaction proceeds smoothly.

Referral fee. If the buyer chooses buyer representation in the absence of any broker relationships, it's in everyone's best interest for your listing broker to step aside and introduce the buyer to a local buyer broker for the purpose of representation on your property (someone from their own firm is acceptable). If the buyer chooses buyer representation recommended by your listing broker, then, your broker may possibly receive a referral fee in return. Don't let this information spoil your experience.

Referral fees between brokers are a vital part of the real estate industry. When a broker refers a client to another licensed broker, they are entrusting them to provide the highest level of service, professionalism, and expertise. The referral fee—a way to acknowledge and compensate the referring broker for connecting the ready client with a trusted professional who will perform in their best interest—doesn't affect the quality or cost of the services you receive but ensures the buyer works with another professional vetted and recommended by your broker (who represents you and your interests). If each party has professional representation, this is a pathway to a satisfying experience and reduces conflicts of interest and the chance of a future lawsuit.

For sale by owner (FSBO). If you choose to implement an app for marketing and selling on your own, know an app does not prioritize all your best interests and is often a mistake for many reasons. An app does not offer an objective perspective, strategies for success, nor help you make rational decisions but instead leaves you on your own to make emotional ones. Apps also offer a false sense of convenience/best interest and lack the comprehensive personalized service professionals morally execute. An app can leave you exposed; without licensed representation, you are 100% responsible for being legally compliant, completing all mandatory state disclosures, and presenting property data accurately. These aren't just details but indeed legal obligations, and mistakes can carry serious financial consequences.

What may seem like savings in upfront compensation costs can quickly be offset by unexpected fees buried in the app's agreement or costly missteps due to limited/no guidance. A lack of professional advocacy can leave you vulnerable to contract oversights, repairs, or negotiations that could have been anticipated and addressed earlier. Because real estate transactions are time-consuming and involve complex contracts, addenda, and multiple contractual obligations with legal requirements, you risk all required paperwork being completed on time and legally complying to reduce your stress and avoid potential liabilities. Sellers, be aware that apps might charge fees that don't necessarily correlate with the level of service or expertise you receive: their clever legal language in their own best interest to serve their financial beneficiaries (stockholders) rather than *you* when something goes awry.

While selling without a local professional or using an app might seem cost-effective, it more often leads to less favorable outcomes. Feel confident in an agency relationship and hire real estate representation that keeps you expertly informed of the market, guides you with legal knowledge, and collaborates to prepare both you and your property for a compliant sale.

Preparing for Market

Signing a listing agreement marks the beginning of the #B4MA phase **with a partner.** You will execute and honor your commitment to prepare for market, make any improvements, complete all mandatory disclosures, and gather additional information to attach to the listing. Next, your broker will honor your marketing campaign expectations related to photography, videography, etc. If you haven't already, a week or two before your broker intends to go live and active on the market, you will provide extra keys/necessary codes, create cooperative showing directions (e.g., arrangements for anxious pets), and finalize the placement of the key box and yard sign if one will be installed.

ALIGN

Before Mutual Acceptance (#B4MA)

Expectations and Strategy. Now it's time to focus on reaching a ready buyer. Like you, buyers have acclimated and are mindfully prepared for market conditions regarding locations accommodating their needs: having imagined the condition they want of a property and ready to remove doubts or future remorse in order to protect their earnest money.

They've partnered with a buyer's broker who's conditioning them for due diligence and to make multiple decisions *before* and *after* #MA, when emotions or doubt might creep in. This preparation helps demonstrate their *able-ness*—their readiness and reliability to perform—which strengthens confidence, supports negotiation, and ensures they can follow through to closing.

Responsibilities. You and your broker share the responsibility of accurately preparing the listing to ensure your property is represented to the highest standard. As the seller, you are mandated to disclose material facts and known defects to the best of your knowledge; it's in your best interest to do so #B4MA.

As explained in the <u>Download</u> section, providing these disclosures in advance—either directly within the listing or as MLS attachments (consult with your broker)—can help expedite the buyer's verification period and perhaps reduce the likelihood of a buyer rescinding their offer during due diligence *after* #MA.

Rescission? *A rescission is a formal cancellation or termination of an agreement or contract.* Buyers may elect this option if they believe (*after* #MA) the seller misrepresented the listing, failed to deliver mandatory disclosures, or did not perform per the specific terms outlined. Providing clear, timely, and accurate disclosures protects you and helps create a smoother, more grounded experience for everyone involved.

To receive an offer, you generally need to provide buyer access to the property—unless tenants occupy it, in which case landlord-tenant law applies. Get your head in the game and set the intention to accommodate to:

1. **Attract** a ready buyer and receive an offer

2. **Negotiate** to move forward and reach #MA

3. **Prepare** for what a buyer may reject *after* #MA

4. **Collaborate** and act to not lose them during the contingency phase (grounded in #3)

Showing your property and negotiating offers is often challenging and disruptive. That's why adopting a mindful approach and intentional habits when accommodating buyers and their schedules is essential. By practicing active listening and objectively evaluating feedback (knowing it's not personal) or offers, you generate the positive spirit needed to reach #MA. This mindset will also support you through the buyer's contingency periods. Stay tethered to your *why* to ensure all agreed-upon contingencies are met and waived, maintaining momentum towards your ultimate goal: closing and collecting your net proceeds.

Improve or fail. Price is a choice, and buyers communicate their decision with an offer—or the absence of one. If you haven't received an offer after seven to ten willing and able buyers have been through and your broker has collected feedback, there is no excuse to either not make an effort to improve the condition or adjust the price. If your property is not receiving showings and has surpassed the average DOM, it has tested the market and failed.

The market notices when a seller resists reality. Don't become the listing that sits unchanged, unresponsive, and ultimately overlooked. A "stale" listing is one where feedback is ignored, improvements are dismissed, and pricing concerns are not corrected and brushed off with a casual "Just make an offer."

It's not your broker's job to explain away resistance. Modern buyers are informed, observant, and strategic and will walk away from a listing that refuses to align with the market. Don't shift the burden. Be proactive and calculated, and meet the market with intention.

An exception with respect to exceeding the average market time applies to luxury, unique, or destination properties as these require patience to appeal to a smaller pool of qualified buyers who are both willing and able to purchase.

Contingent vs. Contingent

If you receive **a "contingent" offer**—*one dependent on the net proceeds of the buyer's current property*—before accepting an offer, strategize with your broker to verify the contingent buyer's property is priced to align with their location and condition.

Your broker will likely request to review the contingent buyer's CMA and analyze their BPO. If the property is local, your broker may request to view it to verify and assure you that it's likely to receive an offer (or not); if you choose to accept the contingent offer, you must deem the buyer, their offered terms and their property worth waiting for. Contingent offers are not unusual and often successful but simply require collaboration and open communication to devise plans to organize future closing and possession dates in the case of multiple stacked transactions.

Multiple closings, multiple hurdles. If you receive an offer contingent "upon the closing" (not "sale") of the buyer's property, this specific condition claims your potential buyer's property is already in "pending" status—different from a general "contingent" offer that still needs to find a buyer. Before accepting, seek clarification on which stage of the transaction the "pending" property is in. Has their "pending" buyer completed their inspection and waived that contingency? Has underwriting approved the financing? These are common hurdles, but remember—these are in addition to the requested contingencies (hurdles) in your buyer's "upon the closing" offer for your property. Accurately assess the risks versus the option of staying on the market.

> **Author's Stacked Experience:** *I once had seven transactions stacked as a result of contingent "upon closing" offers—yep, seven properties lined up to close like dominoes, each relying on funds from the other. I represented two of these properties: numbers six and seven, meaning my sellers (Property No. 6) were buying Property No. 7 and needed the net proceeds from the stacked closings of Nos. 1–5 to honor their contract.*
>
> *This may sound messy, but it wasn't—just unusual and complicated, requiring ALL seven buyers and sellers (and their brokers, lenders, and escrow officers) to be aware, vested, and proactive while taking pride and staying flexible during this sophisticated brainteaser.*
>
> *Property No. 7—vacant and relying on all transactions to close before they benefited—was the first one to extend trust and allowed my buyer to move in a few days before closing. It was a tough sell at first, as it was an estate; the attorney representing the estate naturally advised against allowing the buyers to take early possession. The executor, however, decided to grant approval upon understanding the parties affected and the why behind many of the moves.*
>
> *Once the buyer for Property No. 1 received loan approval, No. 7 took the risk with No. 6 and allowed them to move in prior to owning the property: a display of trust*

extending to transactions one through five, reversing the domino effect and ultimately motivating these parties to coordinate a move-out/move-in schedule and adjust closing dates to receive funds and transfer for complete alignment.

It took some time, but each buyer's broker forwarded a copy of their contracts for all to strategize a plan. Email communication between brokers then bonded us to track all moving parts: appraisals, walk-throughs, loan approvals, signings, the timely wiring of funds, cleaning, and finally the transition to the final transfers.

The coordination was extraordinary—the trust extended was outstanding with so much at stake. We had a family moving from coast to coast with children, a military move across states with large pets and belongings housed in storage post-deployment, a contentious, difficult divorce (that broker was a saint), and a grieving estate with no support from heirs. So much could go wrong, but instead, everything went smoothly.

All real estate professionals merely did what was expected of us, and by osmosis, our clients took pride in focusing on their responsibilities. When sellers were flexible and extended trust (e.g., No. 7), this provided a reprieve for the No. 1 buyer to close and its sellers to stay put until the moving coordination played out for Nos. 2–6—which took roughly 4 to 5 days. When No. 1 closed, the buyer's and seller's brokers both remained tethered to the outcome and cheered us all on until my No. 6 closed on No. 7

simultaneously. Every broker was elated for all clients;
it was one of the most satisfying experiences of my career
and would not have happened without the confidence
and competence of the real estate professionals who made
it all happen despite so many moving parts.

Staying Tethered to Your Why

Counteroffer. Be purposeful to secure #MA with a buyer and exercise predetermined alternative strategies. Depending on their circumstances, most offers propose a closing date between 30 and 60 days. Once you go live on the market, if you haven't already, create a tentative move-out plan.

After an offer is presented, then, strategize to align the buyer's offered price with a closing date to achieve #MA (just like how you strategize to align an asking price with your location and condition #B4MA). If you're considering a counteroffer, seek your broker's guidance (to weigh risk) on what is considered a "minor" versus "major" counter—choosing a strategy wisely, especially if you want a particular buyer, knowing any counter is an opportunity for the other party to not move forward.

Also, consider the buyer's *able-ness*—their readiness, reliability, and demonstrated capacity to perform. A slightly lower offer from a well-prepared, financed, and decisive buyer may ultimately present less risk and a higher likelihood of closing than a stronger offer with uncertain ability or delayed responsiveness.

Legal outs? A traditional offer may request additional contingencies. Ask your broker the following questions: How many conditions or legal "outs" does the buyer reserve for themselves within the offer? (Answers will vary depending on the market you're competing in. If the absorption rate is high, you may have the luxury of choosing from multiple competitive offers with fewer contingencies. If the absorption rate is low, the more contingencies you're likely to accept.) What if a buyer—in "good faith"—works through their contingencies one by one and the conditions are met or waived, leaving one remaining obligation for them to close per the terms of the contract but they fail to do so? What risk(s) do you take by accepting this offer from a buyer in your market? Contingencies are not uncommon, but this is about your experience—be curious, gain knowledge, and have clarity so you can better understand your possible outcomes.

Earnest money. Depending on the terms you agreed to, the earnest money may be the only damages you're awarded if a buyer fails to close. Think of it as a security deposit: a financial commitment from the buyer to demonstrate they are ready, willing, and able. You are making a calculated decision based on your strategy and property condition, but what if the buyer changes their mind and chooses to back out after they met or waived their contingency obligations in "good faith"? Before accepting the buyer's offer, you need to confirm that the offered earnest money is sufficient to compensate you for the time (consider the length of the contract) and risk (hurdles) you take in accepting their offer. If the buyer forfeits the earnest money, the listing agreement may have language saying the listing firm and their broker reserve the right to share in this compensation for their professional time and services on your behalf during the transaction. Don't get hung up on this; simply be aware. Fingers crossed you will not encounter this buyer! *After* all terms are aligned and accepted by both you and the buyer, **congratulations are in order.**

After Mutual Acceptance (#MA)

You have achieved "mutual acceptance," triggering the contract's specified timelines. Your broker will monitor the transaction throughout your "pending" status to ensure compliance; you, in turn, can focus on answering any buyer questions, fulfilling your seller obligations, and preparing for a move. As the transaction proceeds forward, remember your broker is there to facilitate its navigational flow, track your buyer's progress, and will remind you of predetermined strategies to implement (if needed) as you work to collaborate through any buyer contingencies and obligations to reach a successful closing you can celebrate.

Buyer Performance

If the buyer's offered terms you accepted are conditional on you providing specific information to satisfy their verification period during due diligence, this obligation becomes your day-one priority. The sooner you fulfill obligations to collaborate, the more you reduce the risk of delays, strengthen the buyer's confidence, remove hurdles, and keep the transaction on track toward closing.

Reminder: Purchase and/or sale contracts include terms designed for the buyer to perform due diligence to verify the listing and disclosures *after* #MA, as mentioned. If they are not satisfied, the buyer may terminate (cancel or rescind) within the specified timeline and retain their earnest money.

Other than due diligence, the pressure is on the buyer to perform in "good faith" their contractual obligations within the specified timeline per the contract and…

1. Deliver the earnest money.

2. List and get their property "active" or "live" in their MLS per the terms of your contract (if you accepted a "contingent" (net-proceeds) offer).

3. Organize and schedule to perform on remaining contingencies (e.g., an inspection) and commit to a lender and make loan application.

Recall your past consultations and how they educated you for potential buyer obligations to be prepared for the transaction experience. Stay calm, remain patient, and answer any questions in a timely manner while the buyer performs their commitments.

Backup Offers

When you're "pending," another ready, willing, and able buyer may submit a "backup" offer in the hopes your "first-position" buyer does not perform and close.

Accepting a backup offer is in your best interest as it does not affect your current pending contract while providing you with valuable future leverage. If the backup buyer's terms are acceptable and #MA is reached, they secure "second position" behind your pending buyer.

Should the first-position buyer attempt to renegotiate price or request repairs/concessions towards their closing costs after inspection, your listing broker can strategically mention to the first-position buyer's broker that you've accepted a backup—signaling their pending buyer has new competition. This may pressure the first-position buyer to proceed "as-is" rather than risk losing the property due to attempts to renegotiate the price, request repairs, etc.

Keep in mind, however, that a backup buyer is not always a sure thing. Buyers in second position reserve the right to continue their search and can withdraw from second position at any time before the first-position buyer fails to close. Your leverage with the first-position pending buyer is only effective as long as the backup buyer remains in place.

Contingent Status

Contingent. If you accepted a contingent offer and depending on the rules of your MLS, "contingent" rather than "pending" status discloses to the public that your property is under contract with a buyer who cannot close per the terms of the contract until they sell, close, and collect net proceeds on another property: alerting active buyers that they may present an offer in an attempt to "bump" the first-position contingent buyer. *Attempt* is the key word here as the second buyer making the new offer is not guaranteed to shift into first position even if you accept it.

The Bump. If the second offer is accepted and the first-position contingent buyer hasn't waived or satisfied their contingency—gone into "pending" status—your broker will give the first buyer "bump notice" that you've accepted a second offer. Now, the contingent buyer in first position has two choices and is required to either:

(A) acknowledge being "bumped," stepping aside and terminating their agreement, or

(B) waive their contingency in order to not be bumped and remain in first position.

Let's say they choose Option B but don't have a buyer yet and instead bet on their property to sell (with their earnest money), therefore waiving their contingency in the hopes that a ready buyer will come along to reach #MA so they can close on yours. This is rare, but it happens. If you're considering accepting a contingent offer, make sure the buyer's earnest money is strong. In these cases, after the first buyer waives their contingency but is unable to perform (close) on the contract, then as the seller you are likely stuck with the earnest money as your sole remedy for damages and forced to go BOMK–unless the second ("bump") buyer chose to be in back-up position. Pay attention to the earnest money in all offers! This is not to discourage accepting a contingent offer but simply a reminder to pause, strategize, and understand the risk (and reward) before moving forward.

Typical Conditional Contingencies

Inspection. If you accept an offer contingent on an inspection, your duty (per #selleretiquette) is to provide the buyer access to all areas of your property including the attic, basement, or crawl space where old stuff is stored and forgotten. Smaller spaces, such as under sinks, may contain personal stuff hiding among the exposed plumbing. Clear or simply organize these spaces for the scheduled inspection, making codes and keys to locked spaces (e.g., storage sheds) available and accessible so the buyer doesn't need to return to complete their due diligence. Turn fuel on for any built-in features such as fireplaces or BBQs. If home entertainment equipment has been negotiated and intended to convey, then leave out remotes. You get the point. Seek advice from your broker about whether to provide a binder sharing insurance carriers and property vendors (e.g., landscaping and pest services) so the buyer can choose to continue their services or not.

Financing. If you accepted an offer contingent on financing, keep the property in showing condition for the appraiser's visit. If the contract terms claim "Cash" at closing with the buyer obligated to provide proof of funds, hold your broker accountable to verify proof was delivered per the terms of the contract.

Title. If you accept an offer contingent on title, carefully review the preliminary title report for accuracy as soon as you receive it. It is your responsibility to click through every blue (hyper) link and thoroughly review each attached document as well. Work closely with the title officer and your broker to promptly address and correct any errors, omissions, or misrepresentations. Remember, the title report reflects not just the property's current status but everything since it was officially mapped and divided into lots and streets (AKA platted). Verify that all agreements, easements, access rights, and restrictions are accurate and accounted for, as the buyer is verifying and relying on this report as part of their due diligence.

Patiently Objective & Curious. Preventing a failed sale should be your priority; you don't want to go from "pending" to BOMK status, after all. Stay curious, practice active listening, and approach contingency negotiations without assumptions, but to collaborate. Buyer requests made during contingency periods are not personal and may require creativity to stay patient so you and your broker can objectively revisit predetermined strategies to consider (or pivot) rather than let prideful emotions take over the negotiations.

Contingencies are meant to satisfy the buyer, not you as the seller. Rather than dismissing the buyer's concerns, approach them with objective curiosity. Be open to problem-solving to keep the transaction moving forward. Review with your broker the most recent market trends and heed their advice on emerging patterns. Are competing listings making price reductions? Do new listings offer superior features? Understanding the bigger picture can help you make informed decisions that protect your sale. If you go BOMK, you may face a shifting market with tougher, more motivated competition. Let this reality drive your collaboration and willingness to find a solution that will satisfy your goal of selling and receiving funds.

Obligations. The first 15 days *after* #MA is the most challenging time period. By now, you've received feedback from previous showings, you and your broker have devised strategies around the condition of your property, and you're fully prepared for this phase. Let your broker absorb the pressure so you can concentrate on your responsibilities and the closing.

It's not unusual to hold your breath until the last contingency is met—typically the finance contingency if the buyer needs a loan. The lender is assigned an appraiser, whose role is to provide an appraisal: an unbiased assessment of your property's condition and market value on behalf of the buyer to satisfy their lender. This third-party opinion ensures the property's *value* aligns with the agreed *purchase price* and is typically a lender requirement for issuing a mortgage satisfying the finance contingency. Zooming out, the appraiser's evaluation protects the lender by confirming the property is a sound investment should the buyer default on the loan and task the lender with foreclosing and repossessing the property.

Extension. Every once in a while, a party is unable to meet the contract closing date and will request an extension—hopefully this doesn't happen to you! If the buyer requests an extension, you and your broker will need to weigh your options to compare and decide what's in your best interest.

Good Faith. More often than not, a buyer (who's performed and promptly shown good faith towards contractual obligations) justifiably needs a few extra business days to close. In this case and after consideration, it will likely make sense to grant said extension.

Seller's Market. If a buyer has *not* shown good faith, however, due to poor communication or an unwillingness to collaborate (for example), do not feel obligated to extend unless it is in your best interest to do so; this might be the case, especially if you have a back-up in second position, but evaluate all your options if your property lacks this luxury.

If the market has shifted in your favor (with supporting data), a stronger, more motivated buyer may be willing to pay more. Your broker will have an opinion here, so ascertain the risk involved in attracting this buyer and negotiating better terms (e.g., a higher price) against the time required to extend the existing contract. Since your property went "pending", the competition has likely changed, and new sellers may have entered the market.

Evaluating your options requires assessing how inventory is being absorbed and how your property's condition compares to current listings. If inventory is low and your property is equal to or better than the current competition, you may consider declining an extension—especially if your broker believes the current buyer has a slim chance of performing. This is not an easy decision, however. In my experience, most sellers choose to grant an extension; in rare cases, though, sellers welcome the opportunity to move on and find a stronger buyer.

Industry Professional Extension Requests. If the extension request is coming from the buyer's side due to their lender requesting additional time, then granting this based on a positive lender update is likely reasonable.

If the extension request is coming from the buyer's side due to a delay during the due diligence phase, and the buyer's inspector reveals a surprise finding (requiring a second opinion and therefore delaying collaboration to remove the contingency), then the extension can be negotiated.

Did the inspector waste everyone's time? If their finding was a mistake and delayed the due diligence phase, your level of frustration may fuel a need to feel out some form of compensation for the extension request.

Concession Solution. If the extension is due to delays on the buyer's side—not yours—consider discussing a buyer concession with your broker; converting the held earnest money into a non-refundable deposit, delivered to you, is a viable negotiation point. As the old saying goes, "You scratch my back, and I'll scratch yours." Verify how this adjustment affects the remaining contract terms before proceeding. In most cases, the deposit will still apply toward the buyer's down payment unless otherwise agreed upon, but at least you've received compensation for granting an extension.

Concession from the Buyer's Perspective. Be prepared for pushback from the buyer and their broker when requesting the earnest money (or a portion) become non-refundable. For example, if the buyer originally agreed to a shorter closing timeline during your negotiations only to realize they need those extra days, they may argue that an extension should be granted without additional concessions. This is especially true if a third party (e.g., an appraiser for a financing contingency) was unable to meet the accelerated negotiated timeline.

Seller Obligations and Closing. Once the buyer has performed and satisfied all their contingencies, the attention pivots to seller obligations, any repairs or improvements you agreed to following the buyer's inspection, or the lender's appraisal. These must be completed before the buyer's final walk-through unless otherwise agreed to, and it's best to forward any documentation such as receipts and warranties for the buyer's file (prior to the walk-through, if possible). Depending on the timeline, it's common to juggle these improvements as you execute your final obligation to clean, pack, move out, and coordinate the transfer of utilities— but well worth the effort. Once the buyer completes their walk-through, escrow will establish signings, convey wiring instructions for funds, and prepare the transaction for final payoffs to close per the terms of the contract.

Escrow Side Note: If your agreed to the buyer's inspection requests, and hired a contractor who agrees to delay receiving your payment when the job is completed, and instead will accept payment from your net proceeds at closing, both you and the broker, are responsible to forward any unpaid invoices with clear instructions to escrow (or the attorney handling the closing) to pay from your net proceeds. You and your broker will have an opportunity to review the settlement (accounting) statement to verify the line item(s) is in your column and the contractor (industry partner) is paid per your arrangement!

The Transfer. Most contract terms have the buyer taking possession and receiving keys, openers, and codes the same day the property closes; transfer is recorded and the seller receives their net proceeds. Have a clear date and time of the transfer of possession. If the language states two separate dates—closing on one date and possession on another—either you, buyer or tenant—set to occupy the property in between the different dates, it's in everyone's best interest to have a temporary rental agreement in place spelling out who will occupy the property, whose insurance will cover occupancy, who is responsible for utilities, etc.

Rent, if any, depends on the market:

○ **Seller's market:** Because the buyer was motivated to get you to accept their offer, they negotiated terms allowing you to remain in the property after closing (e.g., for three days) without taking possession. In this situation, there's a good chance the buyer will not charge you a per diem rent fee.

- o **Buyer's market:** If you negotiate to remain in the property for three days after closing, the buyer will likely charge you a per diem rent rate since the market is in their favor. This is commonly calculated based on the buyer's new mortgage (principal, interest, taxes, and insurance—PITI) rather than your existing mortgage.

With all obligations met, congratulations on your successful closing! Leave your keys, devices, openers, and codes behind, and then celebrate your net proceeds, using them wisely— perhaps towards another property. I hope your journey was predictable and satisfying!

Postscript: Capital Gains & 1031 Exchanges

If you're in the United States, it's important to seek professional accounting advice to determine whether capital gains taxes apply to your situation. If you've owned and lived in the property as your primary residence for at least two out of the last five years prior to the sale, you may qualify for a primary residence exclusion.

If you're considering selling or purchasing an investment property, consult both an accountant and a 1031 exchange specialist or intermediary before entering the market. A 1031 exchange can allow you to defer capital gains taxes, but the process must follow specific IRS rules, timelines, and procedural steps in order for you to qualify. Working with a qualified 1031 facilitator is essential to ensure compliance and protect your tax benefits.

REflection

After closing, most sellers move on quickly from the transaction and rarely pause to reflect on the decisions they made, the timeline they followed, and how their mindset throughout it all may have shaped the outcome. Yet hindsight often reveals where emotion, resistance, and/or a lack of preparation interfered with progress—whether it involved dismissing early feedback, overpricing, or relying too heavily on the broker to take on all responsibilities, or not trusting the partnership and strategy.

Some sellers underestimate the value of the acclimation period, essential time to understand the market and buyer behavior and then objectively assess how their property compares in location and condition: aligning expectations and price before going live. When this work is skipped or approached in a reactive way, sellers may miss critical opportunities to position themselves for a smooth experience and receive the most money in the least amount of time.

There's also a tendency for some sellers to assume their listing broker will simply "handle everything" (after all, *that's what they're getting paid for*, right?)—without recognizing that a successful transaction relies on shared responsibilities. When sellers avoid decisions, resist price alignment, shift the burden of preparation, or hold unrealistic expectations, disappointment often follows. Too often, frustration is then misdirected toward the very broker who was hired as a trusted advisor—one who is working without upfront compensation, yet remains deeply invested in the seller's success.

But the experience doesn't have to unfold that way.

I hope this Mindful Guide doesn't just help you sell a property—but helps you *REclaim your place* in the experience. If a past transaction left you feeling rushed, sidelined, or unsure of what truly happened, may this journey *REcode* that narrative. You now have the tools to set clear goals, choose the right broker partner, and attract buyers who see the value you've stewarded. With preparation, pricing alignment, and collaborative agency, you can move through the process with clarity, confidence, and calm authority.

If you've also explored the Buyer section, you've expanded your perspective to see both sides of the experience, released outdated beliefs, and gained a holistic understanding of how thoughtful collaboration, strategy, and due diligence lead to deeply satisfying outcomes.

Beyond closing, my hope is that you walk away not only with net proceed funds but with renewed pride—pride in contributing to a thriving community, in strengthening your personal wealth road map, and in modeling to younger generations that ownership is not reserved for the privileged— it is possible, repeatable, and worth passing on.

A final bonus section on Industry Partners awaits—designed to complete your mindful real estate journey and reinforce the power of surrounding yourself with the right people, at the right time, for the right reason.

INDUSTRY PARTNERS

…are the essential support system — the heart—of a real estate transaction.

These trusted advisors, problem-solvers, and facilitators align all parties with professionalism, integrity, and trust.

Their collaboration ensures the process flows smoothly and efficiently, creating a balanced and positive experience for both buyers and sellers.

A discerningly connected broker curates a network of high-caliber, ethical professionals as trusted industry partners who share a commitment to integrity and excellence. These relationships create opportunities for better service, proactive solutions, and strategic referrals that benefit *you*. The right team doesn't just facilitate a transaction; it enhances your understanding and helps you strategize to formulate more confident decisions. When you choose to partner with a wise and competent broker, you will—by osmosis—meet thoughtful, proficient professionals who uncomplicate the complexities and instead streamline operations *before* and *after* mutual acceptance (#B4MA and #MA), keeping you focused and empowered as you work toward success.

Real estate industry partners include attorneys, financial advisors, stagers, photographers, lenders, inspectors, insurance brokers, title and escrow officers, and more—each playing a critical role in supporting your real estate journey. While competition among professionals keeps standards high, their collaboration on behalf of buyers and sellers takes the experience to a whole-new level.

The Money Group

Money partners are trusted coaches, advisors, and professionals who help you build wealth and ensure funds are properly verified, handled, and delivered per contractual milestones.

Money #B4MA

Money coaches are financial mentors who help individuals develop a healthier relationship with money and provide guidance on budgeting, saving, and investing with their clients' overall financial well-being in mind. Unlike traditional financial advisors who focus on managing wealth, a money coach empowers clients to shift their mindset, break unhealthy spending habits or inherited beliefs, and create sustainable financial strategies to achieve wealth. They offer support, accountability, and education to quell financial stress and build long-term financial confidence throughout the real estate purchase process.

Financial and investment planners or tax advisors should be the buyer's and seller's first call when preparing for a real estate transaction. These professionals assist buyers with liquidating assets, securing gift funds, and aligning financial goals. Sellers can specifically benefit from strategic financial planning by confirming mortgage payoff amounts and any outstanding property-related debts to understand potential tax implications (e.g., capital gains). They can also seek deferred tax advice regarding a 1031 exchange as the process must follow specific IRS rules, timelines, and procedural steps to qualify (if applicable). These partners help ground you, shift you away from any outdated financial beliefs, and provide guidance for financial preparedness.

Money obligations. Buyers, meanwhile, need a clear strategy and timeline to ensure funds are available when needed. During buyer-agency consultations, your broker may recommend or introduce you to trusted local mortgage brokers: professional lenders often affiliated with national *institutions* who can provide personalized loan service if you need financing. Unlike impersonal national lending web *platforms* and related apps, local mortgage lenders are deeply invested in their communities, provide buyers with customized financial assistance timelines, and are the most motivated to build lasting local relationships by offering guidance, quicker responses, and tailored financing options aligning with their clients' best interests. If a referring broker has a non-business relationship with a recommended mortgage lender, they must disclose this (and any potential compensation or referral fees) in advance.

Lenders. A buyer's financing approval process begins with loan qualification verification that typically involves submitting a loan application. Securing a pre-approved loan in today's competitive market positions a buyer as a strong performance-able contender, not only reassuring sellers but also ensuring the buyer's broker can confidently negotiate on their behalf.

When choosing a local mortgage lender, it's important to understand the difference between aggressive vs. assertive lending practices. An aggressive lender may operate from a place of self-interest, focusing on control and competition rather than service and seeking dominance in negotiations to create unnecessary stress for buyers. In contrast, an assertive lender is a faithful advocate: resilient, solution-oriented, and dedicated to overcoming obstacles in pursuit of loan approval. Assertive lenders stay patient and committed to navigating underwriting and appraisal challenges with perseverance to ensure you secure the financing you need. Pause, evaluate, and choose an *assertive* local mortgage lender.

Money After #MA

The purchase and/or sale contract is an instrument of instruction. Once a buyer and seller reach #MA, the money group shifts from preparation to execution: ensuring all financial obligations are met on time to keep the transaction moving along toward closing.

The closer. In the United States, the closing process for real estate transactions varies by state but generally falls into one of two categories: **escrow** or **attorney**. Practices can differ even within each state, with methods allowed based on regional customs or other unique circumstances. In other countries, closing practices may look very different, guided by their own legal systems and cultural customs.

In **escrow states**, title companies with licensed escrow officers or Limited Practice Officers (LPOs) handle the transaction with no attorney involvement. LPOs perform specific legal functions related to the closing without being fully licensed attorneys, helping to streamline the process while ensuring legal compliance. These professionals act as neutral third parties or intermediaries.

In **attorney states**, attorney involvement is mandated or customary—with lawyers often required to draft or review key documents such as deeds and mortgage agreements.

The closer typically holds the buyer's earnest money and—after obligations are met per the terms of the contract—prepare closing documents, ensure legal compliance, and facilitate the safe transfer of funds.

Financing

For buyers acquiring financing, this is where the mortgage process intensifies. The lender will finalize underwriting by verifying employment, credit, assets, and debt—confirming the buyer still qualifies per the agreed terms. Buyers should be highly responsive to any lender documentation requests during this time to avoid delays, missed contractual deadlines, and/or the chance of putting their earnest money at risk.

Appraisal. The lender will typically order an appraisal, a report confirming the property's value supports the loan. Many lenders use appraisal management services with advanced tools to gather preliminary data before assigning the file—allowing appraisers to evaluate the property's complexity and determine if the assignment fits their scope, timeline, and fee expectations. If the property has unique features or challenges, the appraiser may adjust the fee to ensure an accurate, on-time valuation. Thanks to advancements in technology, analytics, and AI, the appraisal process is now much more efficient than it once was, leading to fewer errors/ reinspections and quicker turnaround times.

Access. Sellers should ensure the property is clean, accessible, and well-maintained so they can provide timely, on-request access to key industry partners (e.g., the appraiser for valuation and, in some cases, an insurance representative) to assess the property's condition, safety, and key functional elements. This is a critical step in the buyer's loan process, helping to confirm the property poses no unexpected risks and meets underwriting requirements for both the buyer's financing and insurance. Delays at this stage can jeopardize closing timelines.

Legal advice. Your broker may refer an attorney for advice outside their scope to review unique financial terms, legal obligations, agreements, and closing documentation. The ability to meet money-related obligations on time is a direct reflection of a buyer and seller's performance ability to move forward.

Taken altogether, the money group plays a pivotal role in setting clients up to meet all financial obligations in a timely manner. If you choose to seek any advice or professional services, expect additional fees beyond traditional closing costs.

The Due Diligence Group

Due diligence partners are experts who help buyers and sellers identify potential risks, verify property details, and provide critical insight to prepare for complications or costly oversights—all to safeguard major decisions.

Common due diligence partners:

- **Home Inspector**: Evaluates the property's structure, systems, and condition and then provides a written report with photos for reference

- **Pest Inspector**: Checks for wood-destroying organisms (WDOs) such as termites, carpenter ants, or moisture and then provides a written report with photos for reference
- **Sewer Scope Technician**: Inspects the condition of the property's sewer line via camera and often provides a video report for reference
- **Structural Engineer**: Assesses foundation or framing concerns beyond a general inspection and then provides a written report with photos for reference
- **Roofing Contractor**: Provides condition reports and estimates for repairs or replacement
- **HVAC Specialist**: Evaluates heating, ventilation, and air conditioning systems and provides repair estimates as needed
- **Environmental Consultant**: Tests for mold, asbestos, radon, or soil contamination and offers professional opinions and repair estimates as needed
- **Well and Septic Inspector**: Evaluates the functionality and safety of private water and waste systems and is sometimes authorized to report findings to local health departments/governing agencies if certification or compliance steps are required
- **Electrician/Plumber**: Offers professional opinions and repair or replacement estimates as needed

- **General Contractor**: Offers opinions on repairs/renovations and furnishes estimates to inform negotiation or planning as needed

- **Title Officer**: Identifies legal ownership, liens, and encumbrances on the property and explains any conditions tied to the title (e.g., shared well agreements, ingress or egress easements, or recorded encroachments) that may affect use/transferability for the new owner

- **Insurance Broker**: Assesses insurability and provides early premium estimates

Due diligence partners for buyers are professionals who uncover unknown conditions, validate disclosures, and assess any factors that could impact the property's value or future ownership. Their findings often include professional opinions or estimates that can verify and clarify to support the buyer's position during negotiations.

Due diligence partners for sellers are partners who assist in preparing the property for market, ensuring transparency, and mitigating potential liabilities that could arise during negotiations. Their evaluations may also provide pricing context or improvement estimates that help set realistic expectations and avoid surprises during the transaction.

Due Diligence #B4MA

Title

Title representatives and officers are among the most diligent professionals in the real estate industry, working behind the scenes to ensure each transaction is legally sound and protected. These industry partners serve both the principals in the translation and their brokers, their role critical in identifying potential risks and clearing the path for a clean, insurable transfer of ownership.

The agreed-upon title company for the transaction assigns a title officer to verify legal ownership and check for any liens or encumbrances associated with both principals involved. A preliminary title report is then generated for all parties to review.

Title Report: Taking subsequent responsibility—reviewing the preliminary title report as early as possible for recorded agreements, easements, access rights, and restrictions affecting ownership—will ensure there's enough time to address any surprises or unresolved issues before they become last-minute delays. This is a big reason why it's included in the recommended documents to download and review before mutual acceptance.

Once escrow has cleared the report—confirming no unresolved title issues exist—the title company is in a position to issue title insurance. Two policies may be issued at closing:

- **An owner's policy** protecting the buyer from any issues such as undisclosed liens, claims from heirs, or other recorded encumbrances.

- **A lender's policy** protecting the lender's best interest and ensuring they hold the first lien position in the event of foreclosure.

Insurance

Buyers understanding risk. Buyer due diligence begins with understanding regional risk factors. Some call insurance providers as a resource to dig into an area's past claims history, assess weather-related hazards that may require separate/additional policies, and determine whether an area is well-served or otherwise has limited emergency response or fire protection that could impact coverage. Gaining this insight early on helps buyers evaluate potential risks and identify which professionals to consult before entering negotiations.

Sellers understanding risk. Owners must do their best to maintain, improve, and protect their property. When possible, avoid unnecessary insurance claims that can raise red flags and jeopardize a potential buyer's ability to secure homeowners insurance. This happens.

Author Risk REflection: Throughout my career, I've encountered hillsides that slip, waterfronts that erode, rising rivers that flood, and century-old post-and-beam homes that settle over time—quite dramatically, in fact. Each of these elements has its own unique charm and appeal yet also demands awareness and due diligence to fully understand related implications.

The takeaway? Every property tells a unique story shaped by its environment and history. Unique characteristics require buyers to look beyond charm and aesthetics, but with proper diligence, expert insight, and proactive planning, you can help ensure that what initially draws you to a property doesn't become a costly surprise down the road.

Due Diligence After #MA

Home inspectors are industry partners who assess the property's condition and identify structural, mechanical, and safety concerns. Reported findings often lead to recommendations to seek the opinion of a specialized professional to evaluate areas beyond the scope of a general inspection. Common specialized opinions investigate environmental hazards, mold, radon, pests, sewer lines, pools, and more—this professional insight sometimes leading to estimates from contractors and tradespeople who perform repairs or improvements.

Connection. Buyers must verify access to essential infrastructure as some properties lack direct connections to public roads, water, or sewer lines. While sellers are required to disclose any lack of access, they may forget to do so or otherwise assume an agreement is already in place. If a property relies on a private road, easement, shared well, or septic system located on another property, buyers should confirm that legal, recorded documentation grants access. If access is based on an informal or verbal agreement, sellers must consult legal counsel to formulate and record the necessary documentation to secure buyers' confidence and prevent future legal disputes.

> **Author's Connection REcall:** *Years ago, I sold a property that was part of an estate. The executor, who'd grown up there, hadn't lived on the property for 25+ years. The water source was a neighboring well with a recorded agreement identified in the title report. Everything seemed in order, right? Not so fast…*
>
> *No one knew the executor's late father had had a dispute with the original well owner and—rather than resolve the matter—the late father made a new, unrecorded agreement with a different neighbor for water access. Fast forward to the sale. After the new owner moved in, they installed a sprinkler system that eventually drained the second neighbor's well. Furious, that person cut off the water supply, leaving the new owner high and dry.*
>
> *It was a mess. The buyer's attorney had to get involved, and the title company stepped in to help cover the costs of securing a new recorded agreement. The situation blindsided everyone—except the two neighbors who owned the wells.*

The takeaway? Buyers should always read recorded agreements carefully and require the seller to verify they are still in effect. Sellers, meanwhile, should review the preliminary title report and ensure all recorded documents are valid and enforceable.

A little extra diligence in the short term can prevent a major dispute down the road.

When property boundaries, easements, or encroachments are unclear, a surveyor can confirm legal property lines for an additional fee.

> *Due Diligence Reminder; Sellers must disclose any material facts—including established ingress or egress (legal rights allowing someone to enter or exit the property) or pending adjustments, agreements, or assessments— while buyers purchasing within a homeowners association (HOA) should proactively contact the HOA president/ manager to review community rules, financials, and upcoming assessments. Professional management or elected HOA representatives play a crucial role in properly informing and ensuring transparency.*

The Closing Group: What to Expect

If the buyer is receiving financing, the lender and insurance broker will finalize closing documents (including the loan paperwork and insurance binder) after final loan approval is issued. The buyer broker, meanwhile, will begin coordinating with the closer to prepare for the transaction's final steps.

Buyers should prepare to wire their down payment and closing costs in advance to ensure funds are received by the closer before the scheduled closing.

Sellers should also plan how they'll receive and distribute their net proceeds, whether based on guidance from a financial advisor, tax professional, or estate/divorce attorney (if applicable). If they're purchasing another property, sellers may need to coordinate a simultaneous closing whereby net sale proceed funds are wired directly into their next transaction.

This is a common occurrence, and both your broker and the closer will assist in ensuring everything is timed and handled properly.

"Closing Day" Anticipations

Your broker will prepare and guide you through this final stretch along with your team of industry partners. For many buyers and sellers, closing day feels more administrative than ceremonial. You may envision a moment where keys are exchanged and everything feels final, but in reality, both parties typically sign the closing documents in different locations, and closing is not officially complete until several steps are executed behind the scenes.

Depending on how your specific location handles funding and recording, the buyer may not receive keys, and the seller may not receive their net proceeds immediately after signing with the closer. In many cases, the lender reserves the right to review and approve the final signed closing documents before authorizing funding; only then can the transaction be released for recording of the deed, formally transferring ownership from the seller to the buyer.

Navigating a real estate transaction is about more than paperwork and negotiations; it's about making informed, confident decisions with the right professionals by your side. The strength of your broker's industry partnerships ensures you have access to the best resources, insights, and solutions at every stage. By embracing these experts as part of your team, you gain not only a service but collaborative relationships committed to your success. Even in the final moments of the transaction, these relationships matter. The terms of the purchase and/or sale contract determine when the buyer will take possession (keys) and when the seller will vacate (often later the same day or on the next business day, depending on what was negotiated). While closing day may feel formal, the call confirming the recording is complete and funds are available is the moment it all becomes satisfying—and worth every ounce of energy spent up until that point.

Mindfully Speaking…

Each industry partner—whether lender, inspector, title representative, or closer—is an aligned professional, working in concert with the broker to uphold shared standards of service, accountability, and care for the client. These relationships are built on trust, performance, and mutual commitment to the client's success. Most brokers cultivate these partnerships through consistent collaboration, ensuring that each partner performs at the highest level and shares the same dedication to timeliness, communication, and ethical standards. Because these professionals value the ongoing relationship, they're vested in keeping it strong—knowing that mutual respect and excellence lead to continued referrals and a thriving local economy where dollars cycle back into the community.

Ultimately, it remains the client's responsibility to select the professionals best suited to their circumstances, comfort level, and budget—those capable of performing responsibly and on time to meet marketing agreements or contractual obligations. When all parties approach the process with accountability and care, the collective effort creates a seamless, trustworthy, and deeply satisfying real estate experience.

Summary
REcapping It All to Move Forward

Real estate transactions are more than just a series of legal and financial steps to connect a buyer with a property; they are transformative experiences that build relationships, shape lives, strengthen communities, and unlock pathways to financial growth.

A seamless and satisfying transaction is not a matter of luck but instead the result of a mindful approach that involves preparing intentionally, taking personal responsibility, and engaging in the process with clarity and a commitment to achieve your intended outcome. The strength of CORE (Comprehension, Orientation, Relationships, and Etiquette)—the four pillars that guide the Mindful Approach—lies in their ability to prepare you to actively participate in your journey. Supported by the Triple A principles (Acclimate, Agency, and Align), this framework helps you enter the market as a grounded, informed, and well-represented contributor to a more mindful real estate experience.

With the industry's evolving commitment to agency, compliance, and contract law, you now have the context to recognize what quality representation truly looks like. Partnering with a local professional broker leverages that knowledge, building a foundation of trust to help you navigate both the market and your transaction with clarity and strategic intent.

Strategizing both #B4MA and *after* #MA—particularly around due diligence, contingencies, and contractual obligations—removes uncertainty and prepares you to move forward with thoughtful action rather than out of emotion. When paired with expert insight and a commitment to make decisive, informed choices, an often-overwhelming process becomes an intentional and rewarding journey.

Beyond the transaction itself, real estate represents something far greater as a pathway to stability, financial security, and generational wealth. Everyone who desires to own property should have access to this opportunity—not just to build personal wealth but to invest in the communities we call home or work. When more individuals engage from a place of knowledge and alignment, neighborhoods thrive, disparities shrink, and communities become stronger.

As you move forward, remember: real estate isn't just about property but *people*. It's about securing futures, building equity, and creating opportunities that ripple through generations.

Let this be your invitation to take ownership over not only property but your own personal role in shaping a more robust, more connected community.

In *REcoding the Real Estate Experience*—replacing confusion with clarity, transforming passive participation into strategic engagement, and creating a shared language between clients and professionals—buyers and sellers can better understand the journey on both sides of mutual acceptance to align without hesitation and participate without fear.

Laws and best practices will likely evolve over time, so always consult with a local expert who understands your current market and regulatory landscape whether you're buying or selling. Please share this book with others who may benefit as well, consider gifting funds to help others you care about with their down payment and closing costs as necessary. In doing so, you're not only supporting their path to ownership but also helping to close the wealth gap that limits opportunities for many aspiring buyers (while likely enjoying meaningful tax advantages for both the giver and the receiver as a powerful way to build generational wealth within your family and community). Together, we can build thriving communities through shared investment in the dream of property ownership.

Mindful Real Estate
GLOSSARY

Able-ness: The buyer's readiness and reliability to perform through all phases of the transaction to closing. A buyer who has begun financing, verified funds, and is prepared to make timely decisions demonstrates strong able-ness—instilling confidence, strengthening offers, and helping both parties move decisively toward mutual acceptance (#MA). Demonstrating able-ness reassures the seller and their broker that the buyer is credible, prepared, and responsive—even when earnest money is modest.

Absorption rate: A market pace indicator that measures how quickly "available" properties are going under contract compared to total inventory.

Absorption rate formula:

Pending Properties ÷ Available Listings = Absorption Rate

> The formula is typically based on Pending sales within the last 30 days.

Above 20% absorption rate suggests a *seller's market*

Between 15 and 20% is a *balanced market*

Below 15% absorption rate suggests a *buyer's market*

This rate helps buyers, sellers, and brokers understand the speed of demand, guiding strategy, pricing, and expectations for how quickly a property may sell under current market conditions. *See also: Inventory Status; Buyer's Market; Seller's Market.*

Acclimation: The process of becoming aware of the market's pace: gaining general market knowledge, learning about its inventory without specific influence or emotional attachment, and developing a feel for market activity as it unfolds in a neutral, unbiased manner.

Actual Damages: The proven financial loss one party experiences when the other fails to fulfill the terms of a contract. To be awarded, actual damages must be supported by evidence such as receipts, invoices, or market data showing measurable harm. In real estate, this may include lost deposits, inspection or appraisal fees, or the difference between the agreed purchase price and the property's market value when the contract failed. Actual damages aim to restore the injured party to the financial position they would have held if the contract had been performed—no more, no less. *See also: Specific Performance; Liquidated Damages; Purchase and/or Sale Contract.*

Addendum (addenda): An addition or supplement to a real estate purchase and/or sale contract that modifies, clarifies, or adds terms to the original agreement. An addendum becomes a legally binding part of the contract once all parties agree to and sign it. Common addenda address contingencies, responses to contingencies, or required notices. Each addendum should be specific—clearly stating any applicable time frames and consequences—and remain consistent with the intent of the original contract to ensure transparency and mutual understanding. *See also: Amendment, Purchase and/or Sale Contract.*

Adjustable-Rate Mortgage (ARM): Also known as a "hybrid loan," this is a type of real estate loan with an interest rate that changes at specified intervals after an initial fixed period—typically every six months or annually. Rate adjustments are tied to economic indicators such as the U.S. Treasury bill, the Secured Overnight Financing Rate (SOFR), or other published financial indexes, which reflect broader market conditions. These changes can increase or decrease the borrower's monthly payment. Buyers often choose ARMs for their lower initial interest rates compared to fixed-rate loans.

Agency: Refers to the formal relationship established between a client (buyer or seller) and a licensed broker (AKA "agent") and their firm, authorizing the broker to act on the client's behalf in a real estate transaction–commonly known as "representation." Agency is established through a written agreement—such as a buyer agency agreement or a listing agreement—that defines the scope of services, compensation, and responsibilities. The nature and limits of agency may vary by jurisdiction, but universally serve to protect the client's best interests through authorized advocacy and compliance.

Agreement: A formal, written mutual understanding between two or more parties that outlines responsibilities or commitments but does not necessarily meet all the legal requirements of a binding contract. In real estate, agreements such as a **listing agreement** or a **buyer agency agreement** formalize the working relationship between a client and a broker. These documents set expectations and define duties, but they do not, on their own, transfer ownership of property. Agreements may vary by state and, internationally, by country.

Amendment: A formal change made to an existing real estate contract after it has been fully executed. An amendment modifies agreed-upon terms—such as price, closing date, or repair obligations—and becomes legally binding once all parties consent in writing. Unlike an addendum, which supplements the original agreement, an amendment alters the original terms. Clear communication and timely documentation are crucial for maintaining transparency and ensuring mutual understanding throughout the transaction. *See also: Purchase and/or Sale Contract.*

Annual Percentage Rate (APR): The total cost of a loan expressed as a yearly rate. APR includes not only the interest rate but also points, mortgage lender/broker fees, and certain other credit charges a borrower must pay. *See also: Points.*

App-Driven (or Web-based): Extraction Platforms that promote speed, convenience, and savings by bypassing transparent traditional broker representation. While they may appear to reduce costs, these platforms often distract buyers and sellers from the risks of proceeding without advocacy, such as incomplete due diligence, a lack of negotiation strategy, and limited protection against contractual pitfalls. Unlike community reinvestment, profits from these models are extracted rather than cycled back into local economies, removing wealth and resources that could otherwise support clients, and strengthen local neighborhoods.

Application Fee: A fee charged by a mortgage lender or broker when a borrower applies for a mortgage, intended to cover administrative and processing costs associated with the loan application. The amount and refundability of this fee vary by lender and loan program. *See also: Loan.*

Appraisal: An unbiased, professional assessment of a property's market value, conducted by a licensed appraiser. The appraisal is typically required by a lender to confirm that the property's value supports the loan amount and is often part of a financing contingency within the purchase and/or sale contract. Appraisers evaluate comparable sales, location, condition, and features to determine fair market value at a specific point in time. While primarily used for financing, an appraisal also provides both buyers and sellers with an objective perspective to guide informed pricing and negotiation decisions. *See also: Appraiser, Fair Market Value.*

Appraiser: A licensed or certified professional responsible for providing an independent, objective opinion of a property's market value. Appraisers evaluate recent comparable sales, property condition, location, and market trends to ensure fairness and accuracy in the valuation process. Though the lender orders the appraisal, appraisers do not work for banks or lending institutions directly—they are regulated to remain impartial and free from influence. Their report helps confirm that the property supports the loan amount and protects both buyer and seller by promoting a fair, transparent transaction. *See also: Appraisal.*

Appreciation: The increase in a property's value over time, which builds *equity* for the owner. Appreciation may result from market demand, inflation, improvements, or changes in the surrounding community. It is one of the primary ways real estate supports *wealth building* and long-term financial *growth*. Appreciation reflects sustained value, allowing owners to strengthen financial security and create generational stability.

Asbestos: A naturally occurring mineral once widely used in construction materials for its strength, insulation, and fire resistance. Common in homes built before the 1980s, asbestos can be found in insulation, flooring, ceiling tiles, roofing materials, and older textured wall finishes. While asbestos use has been restricted or banned in many countries, older properties may still contain it. Sellers are expected to disclose any known asbestos materials or past remediation. Buyers are encouraged to test before renovation or demolition, and if identified, asbestos is best managed or removed by licensed abatement professionals. *See also: Disclosure; Environmental Hazard; Material Fact.*

Assessed Value: The value a local government assigns to a property for purposes of taxation. This figure is used to calculate the amount of property tax owed by the owner and is often derived from the property's market value using an assessment ratio or formula. Unlike market or appraised value, the assessed value may differ from current market conditions—sometimes higher, sometimes lower—depending on the timing and method of assessment. *In some countries, similar terms include "valuation for tax purposes" or "cadastral value."*

Assessments: Fees or charges imposed on property owners by homeowners associations (HOAs), condominium boards, community developments, or local municipalities. These assessments fund shared expenses, improvements, or infrastructure that benefit the property or community. HOA or community assessments typically cover maintenance, reserve funds, or capital projects, while municipal assessments may be levied for public improvements such as new roads, sidewalks, lighting, power lines, or sewer systems. *See also: Per Diem; Property Taxes; Prorations; Reserve Account.*

Not to be confused with a ***Special Assessment,*** which is a one-time or limited-duration charge for a specific project—such as a roof replacement, road resurfacing, or unexpected capital repair—that falls outside the regular budget. Special assessments are usually divided among owners based on ownership percentage, lot size, or other governing formulas.

Buyers are encouraged to review and question both community and municipal assessment records during due diligence to identify any existing or prepare for upcoming costs. Verifying these obligations supports informed decision-making and long-term financial readiness.

Asset: Anything of monetary value owned by an individual or company. Assets include real property, personal property, savings, stocks, mutual funds, and other investments. Real estate is a powerful asset—equity through appreciation, generating potential income, and contributing to long-term wealth.

Balanced Market: This occurs when there is three to six months of inventory. Neither side holds a distinct advantage. Homes sell at a steady pace, prices remain relatively stable, and negotiations are often collaborative. *See also: Buyer's Market/ Seller's Market.*

Before Mutual Acceptance (#B4MA): The window of opportunity to study how location and condition affect price, create a strategy to perform, initiate due diligence, and negotiate agency terms to enter a representation partnership, and prepare for a future purchase and/or sale contract.

Before-Tax Income (Gross Income): The total amount of money earned by an individual or household before any taxes or deductions are withheld. This figure reflects true earning capacity and is often used by lenders to assess financial qualifications, affordability, and overall ability to sustain homeownership.

Bona Fide Offer: An offer made in good faith, with genuine intent and the financial ability to perform. A bona fide offer is both credible and performance-able—free from fraud, misrepresentation, or deceit. It reflects a buyer's serious commitment to purchase and demonstrates readiness to fulfill the terms of a real estate contract once accepted. *See also: Performance-Able.*

Breach of Contract: The failure of one party to uphold their obligations under a legally binding agreement. In real estate, a breach can occur when a buyer or seller does not meet deadlines, contingencies, or conditions outlined in the purchase and/or sale contract—such as delivering funds, completing repairs, or closing as agreed. A breach may lead to remedies including actual damages, liquidated damages, or specific performance, depending on the contract terms and jurisdiction. *See also: Specific Performance; Actual Damages; Liquidated Damages; Purchase and/or Sale Contract.*

Bridge Loan (also called Interim Loan or Swing Loan): A short-term loan that helps a homeowner purchase a new property before selling their current one. The loan "bridges" the financial gap between transactions by using the equity in the existing home as collateral. Bridge loans provide flexibility for sellers who find their next property first but may carry higher interest rates and shorter repayment terms. They are typically repaid when the current property sells or from the proceeds of the new mortgage.

Broker (AKA Agent): A licensed real estate professional who brokers a buyer and a property, typically through either a **buyer agency agreement** or a **listing agreement** (seller agency). Depending on the country or region, this role may also be called an *estate agent, property consultant, negotiator,* or *solicitor.* When agency relationships vary, the broker may represent one party exclusively or, in limited dual agency situations, facilitate the transaction without exclusive representation. Regardless of structure, the broker's role is to ensure transparency, compliance, and ethical integrity throughout the process. *Not to be confused with the Designated Broker, who holds supervisory responsibility within a firm or branch.*

Broker's Price Opinion (BPO): An estimate of a property's market value prepared by a licensed real estate broker or agent. A BPO is typically based on comparable sales, current listings, and the broker's knowledge of local market conditions. It may be presented as a letter or incorporated into a Comparative Market Analysis (CMA). While not as formal or regulated as an appraisal, a BPO offers a practical, experience-based perspective often used by sellers to determine listing price or by lenders for portfolio evaluations. A BPO reflects the broker's professional judgment and market expertise but should not be mistaken for an independent appraisal. *See also: Comparative Market Analysis (CMA).*

Buyer: A party to the purchase and/or sale contract who seeks to acquire property through an agreed-upon price and terms. A mindful buyer approaches the process with acclimation, agency, and alignment—collaborating to complete due diligence, fulfill contractual obligations, and close the transaction with preparedness and satisfaction. *See also: Principal.*

Buyer's Broker (AKA Selling Agent): A licensed real estate professional who provides representation upon entering a buyer agency agreement and becomes a short-term partner in the buyer's journey. Duties include sharing market insight and contract knowledge, strategizing due diligence, preparing for negotiations, ensuring compliance with disclosure and legal requirements, and managing contractual obligations—ultimately advocating for the buyer throughout the purchase transaction. In some regions, this role is referred to as the buyer's agent. *See also: Agreement; Purchase and/or Sale Contract.*

Buyer's Market: Occurs when there is a high supply of homes—typically more than six months of inventory. Buyers have more choices, absorption slows, and sellers often need to lower prices or improve property conditions to attract offers. Buyers generally hold greater negotiating power in a buyer's market. *See also: Balanced Market/Seller's Market; Inventory.*

Buydown: A mortgage financing strategy used to reduce the borrower's interest rate for a set period—or for the life of the loan—by paying an upfront fee known as discount points. This one-time payment is typically made at closing and lowers the borrower's monthly mortgage payments, making homeownership more affordable. In some cases, sellers or builders may offer to fund a buydown as an incentive to help buyers manage costs and improve affordability in higher interest rate markets.

Bylaws: The governing rules adopted by a homeowners association (HOA), condominium association, or cooperative to define how the organization operates. Bylaws typically outline procedures for meetings, elections, board member duties, budgeting, and enforcement of community standards. They provide a framework for transparency, accountability, and fair decision-making within the association. Buyers are encouraged to review these documents during their due diligence period to understand community obligations, restrictions, and financial responsibilities before closing. *See also: Homeowners Association (HOA); Codes, Covenants, and Restrictions (CC&Rs).*

Caveat Emptor (Buyer Beware): A principle that places responsibility on the buyer to perform due diligence. This includes conducting research, verifying information, and completing inspections to ensure fully informed decisions before purchasing.

Certificate of Eligibility: A document issued by the U.S. Department of Veterans Affairs (VA) verifying a veteran's eligibility for a VA-guaranteed mortgage loan. *See also: VA Loan.*

Clear Title: Legal ownership of real property that is free from liens, disputes, defects, or other encumbrances that could challenge or restrict transfer of ownership. A clear title confirms that no other party has a legal claim, outstanding debt, or unresolved interest in the property. Before closing, a title company or attorney typically conducts a title search to verify the chain of ownership and ensure the title can be transferred without issue. Achieving clear title assures both buyer and lender that ownership is valid, transferable, and protected against future claims.

Closer/Closing agent/ Escrow officer/ Settlement Agent: The person or entity that collects, chronicles, and coordinates the preparation and recordation of closing documents and the disbursement of funds. Typically, the closing is conducted by title companies, escrow companies, or attorneys.

Closing: The final step in a real estate transaction where ownership of the property is legally transferred from the seller to the buyer. If the buyer is receiving **funding** from a lender, those funds are disbursed to the escrow or closing agent to complete the financial exchange. At closing, all contractual obligations are fulfilled, funds are distributed, and documents—such as the deed and mortgage—are signed and recorded. In the United States, closings generally follow either an escrow process or an attorney-led process. Internationally, closing practices may differ, reflecting regional legal systems, customs, and professional roles. *See also: Funding.*

Closing Agent/ Escrow officer/ Settlement Agent/ Closer: The person or entity that collects, chronicles, and coordinates the preparation and recordation of closing documents and the disbursement of funds. Typically, the closing is conducted by title companies, escrow companies, or attorneys.

Closing Costs: The collective expenses associated with finalizing a real estate transaction, typically paid at closing when title transfers from seller to buyer. These costs may include fees for representation, title and escrow services, attorneys, prorated portions of property taxes or homeowners association (HOA) dues, and recording fees. Closing costs vary depending on the location and negotiated terms between the parties, and are itemized in the Closing Disclosure or settlement statement provided prior to closing.

Buyer Closing Costs: Expenses paid by the buyer to complete the purchase of a property. These often include any agreed-upon compensation for agency representation, title insurance, escrow and/or attorney fees, recording fees, prorated portions of property taxes or homeowners association (HOA) dues, prepaid taxes and insurance, and loan-related fees such as underwriting, appraisal, and credit report charges. Buyers may also pay discount points or a rate buydown to reduce their mortgage interest rate. The exact costs depend on the loan program, purchase price, and local regulations. Buyers are encouraged to review their Loan Estimate early in the process and compare it with the final Closing Disclosure to ensure accuracy and transparency.

Seller's Closing Costs: Expenses paid by the seller to complete the transfer of ownership to the buyer. These often include any agreed-upon compensation to the listing broker and buyer's broker, title insurance for the buyer, escrow and/or attorney fees, recording fees, and prorated portions of property taxes or homeowners association (HOA) dues. Sellers may also fulfill agreed-upon repairs, credits, or concessions toward the buyer's closing costs as part of negotiated terms. In most transactions, sellers must also satisfy liens and pay any outstanding utility balances. The exact costs depend on the property location, purchase price, and negotiated contract terms. Sellers are encouraged to review an estimated net proceeds worksheet early in the process to anticipate and prepare for these expenses prior to negotiations and closing.

Closing Date: A negotiated term of the **purchase and/or sale contract.** It represents the day when all contractual obligations are fulfilled, funds are transferred, and ownership of the property legally transferred. While the closing date is set in the contract, it can sometimes shift due to financing delays, appraisal or inspection issues, or other contingencies. Understanding this flexibility helps you prepare with realistic expectations while keeping your transaction on track.

Closing Disclosure Statement(CD): A standardized form provided by the **lender** that gives a detailed breakdown of all closing costs, credits, loan terms, and the final cash needed to close. It allows buyers to review the full financial details of their transaction, compare them to the initial Loan Estimate, and budget accordingly. Federal law requires that buyers receive the Closing Disclosure at least three business days before closing.

Clouded Title: A property title that has defects, disputes, or unresolved claims that prevent it from being considered clear and marketable. Common causes include outstanding liens, recording errors, boundary disputes, undisclosed heirs, or missing signatures in the chain of ownership. A clouded title must be resolved—often through a title company, attorney, or legal action—before the property can be transferred or financed. Clearing title issues protects all parties by ensuring ownership rights are valid, enforceable, and free from future challenge.

Codes, Covenants, and Restrictions (CC&Rs): The recorded legal documents that outline property use, architectural standards, and behavioral expectations within a community governed by a homeowners association (HOA). CC&Rs are binding on all property owners and are intended to preserve property values, ensure aesthetic consistency, and promote harmony within the neighborhood. They are enforceable by the HOA in accordance with its bylaws. Buyers are encouraged to review these documents during their due diligence period to understand community obligations, restrictions, and financial responsibilities before closing. *See also: Homeowners Association (HOA); Bylaws.*

Commission/Compensation: The fee charged by a real estate firm on behalf of an agent or broker for services performed, usually based on a percentage of the final sale price or a negotiated flat fee. There are no standard compensation rates—compensation is fully negotiable and not set by law.

Under the terms of a **Buyer Agency agreement**, if the buyer purchases a property and the sale closes, the buyer is responsible for paying the agreed-upon compensation—unless the seller offers an amount that fully covers it. If the seller offers less, the buyer is responsible for covering the difference. This obligation may be fulfilled directly or negotiated as part of the purchase offer. Depending on the Buyer Agency Agreement, if the sale fails to close due to the buyer's breach of its terms, the broker may still be entitled to the agreed-upon compensation.

Commission Split: A historical compensation model in which the listing firm, after entering into a listing agreement with a seller, agreed to share a portion of the contracted fee with the firm representing the buyer. The split was identified in the Multiple Listing Service (MLS) and intended to encourage cooperation between firms. Once a longstanding industry norm, the commission split model has since evolved—replaced by modern practices that prioritize transparency, client-specific negotiation, and separate agreements outlining compensation for both buyer and seller representation.

Community Reinvestment: The practice of local brokers and industry partners earning through real estate activity and then reinvesting their income, resources, and expertise back into the very neighborhoods and districts they serve. Rather than extracting profits, community reinvestment creates a "local wealth cycle," where money circulates within the community—supporting small businesses, sponsoring local events, and contributing to charitable or civic initiatives. This cycle strengthens neighborhood ties, sustains local district economies, and builds long-term wealth and resilience for the community as a whole.

Comparative Market Analysis (CMA): A detailed evaluation prepared by a licensed real estate broker/agent to estimate a property's current market value or value range. A CMA compares recently sold, pending, and active properties similar in size, room count, location, and condition to the subject property. Often provided to sellers when determining a listing price or to buyers assessing fair market value, a CMA combines market data with the broker's professional insight. While more comprehensive than a Broker's Price Opinion (BPO), it is not a formal appraisal but rather a strategic tool used to inform sellers of current market conditions and develop a plan to effectively position the property for market. *See also: BPO.*

Compliance: Obeying the laws, meeting licensing standards, and following ethical practices that govern real estate transactions at every level.

Comps (Comparables): The most recent pending and sold properties used as comparisons to determine the current value of a property, whether for market pricing or appraisal purposes.

Comprehension: Is the awareness of how each party's contribution shapes the transaction. It creates alignment, encourages accountability, and transforms intentions into purposeful action that supports a mindful, successful outcome.

Concessions: Something agreed to or given up during negotiations to help reach mutual acceptance. For example, a seller may agree to reduce the purchase price, pay for inspection repairs/replacements, or contribute toward the buyer's closing costs—collectively known as concessions.

Consideration: In the context of seller disclosures, consideration means carefully evaluating the importance of providing all known information about the property. Sellers should complete required disclosures and gather supporting documentation to the best of their ability, delivering them as early as possible to reduce the buyer's opportunity to withdraw during the verification process. *See also: Contract.*

> **Consideration Note:** *This meaning of consideration differs from its use in contract law, where it refers to something of value exchanged between parties.*

Contingency (AKA Condition): A condition in a purchase and/or sale contract that must be satisfied, resolved, or formally waived before the contract becomes fully binding. Contingencies are not loopholes but agreements—each with its own defined timelines, forms, and protocols designed to provide structure, accountability, and confidence for both parties to move forward responsibly. They create a framework for performing due diligence and proceeding with assurance, or responsibly terminating, canceling, or rescinding if terms cannot be met. For sellers, contingencies require patience and cooperation, remaining steadfast and collaborative throughout the process to support the shared goal of closing.

Contingency Removal (or Resolution): The formal action of satisfying, resolving, or waiving a contingency within the purchase and/or sale contract. Once removed, the contingency no longer protects the party who held it, and the contract advances toward closing with fewer opportunities to terminate. Timely removal or resolution is essential to maintain trust, communication, and the spirit of collaboration, allowing the transaction to flow steadily toward a cooperative and successful closing.

Contingent Sale: A buyer contingency tied to the successful sale of the buyer's current property. In a net proceeds sale, the buyer negotiates with the seller to include this condition, allowing time to list, market, and close on their property before purchasing the seller's property. The purchase and/or sale contract is therefore subject to the buyer's property closing, enabling the buyer to collect sufficient proceeds for their next purchase. While this contingency provides flexibility and financial alignment for the buyer, it also introduces timing risk for the seller; therefore, having clear terms, defined deadlines, and accountability is essential to ensure all parties perform responsibly.

Contract: A legally enforceable agreement that creates binding obligations between parties. In real estate, the **purchase and/or sale contract** establishes the terms for transferring property ownership. The elements: offer and acceptance, consideration, competent parties, legal purpose, and written form, are required to form a valid contract—can vary by state, by country, and internationally. A contract is enforceable in a court of law and must meet specific legal requirements.

Counter-offer: An offer made in response to a previous offer. In other words, any change made to the terms presented by the other party.

Days on Market (DOM) / Cumulative Days on Market (CDOM): The total number of days a property has been actively listed for sale before going under contract. *DOM* measures time on the current listing, while *CDOM* (Cumulative Days on Market) reflects total days across consecutive listings without a significant break in activity. Rather than serving as a simple measure of desirability, CDOM is often a reflection of the seller's pricing discipline and market awareness. Properties priced according to location, condition, and true market value typically experience shorter market times, while extended CDOM can signal a need for adjustment in pricing, presentation, or strategy. When interpreted correctly, DOM and CDOM reveal how closely the listing strategy aligns with current buyer expectations and market conditions.

Deed: The legal document that transfers title (ownership rights) of a property from one party to another. A deed contains the most current legal description of the property and must be signed by the seller (grantor), delivered to the buyer (grantee), and recorded with the appropriate government office to provide public notice of the transfer.

Default: The failure of a party to perform as agreed within the purchase and/or sale contract. Default occurs when a buyer or seller does not meet a required condition, contingency, or deadline—such as delivering funds, fulfilling contractual obligations, or closing per the agreed terms of the contract. It represents a lapse in contractual performance and may carry legal or financial consequences as outlined in the agreement. In a mindful transaction, default is best prevented through clear communication, proactive follow-up, and accountability to timelines and responsibilities. *See also: Forfeiture.*

Depreciation: The decrease in a property's value over time, often caused by deferred maintenance, physical deterioration, changing market conditions, or external factors such as neighborhood decline or oversupply. Depreciation reduces equity and can impact the owner's overall wealth-building potential. Mindful ownership—through timely upkeep, improvements, and market awareness—can help mitigate depreciation and preserve long-term financial stability.

Designated Broker (DB): The broker legally responsible for supervising all brokers within a firm. May also be the firm owner or managing broker. Requires advanced licensing, experience, and education. The DB acts as a dual agent when two supervised brokers from their firm represent different principals in the same transaction.

Discipline: The foundation of being performance-able. It's not about perfection—it's about consistency. For buyers, this means prioritizing needs over wants; for sellers, it means being realistic about the property's location, condition, and pricing. Discipline keeps buyers and sellers aligned with their goals, helps them avoid distractions, and ensures steady progress toward a successful closing.

Disclosure: The act of providing truthful, complete information about a property's known condition, history, and any material facts that could influence a buyer's decision or affect the property's value. Sellers are legally obligated to disclose known defects, hazards, or other significant issues, while brokers must disclose facts within their awareness that may impact the transaction. Case law shows that buyers who prove a seller knowingly withheld material information may be awarded damages.

Some sellers mark disclosures as **"unknown"** or **"don't know,"** often due to lack of residency, familiarity, or fear. While legally permissible, due diligence falls to the buyer to verify whether any omissions obscure critical information, including potential environmental hazards or concealed defects. Disclosure requirements, processes, and disclosure forms vary by state, region, or country, but transparency remains a universal standard—protecting all parties and promoting trust in the transaction. *See also: Due Diligence; Home Inspection; Latent Defect; Material Fact; Seller's Disclosure.*

Down Payment: When a buyer is securing financing to complete a purchase, the down payment represents the portion of the purchase price the buyer contributes upfront at closing. This amount reduces the loan balance, immediately establishes equity in the property, and reflects the buyer's vested interest in homeownership. To the lender, a larger down payment reduces lending risk, as it demonstrates the buyer's financial stability and commitment to the investment. A down payment may come from the buyer's own funds, proceeds from another property sale, grants or assistance programs, or gift funds. Many loan programs allow eligible gift funds to be applied toward the down payment (and sometimes closing costs) when properly documented, offering buyers flexibility while reinforcing financial responsibility and long-term commitment to ownership. *See also: Loan-to-Value Ratio.*

Dual Agency (limited dual agency): Occurs when one (the same) broker represents both the buyer and the seller in a transaction. This arrangement requires the informed consent of both principals, which must be documented in their separate written agency agreements, with both consents acknowledged in the purchase and/or sale contract.

Due Diligence: The process of thoroughly reviewing, researching, and verifying information about a property or area to identify conditions that may impact a purchase or sale. When initiated early, due diligence allows clients to strategize and create a plan, ensuring they proceed with "eyes wide open." This reduces uncertainty, protects their interests, and strengthens their position.

Earnest Money: Also called "good faith" money, this deposit—typically 1% to 3% of the purchase price—is established in the buyer's offer to demonstrate serious intent and commitment to honor the contract terms. Once negotiated and deposited after mutual acceptance, earnest money provides the seller with assurance to proceed in pending status while contractual obligations are fulfilled. The funds are typically held in escrow (or as otherwise agreed) and applied to the purchase price at closing. In short, earnest money may be forfeited if the buyer defaults without valid cause, serving as protection for the seller. *See also: Forfeiture.*

Easement: A legal right to use or access land owned by another for a specific purpose (such as utilities, shared driveways, or pathways) without owning the land itself. Easements are typically documented in the title report. *See also: Legal Description; Encroachment; Survey.*

Encroachment: A physical intrusion onto another's property without permission or legal right (such as a fence, driveway, or structure extending beyond the property line). Encroachments may be identified in a survey and cited in the title report. *See also: Legal Description; Easement; Survey.*

Encumbrance: Any legal claim, restriction, or liability on a property—such as a lien, mortgage, easement, or unpaid taxes—that may affect the owner's ability to transfer clear title. Encumbrances are generally recorded and noted in the title report. *See also: Title; Mortgage.*

Equity: The portion of a property's value that the owner truly owns, calculated by subtracting any outstanding mortgage or liens from the home's current market value. Equity grows through loan paydown, market appreciation, or strategic improvements. It represents financial strength, provides opportunities to leverage wealth for future goals, and can be a foundation for long-term financial stability and community reinvestment.

Escrow: A third, neutral party—often referred to as the *closer*—that collects, documents, and coordinates the preparation, signing, and recordation of closing documents, as well as the disbursement of funds. Escrow ensures all conditions of the purchase and/or sale contract are satisfied before ownership and funds are exchanged. Typically managed by title companies, escrow companies, or attorneys, escrow provides structure, accountability, and protection for both buyer and seller during the closing process.

Escrow Account (AKA Escrow Impound): A separate account maintained by a lender to hold funds on behalf of the borrower, ensuring timely payment of property taxes, homeowners' insurance, or other recurring expenses associated with the property. These funds are typically collected as part of the borrower's monthly mortgage payment, allowing the lender to manage and disburse payments when due. *See also: Reserve Account.*

Escrow officer/ Settlement Agent/ Closer/ Closing agent: The person or entity that collects, chronicles, and coordinates the preparation and recordation of closing documents and the disbursement of funds. Typically, the closing is conducted by title companies, escrow companies, or attorneys.

Etiquette: Real estate has its own code of conduct, often unspoken but always essential. It means respecting time, honoring relationships, practicing transparency and disclosure, and safeguarding client confidence. It's about upholding morals and ethics, treating others with respect—not undermining them—and ensuring every interaction reflects integrity. Etiquette preserves trust, elevates the industry, and helps make each transaction both successful and satisfying.

Buyer Etiquette: *P.R.E.P.A.R.E. to Close*

P: Promptly deliver earnest money.

R: Review and verify documentation.

E: Evaluate the property in one consolidated site visit.

P: Pull details first, cross-reference, seek to understand.

A: Apply for financing.

R: Respect time, implement strategies, and pivot to collaborate.

E: Execute the final steps to close with clarity and confidence.

Seller Etiquette: *H.O.N.O.R. to Receive*

H: Honor the contract, respect the contingency periods.

O: Offer timely access and answers with clarity.

N: Nurture to collaborate and maintain respectful communication.

O: Organize supporting documents, i.e., receipts, warranties, or service records.

R: Ready to fulfill obligations, move out, and leave the property better than expected.

Exclusive (Agency Agreement): A reference to the type of written agency representation in which a client commits to working exclusively with one licensed real estate broker for a specific location and defined period. This exclusive commitment ensures the broker's full dedication to achieving the client's goals, with their time, expertise, and advocacy protected. The agreement also outlines transparent terms and compensation, ensuring mutual clarity and accountability throughout the relationship. *See also: Non-Exclusive (Agency Agreement).*

Extraction Platforms (also called Distraction Platforms): Web-based or app-driven real estate models that promote speed, convenience, and savings by bypassing traditional broker representation. While they may appear to reduce costs, these platforms often distract buyers and sellers from the risks of proceeding without advocacy, such as incomplete due diligence, a lack of negotiation strategy, and limited protection against contractual pitfalls. Unlike community reinvestment, profits from these models are extracted rather than cycled back into local economies, removing wealth and resources that could otherwise support clients and strengthen neighborhoods.

Fair Market Value: The price at which a property would transfer between a willing buyer and a willing seller, both acting with mutual consent. Each party is assumed to have reasonable knowledge of relevant factors such as location, condition, and market activity. Often summed up by the saying, *"A property is only worth what a buyer is willing to pay,"* fair market value represents the point where informed motivation and market reality align. When financing is involved, an appraisal is typically used to confirm this value for the lender.

Fannie Mae (Federal National Mortgage Association): A publicly traded company operating under a federal charter and listed on the New York Stock Exchange. Fannie Mae is the nation's largest source of mortgage financing. It does not lend money directly to consumers but rather supports affordability and liquidity in the housing market by purchasing mortgage loans from lenders, thereby ensuring that funds remain available for borrowers.

FHA Loan (Federal Housing Administration): A government-insured loan designed to help buyers with lower credit scores or smaller down payments qualify for financing. FHA loans require mortgage insurance and have limits based on location.

Fiduciary Duties: In addition to statutory duties, fiduciary responsibilities are often identified and confirmed within agency agreements, where the firm or broker formally acknowledges their commitment to place the client's interests above their own. These duties extend throughout the relationship and typically include loyalty, confidentiality, full disclosure, diligence, and obedience to lawful instructions.

Final Walk-Through: Buyer's final opportunity to ensure the property is in the agreed-upon condition and that all negotiated repairs or contractual obligations have been completed. Typically conducted after all contingencies have been satisfied but before closing, to provide assurance and accountability before ownership transfers. The purchase and/or sale contract typically outlines this condition, requiring the seller to provide reasonable access for the buyer to complete prior to closing.

Fixed-Rate Mortgage: A type of home loan with an interest rate that remains the same for the entire term, providing stable and predictable monthly payments. The fixed term—commonly set for a specific number of years—offers borrowers long-term financial consistency, making it the most traditional and widely used mortgage option in real estate transactions.

Fixtures: Items permanently attached or affixed to the land or structure in such a way that they become part of the real property and convey with the sale. Examples include built-in appliances, light fixtures, and landscaping. Because fixtures are presumed to transfer with ownership unless specifically excluded in the purchase and/or sale contract, they should be clearly identified during negotiations. *See also: Included/Excluded Items.*

Flood Insurance: Insurance coverage that compensates for physical property damage caused by flooding. It is required for properties located in federally designated flood hazard zones and may also be advisable for properties near bodies of water or in areas prone to heavy rainfall. Flood insurance is typically separate from standard homeowners insurance and is often issued through the National Flood Insurance Program (NFIP) or private insurers. *See also: homeowners insurance.*

Forfeiture: The loss of money, property, rights, or privileges as a result of failing to fulfill a legal obligation or term of a contract. In real estate, forfeiture often refers to the loss of earnest money as a remedy available to the seller if the buyer breaches the purchase and/or sale contract. Forfeiture terms are typically outlined in the contract's default provisions and serve as a reminder of the importance of performance, accountability, and honoring commitments. *See also: Earnest Money.*

Funding: The process by which loan proceeds are transferred from the lender to the escrow or closing agent to complete the financial exchange between buyer and seller. Funding occurs shortly before closing, once all loan conditions and contractual obligations have been satisfied. This step enables the final disbursement of funds and the legal transfer of ownership. *See also: Closing.*

Gift Letter: A written statement from a family member or approved donor verifying that a monetary contribution toward the buyer's down payment or closing costs is a genuine gift—not a loan—and does not require repayment. Lenders require a gift letter to document the source of gift funds and ensure compliance with loan program guidelines. *See also: Gift Funds.*

Golden Rule: The timeless principle of treating others as you would wish to be treated, elevated in real estate to mean practicing collaboration, transparency, respect, and mindfulness in every interaction. It calls for honoring time, communicating with clarity, and maintaining integrity so that all parties—clients, brokers, and industry partners—can move toward a trustworthy, ethical, and satisfying transaction.

Government Mortgage: A mortgage loan that is insured or guaranteed by a U.S. federal government agency, providing lenders with added security and often allowing borrowers to qualify with lower down payments or flexible terms. Common types include FHA, VA, and USDA/RHS loans.

Government National Mortgage Association (Ginnie Mae): A government-owned corporation within the U.S. Department of Housing and Urban Development (HUD). Ginnie Mae guarantees mortgage-backed securities (MBS) that are composed of loans insured or guaranteed by other federal agencies, such as FHA, VA, or USDA. This guarantee ensures timely payment of principal and interest to investors, helping stabilize mortgage markets and expand affordable housing opportunities.

Government Survey System (Rectangular Survey System): A standardized method of describing and dividing land, primarily used in the United States, based on a grid of principal meridians (north-south) and base lines (east-west). Land is divided into townships, ranges, and sections, each with defined dimensions. This system provides consistency and precision in describing large tracts of land. *See also: Legal Description.*

Gross Income (Before-Tax Income): The total amount of money earned by an individual or household before any taxes or deductions are withheld. This figure reflects true earning capacity and is often used by lenders to assess financial qualifications, affordability, and overall ability to sustain homeownership.

Gross Monthly Income: The amount of income earned in a single month before taxes or deductions. It may include wages or salary, self-employment earnings, rental income, alimony, child support, public assistance, and retirement benefits. Lenders use gross monthly income to calculate debt-to-income ratios and determine borrowing capacity.

Hard Money: A short-term, asset-based loan secured primarily by the value of the property rather than the borrower's creditworthiness. Typically issued by local or regional private lenders, hard money loans are often used for time-sensitive transactions, such as property flips, bridge financing, or projects that don't qualify for conventional lending. They offer flexibility and fast access to capital, but usually come with higher interest rates and shorter repayment terms.

Hazard Insurance: Insurance that specifically covers physical damage to the structure of a property caused by fire, wind, vandalism, or other covered hazards and natural disasters. While often included as part of a broader homeowners policy, some lenders may require separate hazard insurance to ensure their collateral is protected. *See also: Homeowners Insurance.*

Home Equity Line of Credit (HELOC): A revolving line of credit secured by the homeowner's equity that can be accessed as needed—similar to a credit card but with the property as collateral. A HELOC can be used to fund improvements, consolidate debt, cover unexpected expenses, or support the transition to a new property. Because funds are drawn only when needed, it offers flexibility while helping owners preserve liquidity and maintain control of their financial strategy.

Home Equity Loan (also called a Second Mortgage): A fixed-term loan that allows homeowners to borrow against the equity in their property and receive the funds in one lump sum. Often used for home improvements, debt consolidation, or other major financial goals, a home equity loan enables homeowners to leverage the value of their property as part of a broader wealth-building strategy. Unlike a HELOC, it provides a set repayment schedule and predictable payments, offering stability while utilizing earned equity responsibly.

Home Inspection: A professional evaluation of a property's overall condition, typically conducted by a local licensed home inspector. The inspection includes an assessment of the home's major systems and components—such as plumbing, electrical, heating and cooling, roofing, foundation, and structural integrity—as well as potential concerns like pest infestation or moisture intrusion. Often performed to satisfy an inspection contingency, a thorough home inspection helps clients strategize, negotiate, and make informed decisions, allowing them to proceed confidently toward closing. *See also: Due Diligence.*

Homeowners Association (HOA): An organized group of property owners within a defined community or development whose primary purpose is to maintain common areas, amenities, and shared services for the collective benefit of all residents. Homeowners associations are typically managed by an elected board of property owners responsible for enforcing community standards, managing budgets, and upholding the recorded bylaws, codes, covenants, and restrictions (CC&Rs). Effective HOAs foster well-maintained, cohesive communities through accountability and resident participation. Buyers are encouraged to review these documents during their due diligence period to understand community obligations, restrictions, and financial responsibilities before closing. *See also: Bylaws; Codes, Covenants, and Restrictions (CC&Rs).*

Homeowners Insurance: A comprehensive policy that protects both the homeowner and the lender against financial loss from damage to the property caused by perils such as fire, theft, wind, or certain natural disasters. It also provides liability coverage for injuries occurring on the property and protection for personal belongings such as furniture, clothing, or appliances. In most cases, hazard coverage is included within a homeowners policy. *See also: Hazard Insurance.*

Home Warranty: A service contract that provides repair or replacement coverage for major home systems and appliances due to normal wear and tear. A home warranty may be offered as an incentive by sellers, builders, or developers, negotiated by buyers during the purchase process, or purchased directly by homeowners for ongoing protection during ownership. While not the same as homeowners insurance, a home warranty can provide peace of mind by minimizing unexpected repair costs after closing.

Included/Excluded Items: Items specifically listed in the purchase and/or sale contract as transferring with the property (included) or remaining with the seller (excluded). These may include appliances, window treatments, mounted televisions, garage storage systems, outdoor features, or other items that could otherwise create confusion. Clearly identifying included and excluded items helps prevent misunderstandings and ensures all parties share the same expectations at closing. *See also: Fixtures.*

Industry Partners: Local professionals—such as attorneys, title companies, lenders, inspectors, stagers, and escrow officers—who play an essential role in the success of a real estate experience. While they often have long-standing relationships with brokers and firms, those partnerships are sustained because they consistently provide excellent service, uphold high standards of integrity, and deliver quality results. Their vested presence in the community ensures clients receive reliable guidance and support, while also contributing to the strength and long-term wealth of the community as a whole. *See also: Relationships.*

Interest: The cost of borrowing money, expressed as a percentage of the loan amount. Interest represents the payment made to a lender in exchange for the use of its funds. In a mortgage, the interest rate determines how much the borrower pays in addition to repaying the principal over time. Interest can be fixed (unchanging throughout the loan term) or adjustable (changing periodically based on market conditions).

Inventory: The collective term for all properties within a defined market segment, including those that are active, pending, sold, or expired. In everyday use, "inventory" most often refers to the *available* or *active* listings currently on the market. Inventory levels are a key indicator of market balance—low inventory tends to create competition among buyers, while higher inventory provides buyers with more choice and negotiating power. Tracking inventory helps both buyers and sellers understand pacing, pricing trends, and the overall absorption rate within their market. *See also: Absorption Rate; Buyer's Market; Seller's Market; Inventory Status.*

Inventory Status (Available / Pending / Sold): Inventory status reflects the lifecycle of a listed property—from pre–mutual acceptance (#B4MA) through closing—providing valuable data for analyzing market activity and identifying shifts and trends.

Available (Active): A property currently on the market, seeking a willing and able buyer to reach mutual acceptance (#MA).

Pending: A property that has reached mutual acceptance (#MA) and is progressing through contingencies such as financing, inspection, and other contractual obligations toward closing.

Sold: A property that has closed and legally transferred ownership. Sold data often includes the final sale price, concessions, buyer-paid closing costs, buyer broker compensation, and negotiated repairs—providing the clearest reflection of buyer behavior and overall market performance.

Latent Defect: A hidden or concealed condition in a property that is not readily visible or discoverable through ordinary inspection. A latent defect may exist with or without the seller's knowledge; however, if known and not disclosed, it can become a legal issue involving misrepresentation or nondisclosure. Common examples include foundation cracks behind finished walls, hidden plumbing leaks, or electrical issues within enclosed systems. While proper disclosure and inspection practices help reduce risk, latent defects may still go undetected despite a professional inspection, as they are not observable through non-invasive means. *See also: Disclosure; Home Inspection; Due Diligence.*

Lead-Based Paint: A hazardous material once commonly used in homes built before 1978. In the United States, the manufacture and residential use of lead-based paint was banned that year; however, some builders and painters continued to use remaining inventories until supplies were exhausted. In many regions, sellers of pre-1978 properties are legally required to provide buyers with a *Lead-Based Paint Disclosure* and the opportunity to conduct testing. *See also: Disclosure; Environmental Hazard; Material Fact.*

Lease-Purchase Option: An agreement that allows a tenant to lease a property with the *option*, but not the obligation, to purchase it within a specified period, often at a predetermined price. This arrangement can be initiated by either the seller—who may wish to delay closing for tax purposes or continue generating income—or by a buyer who needs additional time to prepare financing, build equity, or complete the sale of another property. In many cases, a portion of each rent payment is credited toward the future down payment or purchase price. If the buyer chooses not to move forward with the purchase, the option simply expires—typically without penalty beyond the forfeiture of any option fee or rent credits. Because terms and responsibilities can vary widely, both parties should clearly outline payment allocations, purchase timelines, and maintenance obligations to ensure transparency and a smooth transition to ownership.

Legal Description: A precise, formal written description of a property's geographic boundaries and location, recognized by courts, title companies, and public records. Unlike a street address, which can change over time, a legal description uniquely identifies a parcel of land with permanent reference points. Common formats include metes and bounds (using distances and directions between landmarks), lot and block (for platted subdivisions), and the government survey system (referencing township, range, and section). A correct legal description ensures clarity of ownership, accurate title transfer, and boundary integrity in every transaction. *See also: Title; Survey; Parcel/Property Identification Number (PIN); Purchase and/or Sale Contract.*

Lender (Loan Officer / Mortgage Broker): A licensed financial professional who guides buyers through the process of securing a mortgage loan. Acting as both educator and facilitator, the lender explains available loan options, gathers documentation, and ensures the buyer understands their obligations before closing. Some loan officers work directly for a single financial institution, while **mortgage brokers** are licensed to place loans with multiple lenders, helping buyers compare programs and rates. While buyers typically interact with their lender or broker, the actual funds come from the financial institution underwriting and funding the loan.

Lien: A legal claim or charge against a property that secures the payment of a debt or obligation. Liens are typically recorded in public records and identified in a title report. Common examples include mortgage liens, property tax liens, and mechanic's (contractor) liens. In a financed transaction, the lender's lien gives them the right to take title to the property through foreclosure if the borrower fails to make required payments. Before closing, title professionals confirm that all liens are satisfied or properly subordinated to ensure a clear, marketable title. *See also: Title; Mortgage; Encumbrance.*

Liquidated Damages: A predetermined amount or formula outlined in a contract to address what happens if one party fails to perform as agreed. Liquidated damages are intended to simplify resolution and avoid prolonged disputes over actual losses. In real estate, this often refers to the buyer's earnest money deposit, which may be released to the seller if the buyer fails to close without valid cause. A well-structured earnest money amount should reflect a fair and reasonable estimate of potential loss at the time the contract was signed—not serve as a penalty. Sellers are encouraged to advocate for an earnest money amount that aligns with market norms and the level of risk, ensuring fairness and accountability for both parties.

See also: Actual Damages; Specific Performance; Earnest Money; Purchase and/or Sale Contract.

Listing Broker (AKA Seller's Agent): A licensed real estate professional who provides representation upon entering a listing agreement and becomes a short-term partner in the seller's journey. Duties include analyzing market conditions, developing pricing and marketing strategies, managing property presentation, ensuring compliance with disclosure and legal requirements, and overseeing contractual obligations—ultimately advocating for the seller throughout the transaction. In some regions, this role is referred to as the listing agent. *See also: Agreement; Purchase and/or Sale Contract.*

Loan: A sum of money borrowed by a buyer to finance the purchase of a property, which must be repaid with interest over an agreed period. A loan is a financial agreement between the borrower and the lender, often secured by a mortgage or deed of trust recorded against the property. Loan terms specify the amount borrowed, interest rate, repayment schedule, and conditions for default. *See also: Mortgage; Deed of Trust; Funding; Default.*

Loan-able: A term describing a property's readiness to qualify for financing under lender or government-backed loan standards. A loan-able property is well-maintained, free of major deferred maintenance, and meets basic safety and livability requirements—such as intact paint surfaces, functional electrical systems, and secure handrails or fixtures. Preparing or maintaining a loan-able property not only supports smoother underwriting and timely funding, but also extends opportunity to more qualified buyers—especially those using traditional or first-time buyer financing programs. This mindful approach strengthens marketability, contributes to the neighborhood, and continues the cycle of responsible ownership.

Loan Estimate (LE): A standardized form provided by the **lender** within three business days of a borrower submitting a loan application. It gives a breakdown of the estimated loan terms, projected payments, interest rate, and closing costs so buyers can compare loan offers and understand the financial impact of their mortgage. The Loan Estimate is the first major disclosure in the mortgage process and is designed to promote transparency and informed decision-making. The Loan Estimate is specific to the United States under federal TRID regulations. Other countries may have their own mortgage disclosure practices, but they differ in format, timing, and level of detail.

Loan Origination: The full process by which a mortgage loan is created—from the borrower's initial application through processing, underwriting, approval, and preparation for funding. Loan origination includes verifying credit, income, assets, and property details to confirm that the borrower meets the lender's guidelines and the loan can be completed responsibly. *See also: Loan Origination Fees; Buyer Closing Costs; Points.*

Loan Origination Fees: The charges paid to a mortgage lender or broker for processing, underwriting, and preparing the borrower's mortgage loan. Origination fees are typically expressed as *points*—where one point equals 1% of the total loan amount—and may vary by lender or loan program. These fees compensate the lender for the administrative work involved in originating the loan and are disclosed early in the process on the Loan Estimate (LE), then confirmed on the Closing Disclosure (CD). Transparency in loan origination fees allows buyers to compare offers, evaluate value, and make informed financing decisions. *See also: Loan Origination; Buyer Closing Costs; Points.*

Loan-to-Value (LTV) Ratio: The percentage that compares the loan amount to the property's purchase price or appraised value, whichever is lower. Lenders use the LTV ratio to measure risk—the lower the ratio, the less risk to the lender and the stronger the buyer's equity position. For example, a $100,000 property with an $80,000 mortgage has an LTV of 80%. A higher LTV may require mortgage insurance or stricter loan terms. Understanding this ratio helps buyers recognize how their down payment influences loan approval, interest rates, and overall financial strength. *See also: Down Payment.*

Lock-In Rate: A written agreement between a borrower and lender guaranteeing a specific mortgage interest rate—and sometimes points or terms—for a set period before closing. Locking the rate protects the borrower from market fluctuations during loan processing and approval. Lock periods typically range from 15 to 60 days, depending on the lender and market conditions. If the rate lock expires before closing, the borrower may need to extend it for a fee or accept the current market rate. *See also: Interest.*

Lot and Block: A legal description method used primarily for properties within platted subdivisions. Each parcel is identified by a specific lot number and block number, which correspond to a recorded subdivision map on file with the local jurisdiction. This system simplifies the identification and transfer of ownership for residential and commercial developments. *See also: Legal Description.*

Managing Broker: A broker responsible for supervising and supporting other brokers within a branch office of a firm. A managing broker may also hold a designated broker license, depending on state requirements.

Manufactured Housing: Homes built entirely in a factory under a federal building code administered by the U.S. Department of Housing and Urban Development (HUD). Manufactured homes may be single- or multi-section and are transported from the factory to a designated site for installation. When permanently affixed to a foundation, a manufactured home may be classified as real property under applicable state law and financed with a mortgage. Homes not permanently affixed are typically classified as personal property and financed through a personal loan rather than a traditional mortgage. *Manufactured homes differ from modular and mobile homes:*

> **Modular homes** are also factory-built but transported in sections and permanently affixed to a foundation, meeting local or state building codes similar to site-built homes.

Mobile homes (built before 1976, prior to HUD code enforcement) often do not meet current safety or building standards and have more limited financing and resale options.

Material Fact: Any fact that would influence a reasonable person's decision to buy, sell, or lease a property, or affect the price and terms under which they are willing to do so. Material facts include known defects, hazards, boundary disputes, pending assessments, or conditions that could impact the property's value, safety, or desirability. Sellers are legally obligated to disclose all known material facts, and brokers must disclose any material information within their knowledge, regardless of who they represent. Failure to do so—whether intentional or by omission—may result in legal or financial consequences. Transparency about material facts supports fairness, informed consent, and extends trust between all parties. *See also: Disclosure; Asbestos; Due Diligence; Home Inspection; Latent Defect; Lead-Based Paint; Mold; Radon.*

Metes and Bounds: A method of describing land by outlining its boundaries using measurements of distance (metes) and direction or physical features (bounds). Often referencing landmarks such as trees, roads, or rivers, this system is one of the oldest forms of property description. It is commonly used for rural or irregularly shaped parcels not included in platted subdivisions. *See also: Legal Description.*

Mold: A naturally occurring organism that grows in areas of moisture or poor ventilation. In real estate, mold can range from a minor maintenance issue to a significant health or structural concern. Some states classify mold as a pest because it thrives in conditions that also attract wood-destroying organisms. Disclosure laws and remediation standards vary by region, but sellers are generally expected to disclose any known water intrusion, visible mold, or history of remediation. During due diligence, buyers should verify that any prior issues were properly addressed, and learn how to prevent or deter recurrence in the future. *See also: Disclosure; Latent Defect; Material Fact; Pest Inspection.*

Months of Supply is a traditional statistic used to estimate how long it would take to sell *all* available listings at the current pace (assuming no new listings come on the market). Months of supply formula: *Available Listings ÷ Sold Properties = Months of Supply.* The formula is usually based on Sold properties within the last 30 days.

Mortgage: A loan secured by real property, in which the property itself serves as collateral for repayment. The term "mortgage" may refer both to the financing arrangement and to the legal document granting the lender a lien on the property. In practice, the mortgage ensures that if the borrower fails to meet loan obligations, the lender has the right to foreclose and claim the property to recover the debt. The mortgage amount is typically the purchase price minus the down payment. *See also: Loan; Lien; Encumbrance; Deed of Trust.*

Mortgage Broker (Lender / Loan Officer): A licensed financial professional who guides buyers through the process of securing a mortgage loan. Acting as both educator and facilitator, the lender explains available loan options, gathers documentation, and ensures the buyer understands their obligations before closing. Some loan officers work directly for a single financial institution, while **mortgage brokers** are licensed to place loans with multiple lenders, helping buyers compare programs and rates. While buyers typically interact with their lender or broker, the actual funds come from the financial institution underwriting and funding the loan.

Mortgage Insurance (MI / PMI / MIP): Insurance that protects the lender against loss if a borrower defaults on a mortgage loan. Mortgage Insurance (MI) is typically required when the borrower's down payment is less than 20% of the purchase price. *There are two primary types:*

> **Private Mortgage Insurance (PMI):** Applies to conventional loans.

> **Mortgage Insurance Premium (MIP):** Applies to FHA or other government-backed loans.

> While MI protects the lender, it enables buyers to qualify with a lower down payment. Depending on the loan type, PMI may be removed once sufficient equity is verified—typically through an appraisal or refinance—while MIP generally remains for the life of the loan unless refinanced into a conventional loan. *See also: Down Payment.*

Multiple Listing Service (MLS): A cooperative database through which members—traditionally real estate brokerage firms and licensed brokers—list properties to gain maximum exposure and access listing information from other professionals. The MLS enables members to offer compensation, collaborate effectively, and provide buyers and sellers with the most accurate, reliable, and up-to-date market data available. MLS organizations operate under established rules and guidelines designed to maintain accuracy, consistency, and ethical standards across listings—ensuring a trustworthy and standardized marketplace that benefits both professionals and consumers alike.

> Most MLS systems are operated by local real estate associations or regional boards as a joint venture to promote transparency, cooperation, and accountability in real estate transactions. Some are affiliated with the National Association of REALTORS® (NAR), while others are independently owned and operated under their own participation standards.

Mutual Acceptance (#MA): Is when both parties have consented and agreed to the same contractual terms, conditions, and obligations, binding them as principals to a purchase and/or sale contract. This marks the official agreement between the parties.

National Association of Realtors (NAR): The industry's largest trade organization, with over one million members known as *Realtors*. These members are licensed brokers or agents who, in addition to meeting state licensing requirements, commit to NAR's Code of Ethics and professional accountability standards. Not every licensed broker or agent is a Realtor—membership is voluntary. Importantly, this does not mean non-members are less committed to ethics or professional standards; many uphold the same high level of professionalism without belonging to NAR.

Natural Hazard Disclosure (NHD): A report that identifies whether a property is located in an area with known natural risks such as flooding, wildfires, earthquakes, or landslides. In the United States, certain states require sellers to provide this disclosure, often prepared by a professional third-party service using official maps and data. Similar reports may exist internationally under different names or local regulations, but the intent remains the same—to inform buyers of environmental risks, support responsible ownership, and promote transparency in real estate transactions.

Net Proceed Funds: The amount of money a seller receives from closing a real estate transaction after all costs and obligations are deducted from the gross sale price. Deductions may include mortgage payoffs, liens, broker compensation, title clearance, closing costs, taxes, inspection-related repairs, and other agreed-upon expenses. In simple terms, it's the money a seller "walks away with" when the property closes.

> **Negative Net Proceeds (also called "Seller Net Deficit" or "Bringing Cash to Close"):** A situation where the seller's net proceed funds are not enough to cover all costs, obligations, and liens on the property. Instead of walking away with net proceeds, the seller must bring personal funds to closing to cover the shortfall, satisfy the outstanding balance, pay off liens, or meet other required expenses to transfer a clear title.

In other words, instead of walking away with money, the seller must bring money to close.

Net Proceeds Contingency: A buyer's condition in a purchase and/or sale contract stating that their ability to purchase is 'contingent' upon receiving funds (net proceeds) from the sale of another property. In simple terms, the buyer cannot close on their next property until their current one sells and closes. *See also: Addendum, Contingent Sale.*

No Agency: occurs when a principal chooses to waive their right to any representation, opting instead to advocate for and represent themselves. While this option is available, it is generally not advisable as it leaves the principal without professional agency, advocacy, or guidance and rarely serves their best interest.

Non-Exclusive (Agency Agreement): A reference to the type of written agency representation that allows a client to work with multiple brokers simultaneously without being exclusive to one. This arrangement offers the client flexibility to explore various perspectives or markets, but may reduce the client's level of priority service from any single broker. The agreement also outlines transparent terms and compensation, ensuring mutual clarity and accountability throughout the relationship. *See also: Exclusive (Agency Agreement).*

Occupancy: The actual use or utilization of a property by its owner, tenant, or other authorized party. Occupancy reflects how the property functions—such as owner-occupied, tenant-occupied, vacant, or investment-held—and influences factors like insurance requirements, financing eligibility, zoning compliance, and tax classification. Occupancy status is typically disclosed in the loan application and other transaction documents; misrepresentation may impact loan terms, coverage, or legal standing. *See also: Possession.*

> **Owner-Occupied:** A property used as the primary or secondary residence of the legal owner. Lenders often view owner-occupied properties as lower risk, which can result in more favorable loan terms. Ownership occupancy typically requires the buyer to take possession and occupy the home within a defined timeframe after closing.

> **Tenant-Occupied:** A property occupied by someone other than the legal owner under a lease or rental agreement. Tenant-occupied properties may require notice before showings or closing and can carry additional considerations for insurance, financing, and property management.

Offeree: The party to whom the offer is made. The offeree may accept, reject, or counter the proposal.

Offeror: The party who makes an offer in a real estate transaction (for example, a buyer proposing to purchase or a seller countering terms).

Orientation: True orientation goes beyond preparation; it transforms uncertainty into readiness by encouraging clients to be proactive and carefully review, investigate, and ask prudent questions before negotiations and during the transaction. It fosters a calm and confident presence that empowers clients throughout their journey, ensuring they remain prepared, informed, and in control for a more straightforward and successful experience.

Owner Financing: A transaction in which the property's seller provides all or part of the financing for the buyer's purchase, rather than the buyer obtaining a traditional loan from a lender. The buyer makes payments directly to the seller based on agreed-upon terms, which may include interest, an amortization schedule, and a promissory note secured by the property. Owner financing can benefit sellers who wish to broaden their buyer pool or earn interest income. Clear documentation and legal guidance are essential to protect both parties and ensure compliance with lending laws. *See also: Promissory Note.*

Parcel/Property Identification Number (PIN): A unique number assigned by a local taxing authority or land registry to identify a specific parcel of real property for assessment, taxation, and record-keeping purposes. The PIN ensures accuracy in property records by linking legal descriptions, ownership, and tax data to a single, traceable identifier. Depending on the region, this number may also be known as an Assessor's Parcel Number (APN), Parcel ID, or Cadastral Reference Number. Verifying the correct PIN is essential during due diligence to confirm property boundaries, ownership, and tax status before closing. *See also: Legal Description; Purchase and/or Sale Contract.*

Per Diem: A Latin term meaning "per day," referring to a daily rate used to calculate interest, rent, or carrying costs. Per diem charges most commonly apply to interest, taxes, and insurance prorations at closing and, when negotiated, may also apply when a seller remains in the home after closing under a rent-back agreement or when a buyer takes early occupancy/possession. They can also arise from timing adjustments related to loan funding or delayed closings. *See also: Possession. See also: Assessments; Property Taxes; Prorations.*

Performance-able: The readiness and ability of a buyer or seller to move beyond signing an agency agreement and actively fulfill their role in a transaction. This includes being prepared to negotiate, complete due diligence, meet contractual obligations, and act with decisiveness to ensure a successful closing.

Personal Property / Real Property: Personal property refers to movable possessions that are not permanently attached to the land or structure and therefore do not automatically transfer with the sale. Real property includes the land, any permanent improvements, and the rights associated with ownership. The distinction between the two determines what is conveyed at closing; personal property must be specifically included in the purchase and/or sale contract, while real property transfers through the deed.

PITI (Principal, Interest, Taxes, and Insurance): The standard components of a monthly mortgage payment. Principal is the portion that reduces the loan balance, interest is the lender's charge for borrowing, taxes are the property taxes assessed by the local jurisdiction, and insurance covers the property (and sometimes mortgage insurance). Lenders reference PITI when evaluating loan affordability.

Planned Unit Development (PUD): A type of real estate community, often suburban and developed as part of a larger master plan. PUDs typically include residential or condominium properties along with shared amenities such as parks, playgrounds, swimming pools, and tennis courts. These amenities are generally managed and maintained through a homeowners association (HOA).

Points (Mortgage Points): A form of prepaid interest paid at closing to reduce a loan's interest rate or cover loan origination costs. One point equals 1% of the loan amount.

> *Discount points* are optional payments made by the buyer to lower the interest rate and monthly payment over time.

> *Origination points* are fees charged by the lender for processing and originating the loan. Understanding points allows buyers to compare loan options mindfully and determine whether the upfront cost provides long-term value.

Possession: The point at which the buyer gains the right to occupy the property, often symbolized by receiving the keys. Possession typically aligns with the closing date but may occur before or after closing if otherwise negotiated in the purchase and/or sale contract. Clear possession terms—supported by proper documentation, timing, and insurance coverage—help ensure a smooth and secure transition between buyer and seller. *See also: Closing; Per Diem.*

Price per Square Foot (PPSF): A calculation dividing a property's price by its total square footage, often used to compare relative value among properties. While it can serve as a general benchmark, price per square foot is frequently overemphasized and can be misleading without context. Location, condition, lot size, floor plan, upgrades, and amenities all play a vital role in determining true value. PPSF should be viewed as one reference point within a broader market analysis—not as the sole measure of value.

Principal (loan amount): the amount of money borrowed or the amount of the loan that has not yet been repaid to the lender. This does not include the interest on borrowing that money. The principal balance (sometimes referred to as the outstanding or unpaid principal balance) is the amount owed on the loan, minus the amount paid.

Principal (Client): The buyer or seller who is a party to a purchase and/or sale contract.

Promissory Note: A written, legally binding promise by one party (the borrower) to pay a specified amount of money to another party (the lender) under agreed-upon terms, including repayment schedule, interest, and other conditions.

Property Description: A general written description of the property that identifies its location and basic details, such as the street address, parcel number, and sometimes notable features. This everyday description is used to help buyers, sellers, lenders, and agents understand which property is being discussed. Unlike a legal description, it is not precise enough to define property boundaries in a court of law.

Property Taxes: Recurring taxes levied by local or regional governments on real property, based on the property's assessed value. In the United States, property taxes help fund essential public services such as schools, infrastructure, and emergency response. Rates and assessment practices vary widely by state, county, and municipality. Internationally, similar property-based taxes—often referred to as *rates*, *land tax*, or *council tax*—serve comparable purposes but may differ in calculation and collection methods. Property owners are responsible for timely payment, as unpaid taxes can result in liens or other financial penalties. *See also: Escrow Account; Per Diem; Prorations; Reserve Account.*

Prorations: The calculated division of property-related expenses or income—such as taxes, insurance, homeowners association (HOA) dues, or rent—between buyer and seller based on the portion of the billing period each party owns or occupies the property. Prorations ensure fairness and accuracy at closing, with costs or credits allocated according to the closing date. For example, if property taxes are prepaid by the seller, the buyer may reimburse the seller for the unused portion after closing. Prorations are typically shown on the settlement statement and may be calculated using per diem (daily) rates to ensure precise accounting. *See also: Per Diem; Property Taxes; Assessments.*

Purchase and/or Sale Contract: A legally binding agreement between a buyer and a seller that outlines the terms and conditions for transferring ownership of real property. The contract defines key details such as the purchase price, good faith deposit, legal description, property identification number (PIN)—also known in some regions as an Assessor's Parcel Number (APN) or Cadastral Reference Number—financing terms, contingencies, timelines, each party's responsibilities, and the closing and possession dates. Once signed and mutually accepted (#MA), the contract becomes the framework that guides the transaction—establishing the rights, obligations, and potential consequences for both parties until the transaction is closed or terminated. Depending on the jurisdiction, this document may also be known as a purchase agreement, contract of sale, or sale deed. *See also: Addendum.*

Radon: A naturally occurring, colorless, odorless radioactive gas formed by the breakdown of uranium in soil, rock, and water. Testing for radon is often part of environmental due diligence, especially in regions where concentrations are known to be higher. Some states or countries mandate radon disclosure or recommend mitigation systems for elevated levels. *See also: Disclosure; Environmental Hazard; Material Fact.*

Recording: The act of filing finalized real estate documents—such as the deed, mortgage, or lien—with the appropriate public records office, usually through the **closer** (escrow officer, title closer, or attorney). After funding is confirmed, the closer arranges for the documents to be recorded, ensuring the transfer of ownership and any related encumbrances are legally recognized. Recording provides public notice of the property's ownership, establishes lien priority, and marks the official completion of the transaction. Many jurisdictions now use digital or e-recording systems. *See also: Recording Number; Closing; Funding; Title; Deed.*

> **Recording Number:** A unique identifier assigned by the county or regional recording office when a document—such as a deed or mortgage—is officially filed in public records. The recording number includes a timestamp or date component, which establishes the exact sequence and priority of ownership transfers, liens, and other encumbrances. Recording numbers serve as the permanent reference for verifying ownership history and ensuring legal transparency in property records.

Relationships: Intentionally cultivated professional connections who uphold integrity, transparency, and excellence. These relationships enable proactive problem-solving, strategic referrals, and expedient service. *See also: Industry Partners.*

Reserve Account: A separate account established to collect and hold funds for recurring property-related expenses. A reserve account may be used for HOA or replacement reserves in multi-unit or investment properties, but is most commonly maintained by the mortgage servicer on behalf of the borrower for property taxes, insurance premiums, or other required charges. The servicer disburses these funds when due to ensure timely payment and protect the lender's security interest in the property. Also known as an escrow or impound account. *See also: Escrow Account; Property Taxes; Insurance; HOA.*

Real Estate Settlement Procedures Act (RESPA): A U.S. federal law designed to protect consumers during the homebuying process. RESPA requires lenders to provide borrowers with clear information about transaction-related costs before settlement (closing) and ongoing disclosures about loan servicing and escrow accounts throughout the life of the loan. The law also prohibits kickbacks, referral fees, and other unearned compensation in the mortgage and settlement services industry, promoting transparency and fairness.

Refinance (Refi): The process of replacing an existing mortgage with a new loan, often to secure better terms such as a lower interest rate, adjusted loan length, or a different type of mortgage. A refinance can also allow owners to access built-up *equity* through a "cash-out refinance," where a portion of the equity is converted to cash. These funds may be used to build wealth, purchase additional real estate, pay debt, or invest in other opportunities. *See also: Equity.*

Room Count: The total number of rooms in a property, including bedrooms, bathrooms, living and dining areas, offices, dens, media or recreation rooms, and other finished spaces that contribute to livability and flow. Focusing on total **room count**—rather than just the number of bedrooms— encourages a more mindful assessment of how a property functions and adapts to individual needs. This broader view helps buyers and sellers evaluate lifestyle, comfort, and flexibility in how the property can be utilized and enjoyed. Definitions of room count may vary among appraisers, MLS systems, or regional standards, but the intent remains consistent: to provide a clear and comprehensive understanding of a property's functional space.

Seller: A party to the purchase and/or sale contract who offers property for sale and agrees to transfer ownership under specified terms. A mindful seller approaches the process with acclimation, agency, and alignment—collaborating to complete disclosures, fulfill contractual obligations, and close the transaction with responsibility and satisfaction. *See also: Principal.*

Seller's Disclosure: A mandated statement in which the seller provides all known information about the property's condition, including past or present defects that could affect its value or desirability. Disclosures must be completed truthfully and to the best of the seller's knowledge, usually on a standardized form. While sellers are not expected to act as inspectors, failure to disclose known material facts can carry legal consequences. *See also: Disclosure; Due Diligence; Home Inspection; Latent Defect; Material Fact.*

Seller's Agent (AKA Listing Broker): A licensed real estate professional who provides representation upon entering a listing agreement and becomes a short-term partner in the seller's journey. Duties include analyzing market conditions, developing pricing and marketing strategies, managing property presentation, ensuring compliance with disclosure and legal requirements, and overseeing contractual obligations—ultimately advocating for the seller throughout the transaction. In some regions, this role is referred to as the listing agent. *See also: Agreement; Purchase and/or Sale Contract.*

Seller's Market: A market condition in which buyer demand exceeds the available supply of properties. Homes may sell quickly and, at times, above asking price, giving sellers stronger negotiating leverage. In a seller's market, buyers must be prepared, decisive, and strategic to compete successfully. *See also: Buyer's Market/Balanced Market; Inventory.*

Selling Agent (AKA Buyer's Broker): A licensed real estate professional who provides representation upon entering a buyer agency agreement and becomes a short-term partner in the buyer's journey. Duties include sharing market insight and contract knowledge, strategizing due diligence, preparing for negotiations, ensuring compliance with disclosure and legal requirements, and managing contractual obligations— ultimately advocating for the buyer throughout the purchase transaction. In some regions, this role is referred to as the buyer's agent. *See also: Agreement; Purchase and/or Sale Contract.*

Septic System (Private Wastewater Utility): An on-site wastewater treatment system, privately owned and maintained, that collects and processes sewage from a property. Unlike public sewer connections, the property owner is responsible for the system's operation, inspections, and upkeep.

Settlement Agent/ Closer/ Closing agent/ Escrow officer: the person or entity that collects, chronicles, and coordinates the preparation and recordation of closing documents and the disbursement of funds. Typically, the closing is conducted by title companies, escrow companies, or attorneys.

Settlement Statement (HUD-1 or ALTA): A document that itemizes all of the costs, fees, and credits involved in a real estate transaction. While the Closing Disclosure(CD) is required for most consumer mortgage loans, settlement statements—often the ALTA form today—are commonly used by title and escrow companies to show how funds are distributed at closing. Both buyers and sellers may receive a settlement statement for their records.

Short Sale: A property sale in which the seller's lender agrees to accept a payoff amount less than the outstanding loan balance. Short sales typically occur when a homeowner is experiencing financial hardship and lacks sufficient equity, meaning the market value of the property is not enough to cover what is owed. A short sale is not a discount without reason—it reflects the seller's circumstances and the lender's willingness to avoid a foreclosure outcome. The lender must review and approve the offer terms and timeline.

Simultaneous Closing (Concurrent Closing): When two or more real estate transactions—often the sale of one property and the purchase of another—are coordinated to close on the same day. This approach is common and requires thoughtful collaboration among industry partners, including lenders, closers, and brokers, to align timing and funding seamlessly.

Signatures: The formal acknowledgment by which all parties agree to the terms of a contract or document, making it legally binding. Signatures may be **wet** (handwritten in ink) or **electronic** (digitally executed through approved platforms), depending on jurisdiction and document type. Both forms carry equal legal weight when properly executed and verified, ensuring authenticity, consent, and enforceability in the transaction. *See also: Agreement; Contract; Purchase and/or Sale Contract; Mutual Acceptance (#MA).*

Specific Performance: A legal remedy that allows one party to ask the court to require the other to complete the agreed terms of a real estate contract—such as finalizing a sale—rather than accept financial compensation. Because real property is considered unique, courts sometimes allow this remedy; however, it is often difficult to enforce when one party's willingness or "heart" is no longer in it. This reinforces the importance of entering into agreements only when both parties are *performance-able*—ready, willing, and able to complete their commitments in good faith. *See also: Breach of Contract; Actual Damages; Purchase and/or Sale Contract.*

Statutory Duties: The baseline legal obligations imposed by state law that guide how brokers and firms must conduct themselves once an agency relationship is established— whether through a buyer agency or listing agreement, and continuing throughout the transaction. These duties vary by jurisdiction but generally include honesty, reasonable skill and care, disclosure of material facts, and proper accounting of funds. Many states also regulate dual agency within their statutes, requiring written disclosure, informed consent, or, in some cases, prohibiting the practice.

Survey: A professional measurement and mapping of a property's boundaries, dimensions, and physical features, typically performed by a licensed land surveyor. A survey ensures the legal description accurately reflects the property as it exists on the ground and identifies encroachments, easements, and boundary lines. Surveys are often required by lenders or title companies before closing to verify ownership boundaries and avoid disputes. *See also: Legal Description; Easement; Encroachment.*

Title: refers to the legal right of ownership to a property. Having "clear title" means the owner has full, marketable rights to sell, transfer, or use the property without undisclosed claims, liens, or disputes. In the United States, title is typically verified through a **title search** and protected by **title insurance**, ensuring the buyer receives ownership that is legally recognized and free of hidden encumbrances. In some countries, the concept of "title" differs. Instead of private title companies, ownership may be verified and guaranteed by government land registries. These registries maintain official public records, and in many cases, title insurance is not commonly used because the state guarantees ownership.

Title Report: A document prepared by a title company that outlines the legal status of a property's ownership. It identifies the current owner of record, the legal description, and any recorded encumbrances such as easements, liens, mortgages, covenants, conditions, or restrictions that may affect title. The title report also confirms whether the seller can transfer a *clear and marketable title* to the buyer. Because it serves as the foundation for issuing title insurance, buyers, sellers, and brokers review the title report carefully to verify accuracy and address any issues before closing. *See also: Encumbrance, Lien.*

TRID (TILA-RESPA Integrated Disclosure): A U.S. federal regulation issued by the Consumer Financial Protection Bureau (CFPB) that combines and standardizes mortgage disclosure forms. TRID requires lenders to provide borrowers with a Loan Estimate (LE) within three business days of a completed loan application, and a Closing Disclosure (CD) at least three business days before closing. The purpose of TRID is to improve transparency, help borrowers compare loan offers, and ensure buyers understand the true costs of their mortgage before committing. *See also: Loan Estimate; Closing Disclosure; Settlement Statement.*

Transparency: A real estate firm's and broker's responsibility to communicate openly, clearly, and honestly with clients and all parties to a transaction. This includes clarifying agency relationships, disclosing any potential conflicts of interest, explaining compensation, and sharing property condition details. Practicing transparency ensures clients can make informed decisions, strengthens trust, and supports an ethical, fair transaction process.

Truth in Lending Act (TILA): A U.S. federal law that ensures borrowers receive clear, accurate information about the cost of credit. TILA requires lenders to disclose key terms of a loan— including the annual percentage rate (APR), finance charges, total payments, and repayment schedule—so consumers can compare loan products and make informed decisions. TILA promotes transparency, prevents deceptive lending practices, and gives borrowers certain rights, such as the ability to rescind specific types of loans within a limited timeframe.

Underground Oil Tanks (USTs): Storage tanks once commonly used to hold heating oil for residential or commercial properties, often buried below ground. Over time, older steel tanks can corrode and leak, contaminating soil or groundwater and creating environmental and financial liability for property owners. Many regions require disclosure of known or decommissioned tanks, along with documentation of proper removal, soil testing, and remediation if contamination occurred. Buyers are encouraged to confirm whether a property currently or previously had an underground tank and, if so, to obtain inspection records and environmental clearance. Proper management or removal by licensed contractors protects future owners and preserves property value. *See also: Disclosure; Environmental Hazard; Due Diligence; Material Fact.*

Underwriting: A detailed review process that determines whether a loan or insurance policy meets the standards for approval. In mortgage lending, underwriting confirms that both the borrower and the property qualify for financing by reviewing the buyer's documentation and the property's appraisal to ensure the loan can be funded responsibly. In insurance, underwriting evaluates the property's risk profile—considering location, age, condition, and exposure to potential hazards—to determine eligibility, coverage limits, and premiums.

USDA Loan (Rural Housing Service): A government-backed loan offered by the U.S. Department of Agriculture to promote homeownership in designated rural areas. USDA loans often require no down payment and offer competitive interest rates, subject to location and income eligibility.

VA Loan (Department of Veterans Affairs): A government-guaranteed loan program available to eligible veterans, active-duty service members, and certain surviving spouses. VA loans typically require no down payment or mortgage insurance. *See also: Certificate of Eligibility; Mortgage.*

Venture Capitalists (VCs): Investors or firms that provide funding to start-ups and growing companies in exchange for equity (ownership interest). While they can drive innovation and make a difference in many industries, their role in real estate often raises concerns. VCs frequently back technology platforms, institutional landlord models, or AI-driven rent optimization systems—innovations designed to maximize efficiency and returns. However, these models can also drive up housing costs, consolidate property ownership into fewer hands, and reduce opportunities for individual buyers, especially first-time buyers. With a focus on rapid growth and profit, VCs may unintentionally contribute to the wealth gap by prioritizing investor returns over affordability and long-term community stability.

Verification: The buyer's process of confirming that a property matches the seller's representations and that disclosures and documents are satisfactory. This step ensures the information meets their expectations and identifies whether further research is needed. Common areas of verification include lot size, square footage, utilities, easements, encroachments, HOA financial health, litigation, insurance costs, zoning, ordinances, and potential hazards. While a broker can provide guidance, the buyer must complete their verification process to support informed decision-making and protect their interests.

Walk-through (Final walk-through): Typically conducted after all contingencies have been satisfied but before closing, the final walk-through provides assurance and accountability before ownership transfers. It is a buyer's final opportunity to ensure the property is in the agreed-upon condition and that all negotiated repairs or contractual obligations have been completed. The purchase and/or sale contract typically outlines this condition, requiring the seller to provide reasonable access for the buyer to complete the walk-through. This step confirms the property's readiness and alignment with contract expectations prior to closing.

Wall Street Speculators: Investors who buy and sell financial assets, including real estate–backed securities or large property portfolios, with the goal of profiting from short-term market movements. While speculation can provide liquidity and attract investment, in real estate, it often comes at a cost. Speculators encourage bulk acquisitions, may fuel rapid price increases, or pressure rental markets through profit-maximizing models. These practices can push housing further out of reach for individual buyers—especially first-time buyers—and contribute to widening the wealth gap. By focusing on immediate returns for their investors, rather than sustainable housing solutions, speculation can destabilize local communities and limit opportunities for individual long-term homeownership.

Web-based (or App-Driven): Extraction Platforms that promote speed, convenience, and savings by bypassing traditional broker representation. While they may appear to reduce costs, these platforms often distract buyers and sellers from the risks of proceeding without advocacy, such as incomplete due diligence, a lack of negotiation strategy, and limited protection against contractual pitfalls. Unlike community reinvestment, profits from these models are extracted rather than cycled back into local economies, removing wealth and resources that could otherwise support clients and strengthen neighborhoods.

Well (Private Water Utility): A privately owned and maintained system that supplies water to a property, typically drawn from groundwater. Unlike municipal water services, the property owner is responsible for the well's quality, testing, and maintenance.